THE THEOLOGY
OF
DIETRICH
BONHOEFFER

THE THEOLOGY
OF
DIETRICH BONHOEFFER

by
John D. Godsey

WIPF & STOCK · Eugene, Oregon

Wipf and Stock Publishers
199 W 8th Ave, Suite 3
Eugene, OR 97401

The Theology of Dietrich Bonhoeffer
By Godsey, John D. and Barker, Gaylon
Copyright©1960 by Godsey, John D.
ISBN 13: 978-1-4982-2578-6
Publication date 11/1/2015
Previously published by Westminster Press, 1960

Scripture quotations from the Revised Standard Version of the Bible are copyright 1946 and 1952 by the Division of Christian Education of the National Council of Churches, and are used by permission.

Series Foreword
BONHOEFFER SECONDARY STUDY SERIES

When Dietrich Bonhoeffer (1906-45) died at the age of 39, he was relatively unknown, recognized by few outside of a small circle of church and ecumenical leaders. The extent of his involvement in the German Church Struggle and resistance movement had not been explored. His contribution to 20th century Protestant theology was minimal. Today, however, 70 years later, his is one of the most influential theological voices in Protestant, Catholic and Evangelical circles, and interest in his theology and witness continues to grow in the academy, the church and beyond. While the leading theological voices of the mid-twentieth century have been replaced by more contemporary ones, Bonhoeffer remains a seminal figure. As any quick internet search will indicate, there is an ongoing fascination with his life and witness.

Bonhoeffer was introduced to the English-speaking world in the 1950s when the first editions of his writings, edited by Eberhard Bethge (Bonhoeffer's close friend and confidant, biographer, and leading interpreter of Bonhoeffer's legacy), appeared in translation. Shortly thereafter, he captured the popular imagination when his name was attached to the "Death of God" and secular theological voices in the 1960s. Our understanding of Bonhoeffer reached a significant milestone when Bethge's masterful biography of Bonhoeffer was translated in 1970. It was during this time that the first scholarly studies on Bonhoeffer's life and theology appeared. The first generation of scholars and the work they produced helped secure Bonhoeffer's legacy and laid the foundation for the ongoing interest in Bonhoeffer in ways that could not have been imagined 50 years ago.

In the intervening years, scholars have produced a multitude of studies that have explored a variety of themes related to Bonhoeffer's work, his influence in the church and the world, his political resistance and engagement, his contribution to ethics, and his role in the Church Struggle and in Post-WWII Jewish-Christian relations, among others. At the center of this work has been an emphasis on what was most important to Bonhoeffer: what it means to be a Christian and the nature of the church's witness in the world. Both by posing questions about Bonhoeffer's thought and his contribution to the theological conversation, these foundational studies have led successive generations to think about Bonhoeffer's contribution to the church's witness in a changing world. The heritage they have left has been passed on as we continue to see the fruits of their labor in the research being carried out by scholars around the world.

Alongside the widespread interest in Bonhoeffer, new scholarship continues to appear, providing us with new insights that help us to gain a greater appreciation for the many aspects of his life; new studies appear that push and expand our understanding; and conferences and gatherings around the world explore his continuing significance in new contexts. The vitality of interest in Bonhoeffer is displayed no more clearly than in the number of essays and books produced each year. Yet, as we marvel at the richness these texts present, a careful reading of them shows their reliance on the work of previous scholarship, thereby acknowledging their indebtedness to the work of previous generations out of which they grow. While embracing the new insights proffered, the references to previous work contained in them stand as a reminder that we cannot forget the foundations upon which these works are based. As we continue to study and explore the Bonhoeffer corpus and the ever-expanding body of secondary literature, it is also important to maintain these foundational voices. By preserving these voices, and adding them to the ongoing conversation, our approach to Bonhoeffer and his enduring witness will be enriched even more.

We are very pleased, therefore, that Wipf & Stock, which continues to make important classic theological works available, has produced this Secondary Study Series on Bonhoeffer's theology. We welcome this new series that makes available again some of the foundational texts that continue to influence the way we approach and interpret Bonhoeffer's legacy. The books you will find here are works of quality that still hold the power to inform. They represent the best of the early interpretations of Bonhoeffer and his theology.

This series appears at a particularly appropriate time since we have reached another significant milestone. The completion of the 17 volume *Dietrich Bonhoeffer Works*, which makes available all the available primary sources from Bonhoeffer's hand in English, now opens the door to a deepened understanding of Bonhoeffer's theological contribution within its context. In addition, the 70th anniversary of Bonhoeffer's death in 2015 will provide new impetus to explore recurring themes in Bonhoeffer's work, as well find new ways to apply Bonhoeffer's ideas to current conditions.

It is our hope that the renewed interest in Bonhoeffer occasioned by these developments will be enriched by the volumes published here. When these volumes first appeared, they were greeted with accolades from the academic community. Over the years, they have guided and shaped our interpretation. Now with their reissue, they will inspire yet another generation of scholars and church leaders to find within Bonhoeffer's legacy a source for the deepening of faith in Christ crucified and a strengthening of the Christian witness in the world. It is also our hope that, with this series of significant works on Bonhoeffer's theology, the ties between past and future will be strengthened.

H. Gaylon Barker, Series Editor

President of the International Bonhoeffer Society
(English Language Section)

September 2014
Ridgefield, CT.

*To my parents and my wife
 — whose encouragement made this
 work possible*

Genehmigt von der theologischen Fakultät auf Antrag der Herren Prof. Karl Barth, Referent, und Prof. Hendrik van Oyen, Korreferent.

Basel, den 2. Juli, 1958

Der Dekan: Herr Prof. Oscar Cullmann

Contents

Series Foreword	1
Key to Abbreviations	11
Introduction	13
Chapter I. Theological Foundation	19
A. Biographical Introduction (1906–1931)	19
B. Theological Exposition	26
1. *Sanctorum Communio*	27
2. *Act and Being*	55
Chapter II. Theological Application	80
A. Biographical Introduction (1932–1939)	80
B. Theological Exposition	95
1. The Ecumenical Movement	96
2. The German Church Struggle	107
3. Theological Interpretation of Scripture	119
a. *Creation and Fall*	119
b. *King David*	143
c. *The Cost of Discipleship*	151
d. *Temptation*	172
e. *Life Together*	179
f. *The Prayer Book of the Bible*	189
Chapter III. Theological Fragmentation	195
A. Biographical Introduction (1940–1945)	195
B. Theological Exposition	203
1. *Ethics*	204
2. *Prisoner for God*	248

Chapter IV. Theological Evaluation 260
    A. The Problem 260
    B. The Clue to Bonhoeffer 264
    C. Questions 273
    D. Conclusion 279

Bibliography 283

The Author 289

KEY TO ABBREVIATIONS

AS — *Akt und Sein* (2d ed., 1956)
CD — *The Cost of Discipleship*
DB: Einf. — *Dietrich Bonhoeffer: Einführung in seine Botschaft*
DRk — *Dein Reich komme* (2d ed., 1957)
E — *Ethics*
Gebetbuch — *Das Gebetbuch der Bibel*
GS I — *Gesammelte Schriften,* Band I (Oekumene)
LT — *Life Together*
MW I — *Die mündige Welt I*
MW II — *Die mündige Welt II*
N — *Nachfolge*
PFG — *Prisoner for God* (*Letters and Papers from Prison*)
SC — *Sanctorum Communio* (2d ed., 1954)
SchF — *Schöpfung und Fall* (3d ed., 1955)
T — *Temptation*

Introduction

The name of Dietrich Bonhoeffer is becoming known in ever-widening circles. This is as it should be, for he is certainly one of the most interesting figures in the history of modern theology. More than that, his theology is teaching the church how to live and serve in the crisis that appears to be its destiny in our revolutionary era. In God's providence it is given to some men to think ahead of their times, and thus to help prepare the way of the church in the future. The present work is undertaken with the conviction that Bonhoeffer is such a man.

The mere story of Bonhoeffer's life would provide fascinating reading for anyone. Take a young Protestant theological student from pre-Nazi Germany, reared with all the advantages of bourgeois existence; give him a year of life in the United States; then plunge him back into Hitler's Third Reich, and watch him struggle to be a Christian during the ensuing years of church controversy, Gestapo terrorism, and World War II. Dangle before his eyes the opportunity to escape from it all; witness his tormented decision and the final outcome. That is a sketch of Bonhoeffer's life *in nuce!* It is no wonder that here we have to do with an unusual person.

Bonhoeffer was the sort of person who, by his very demeanor, stood out in a crowd. There was a certain aura about this powerfully built man with aristocratic features and gentle eyes, which attracted people to him. He was a man among men, a lover of the full life, and yet he was not gregarious. Instead, he tended to be reserved, and acquaintances were always conscious of an inner discipline and integrity that set him apart. True friendship was something precious to him and could be cultivated with only a very few. Yet there was no question about his loving people with an openness and freedom that was almost disarming. Indeed, "freedom" is a good word to depict the impression one gains of Bonhoeffer — freedom of thought and action springing from a deep faith. In him one catches a glimpse of how commitment to Jesus Christ issues in the freedom of the Spirit.

Neither an unusual life nor a striking personality, however, provides sufficient warrant for writing this book. That can come only from Bonhoeffer's theology *an sich,* and it is our conviction that the theology of this young German is important, first, because it affords one of the best available introductions into the complex field of twentieth-century Protestant theology, and, second, because it is so profoundly Christ-centered that it raises in a sharp and unavoidable way the question of the church's very existence in the modern world.

Dietrich Bonhoeffer's dates are 1906–1945. This is significant, for it means that he lived through a critical period in the history of the Christian church. Indeed, he not only lived through the period, but he participated vigorously in three developments, a knowledge of which is absolutely indispensable for an appreciation and understanding of our present theological situation.

The first of these is the rise of the so-called "dialectical theology," that theological movement beginning in the 1920's which, in opposition to the optimistic, man-centered theology of the nineteenth century, attempted to recover the Reformation doctrine of the Word of God, emphasized the crisis in which God's Word places man, and introduced into theology a dialectical method that recognized the polarity between God and man, eternity and time, life and death. Interestingly enough, Bonhoeffer was not a pupil of any of the theologians most intimately associated with the new movement, viz., Karl Barth, Eduard Thurneysen, Emil Brunner, Friedrich Gogarten, and Rudolf Bultmann. In fact, most of his theological studies were at the University of Berlin, where the theological milieu was still quite "liberal," being under the influence of the "history of religions" approach to Biblical criticism, the "modernism" of Adolf von Harnack, and the "modern positive theology" of Reinhold Seeberg, who attempted to mediate between modernism and confessional Lutheranism. Nevertheless, Bonhoeffer cut his theological teeth, so to speak, on the "new" theology, which was being expounded in the periodical *Zwischen den Zeiten,* and he soon identified himself with its starting point and its general direction. This is clearly evident in his dissertation *Sanctorum Communio,* which was completed in 1927, a noteworthy year marked by the appearance of such influential books as Karl Barth's *Die christliche Dogmatik* and Martin Heidegger's *Sein und Zeit,* and by the first Ecumenical Conference on Faith and Order at Lausanne, Switzerland.

Although Bonhoeffer shared with the dialectical theologians their desire to recapture the Reformation understanding of revelation, he was critical of their method, which he believed was ultimately individualistic and abstract. In contrast, Bonhoeffer advocated a theology that did justice to the fact that revelation is bound to the church. That is, God's revelation has a spatial component as well as a temporal one, and so, while the dialectical theologians were concentrating on the problem of faith and history, Bonhoeffer was concerned with the problem of faith and community. *Sanctorum Communio* was an attempt to develop an ontology of the church, in which the being of the church was interpreted not in static, substantial categories but in living, sociological categories. In his second book, *Act and Being,* he tried to make this ontology fruitful for prolegomena to dogmatics, which, under the influence of the consciousness philosophy of the nineteenth century, had heretofore been dominated by epistemology and philosophy of religion. How Bonhoeffer, as an exponent of the new theology, joins the battle against "liberalism" on the left and Roman Catholicism on the right, while at the same time criticizing the new movement from within, provides an unusual introduction to the main issues facing contemporary Protestant theology.

The second development in which Bonhoeffer participated was the ecumenical movement, that centripetal movement of the churches toward unity which was given impetus by the World Missionary Conference at Edinburgh in 1910 and had formative expression in the founding of the World Council of Churches at Amsterdam in 1948. Between Edinburgh and Amsterdam the work toward ecumenicity was carried forward by three different groups:

Faith and Order, Life and Work, and the World Alliance for Promoting International Friendship Through the Churches. Bonhoeffer began working with the World Alliance in 1931, was co-opted a member of the Universal Christian Council for Life and Work at the Fanö Conference in 1934, and from that time on was one of the leading representatives of the German Confessing Church in ecumenical affairs. Mere interest and participation in the ecumenical movement on the part of a German theologian at that time was unusual, but in Bonhoeffer the "practical Christianity" wing of the movement found a dedicated exponent who could speak of the church with as much theological sensitivity as anyone from Faith and Order. In fact, he leveled some stinging, theologically grounded criticism against the leadership of Faith and Order for their doctrinaire attitude during the German Church Struggle. Through participation in the ecumenical movement Bonhoeffer's theology was refined by the hot flame of encounter with the theologies of many churches, and through his writings one becomes aware of the imperative as well as the problem of church unity. His thought provides an excellent entree into this most significant church phenomenon of our century, a movement that is essential to an understanding of theology today.

A third indispensable key for unlocking the mysteries of current theological attitudes and trends is a knowledge of a development mentioned above, namely, the German Church Struggle. This is the struggle of the evangelical Confessing Church in Germany against the state-supported "German Christians" during the Nazi regime. Although the matter is seldom discussed openly, and indeed reactions are often almost unconscious, Continental theologians are still judged according to their role in or attitude toward this *Kirchenkampf*. The anti-Semitism of the German Christians, the co-operation of this group with Hitler's despotism, the persecution of the church by the Third Reich — all these have left a deep scar on the body of Christ, not only in Germany but throughout the world, and any theology that provides a basis for such a perverted church-state relationship as that of the German Christians to the Nazis is, to say the least, suspect. It is for this reason that the notion of "orders of creation" and "natural theology" are such touchy subjects in post-

World War II theology, and why the Lutheran " doctrine of the two realms " is being called into question.

Dietrich Bonhoeffer lived in the midst of the church struggle and has thereby earned the right to be heard. He discerned from the very first the nature of the struggle, and never wavered in his opposition to accommodating the Christian faith to nazism. His leadership at the Confessing Church's " illegal " seminary in Finkenwalde proved to be a great stimulus for the cause of evangelical Christianity at this crucial time in Germany's history. Furthermore, he was one of the few men who realized that the initial struggle against the German Christians had to give way to a struggle on an entirely different level, namely, the level of politics, because the real enemy of the church was not the German Christians but Adolf Hitler himself. The church today is fortunate to be able to listen to Bonhoeffer and to profit from his experience, for rarely has it had such a theologically perceptive and articulate witness so intensely involved in a crisis of this magnitude.

In addition to the value of Bonhoeffer's theology as an introduction into the contemporary theological situation, it deserves to be read and pondered for a more important reason, namely, because of the profundity of the thought per se. In Bonhoeffer we have a theologian whose thought is as Christocentric as that of Karl Barth, who raised the question of the communication of the gospel as sharply as Rudolf Bultmann, who was led to take the problems of our pragmatic, problem-solving, technological world as seriously as Reinhold Niebuhr, but who, more than any of these men, thought from the perspective of the concrete church. Not that these men are not church theologians, but Bonhoeffer somehow more consistently made the body of Christ the center of his concern and the *terminus a quo* of his thinking. He challenged the church to be the church by bringing into line its word and its act, its faith and order and its life and work. That which the church proclaims must take effect within the proclaiming community. Moreover, Bonhoeffer challenged the church to rethink its own mission to the radically secular world of the twentieth century. The continuance of a " religious " interpretation of the gospel in a " nonreligious " world may be at once a misunderstanding of the gospel itself and a default of the church's responsibility vis-à-vis the world. Bonhoeffer has posed this question in a way that cannot be ignored.

Yes, the name of Dietrich Bonhoeffer is becoming known. His life and thought are a permanent reminder that the church cannot exist on the basis of " cheap grace," but only on that of suffering love, the way of the cross. For this is Christ's way, and it is Christ who takes form in the church. Bonhoeffer would not desire to be remembered for himself, but solely as a witness to Him who is the way, the truth, and the life. What follows should be read with this in mind.

Chapter I

Theological Foundation

Bonhoeffer said to the theologians: Your theme is the church!
(Eberhard Bethge.)

A. Biographical Introduction (1906–1931)

Dietrich Bonhoeffer was born into a cultured, upper-middle-class family in Breslau, Germany, on February 4, 1906. He and his twin sister, Sabine, were the sixth and seventh children in a family of eight. His father was Karl Ludwig Bonhoeffer, a well-known physician and authority on psychiatry and neurology, and his mother was the former Paula von Hase, whose father had been a chaplain to the emperor and whose grandfather was the famous nineteenth-century church historian, Karl von Hase, who "had made Jena an attractive place for theology and men of learning all over the world."[1]

In 1912 the family moved to Berlin, where the father became professor of psychiatry at the University of Berlin, and Dietrich was reared in the pleasant surroundings of Berlin-Grunewald, a suburb in which the families of such distinguished scholars as Adolf von Harnack and Hans Delbrück were neighbors. Growing up in the advantageous atmosphere of Germany's finest liberal tradition and within a family where love and joy of living were coupled with a proper sense of ethical responsibility, young Dietrich waxed strong in both physical and mental prowess. He enjoyed sports and was a natural competitor, he liked music and became an accomplished pianist, and he was a good student, being gifted with what a friend has called "an amazing power of concentration." Beyond these gifts

[1] "Memoir" by G. Leibholz in CD, p. 10, n. 1.

Bonhoeffer had three characteristics that play a perceptible role at every point in his career: a remarkable vitality, an unusually sensitive nature, and a capacity for turning thought into action.

At the age of sixteen, Bonhoeffer decided to enter the ministry of the church, and in the fall of 1923 he entered Tübingen University to begin his theological studies. Here he heard such renowned New Testament scholars as Adolf Schlatter and Wilhelm Heitmüller,[2] studied the history of the new philosophy with K. Groos, and formed a lasting impression of the great theologian Karl Heim.[3] After a year at Tübingen, Bonhoeffer matriculated in 1924 at the University of Berlin, where he completed his education under the tutelage of some of the world's foremost scholars: the aging Harnack, with whom he would ride to the university on the railway and who was so impressed with the brilliant young student that he tried to persuade him to specialize in church history; Adolf Deissmann, the scholar who had revolutionized New Testament studies with his linguistic investigations; Hans Lietzmann, the historian of early church history and editor of the New Testament commentary series *Handbuch zum Neuen Testament;* and Ernst Sellin, the Old Testament professor for whom Bonhoeffer wrote a long paper on "The Different Solutions of the Problem of Suffering in Job" ("Die verschiedenen Lösungen des Leidensproblems bei Hiob").

But above all, the young student's interest turned toward systematic theology, and the two Berlin professors with whom he worked most closely were the leaders of the Luther renaissance, Karl Holl and Reinhold Seeberg. For the former, Bonhoeffer wrote long historical essays on "Luther's Impressions About His Work in the Last Years of His Life, According to His Correspondence from 1540–1546" ("Luthers Stimmungen gegenüber seinem Werk in seinen letzten Lebensjahren, nach seinem Briefwechsel von 1540–1546") and "Luther's Views of the Holy Spirit According to the Disputations of 1535–1545" ("Luthers Anschauungen vom Heiligen Geist

---

[2] Schlatter lectured on the Fourth Gospel and Heitmüller on Paul's letter to the Romans. Bonhoeffer was impressed by Schlatter's so-called "Biblicism" and years later urged his students to read his works and learn from him. See MW I, p. 64.

[3] For one of the best critiques of Heim's theology, read Bonhoeffer's review of the first edition of Heim's *Glaube und Denken* in *Christentum und Wissenschaft*, December, 1932, pp. 441–454.

nach den Disputationen von 1535–1545"). Reinhold Seeberg, who held the chair of systematic theology and who published his two-volume *Christliche Dogmatik* during Bonhoeffer's period of study, was the professor under whom the would-be theologian decided to do his work for the degree of licentiate of theology.[4] For him Bonhoeffer wrote essays on such varied topics as " May a Historical and Pneumatic Interpretation of Scripture Be Differentiated, and How Does This Relate to Dogmatics?" ("Lässt sich eine historische und pneumatische Auslegung der Schrift unterscheiden, und wie stellt sich die Dogmatik hierzu?"); "Reason and Revelation in the Old Lutheran Dogmatics" ("Vernunft und Offenbarung in der altlutherishen Dogmatik"); " Church and Eschatology" ("Kirche und Eschatologie"); " The Doctrine of the Life After Death and of the Last Things in the Old Protestant Dogmatics" ("Die Lehre der altprotestantischen Dogmatik vom Leben nach dem Tode und den letzten Dingen"); and "Frank's Views of the Spirit and of Grace According to His *System of Christian Certainty* and *System of Christian Truth*" ("Franks Anschauungen vom Geist und von der Gnade dargestellt nach dem *System der christlichen Gewissheit* und dem *System der christlichen Wahrheit*").

In 1927, at the age of twenty-one, Bonhoeffer submitted to the Berlin faculty his dissertation, entitled *Sanctorum Communio: a Dogmatic Investigation of the Sociology of the Church* (*Sanctorum Communio: Eine dogmatische Untersuchung zur Soziologie der Kirche*),[5] a work that Karl Barth has called "a theological miracle"[6] and that Ernst Wolf praises as " probably the most discerning and perhaps the most profound handling of the question about the real structure of the church."[7] Already in this work is to be seen the influence of the developing " theology of the Word of God," the chief proponent of which was the Swiss theologian Karl Barth, with

[4] This degree is equivalent to that of doctor of theology and has since been discontinued in favor of the latter.
[5] This work was first published three years later as the twenty-sixth number of the series *Neuen Studien zur Geschichte der Theologie und der Kirche*, edited by Reinhold Seeberg, and in 1954 was republished as Vol. 3 in the Chr. Kaiser Verlag's *Theologische Bücherei* series.
[6] Barth made this comment in a private conversation. Cf. his *Church Dogmatics*, IV, 2, p. 641.
[7] Preface to second edition of *Sanctorum Communio*, p. 5.

whom Bonhoeffer never studied as a student, but whose theological perspectives played an important role in the development of this young German's own theology.

On December 17, 1927, Bonhoeffer publicly defended the following theses, for which the University of Berlin awarded him a promotion to licentiate of theology:

1. The speeches of God in Job, chs. 38 to 41, do not belong to the earliest form of The Book of Job.

2. In Paul the identification of "being in Christ" and "being in the church" stands in an unsolved contradiction to his notion of Christ in heaven.

3. Every evangelical Christian is a dogmatician.

4. The introduction of the concept of potentiality into the Christian idea of God means a restriction of the divine omnipotence.

5. There is no sociological concept of the church that would not be theologically grounded.

6. The church is "Christ existing as community" and is to be understood as a collective person.

7. The church, according to its sociological structure, unites in itself all possible types of social connections and supersedes them in the "fellowship of the Spirit"; this rests on the basic sociological law of representation.

8. Logically considered, faith rests not on psychical experiences but on itself.

9. The dialectic of the so-called "dialectical theology" bears a logical, not a real, character and consequently runs the risk of neglecting the historicity of Jesus.

10. Evangelical preaching and teaching must be dogmatically oriented.

11. There is no Christian teaching of history.

Early in 1928, Bonhoeffer went to Barcelona, where he served a year as vicar [8] in a German-speaking congregation and found in the workaday world of the ministry the synthesis of work and life that

[8] In the German Evangelical Church a *Vikar* is roughly equivalent to an American assistant minister. After a ministerial candidate has completed his formal theological training at the university, he must serve a year of apprenticeship under an experienced pastor. Subsequently he normally must study one or two additional semesters at a *Predigerseminar* of his church.

he had sought for but had never found as a student.⁹ He was especially fascinated by the colorful ritual of the Spanish bullfight, which he regarded as simply an aristocratic expression of an old culture,¹⁰ and he reveled in the daily encounter with men as they are — far from the masquerade of the "Christian world."¹¹ While in Spain he preached every other week, and near the end of his stay he delivered three lectures on the following topics: "Distress and Hope in the Present Religious Situation" ("Not und Hoffnung in der religiösen Lage der Gegenwart"); "Jesus Christ and of the Essence of Christianity" ("Jesus Christus und vom Wesen des Christentums"); and "Basic Questions of a Christian Ethic" ("Grundfragen einer christlichen Ethik").

Bonhoeffer returned to Berlin early in 1929 and worked on his *Habilitationsschrift,* an inaugural dissertation that is required before one can be admitted to a theological faculty in Germany. This work, entitled *Act and Being: Transcendental Philosophy and Ontology in Systematic Theology (Akt und Sein: Transzendentalphilosophie und Ontologie in der systematischen Theologie),*¹² was accepted by the University of Berlin in 1930 and won for Bonhoeffer a position as lecturer in systematic theology, and on July 31, 1930, the new teacher delivered his matriculation address on "The Question About Man in Modern Philosophy and Theology" ("Die Frage nach dem Menschen in der gegenwärtigen Philosophie und Theologie"). Only two weeks earlier he, as a representative of the students, had given a commemorative address on the occasion of the death of his great teacher, Adolf von Harnack. In it he praised Professor Harnack for teaching his students that "truth is born only out of freedom."

Before Bonhoeffer began his teaching duties, however, the Obenkirchenrat (church consistory) granted him a leave of absence in order that he could accept a scholarship to study for one year at Union Theological Seminary in New York City, and in the late sum-

---

⁹ Cf. Bonhoeffer's letter to his friend Helmut Rössler, published in DB: Einf., p. 58.
¹⁰ Bethge's "Einblick in Bonhoeffers Leben und Schaffen" in Gebetbuch, p. 20.
¹¹ DB: Einf., p. 58.
¹² Published in 1931 in the series *Beiträge zur Förderung christlicher Theologie,* 34. Band, 2. Heft, edited by A. Schlatter and W. Lütgert; republished in 1956 as Vol. 5 in the *Theologische Bücherei* series.

mer of 1930 the "brilliant and theologically sophisticated young man"[13] sailed for a new land that was to affect him in a fundamental way.[14] At Union he heard, among others, Professors Webber, Ward, Lyman, and the budding rediscoverer of the doctrine of sin, Reinhold Niebuhr, and he wrote papers on "The Character and Ethical Consequences of Religious Determinism" ("Charakter und ethische Konsequenzen des religiösen Determinismus"); "The Religious Experience of Grace and the Ethical Life"; "The Theology of Crisis and Its Attitude Toward Philosophy and Science"; and "The Christian Idea of God."[15] In general, Bonhoeffer played a significant role in introducing and interpreting the dialectical theology in this center of American theological learning, which was then suffering the frustrations that accompanied the collapse of liberalism.[16]

During his sojourn in this foreign land, however, Bonhoeffer mostly studied, not theology, but America itself! He was passionately interested in becoming acquainted with and understanding this new country, and he succeeded as few foreigners do. He was fascinated by the history and problems of the Negroes in America and spent much time in Harlem gaining firsthand information and making friends and learning spirituals, which he was later to sing in Germany.[17] Eager to see as much of North America as possible, Bonhoeffer and a fellow student, Erwin Sutz, of Switzerland, spent the Christmas holidays in Cuba. After the school year was over in the spring of 1931, he and Sutz and Jean Lasserre, of France, toured all the way across the United States, down into Mexico and back, in an old Oldsmobile that was lent to Bonhoeffer by a family he had met on the ship coming to America.

[13] Reinhold Niebuhr's characterization in the *Union Seminary Quarterly Review*, Vol. I, No. 3, March, 1946, p. 3.

[14] Cf. PFG, p. 119.

[15] "The Christian Idea of God" was published in a somewhat improved form in the *Journal of Religion*, Vol. XII, No. 2, April, 1932, pp. 177–185.

[16] For instance, Paul Lehmann, a fellow student and close friend of Bonhoeffer at Union, attributes to Bonhoeffer a firmer grasp of the substance of Karl Barth's theology and of the fact that this theology was concerned with living issues affecting the understanding and application of Christian faith.

[17] See Bethge's remarks in Gebetbuch, p. 21; for an excellent discussion of the Negro church in America, see Bonhoeffer's "Protestanismus ohne Reformation" in GS I, pp. 323 ff.

In trying to assess the effect of America on this young German, it might be well to say that in the United States he experienced the encounter of his Reformation background with a "Protestantism without Reformation," which was his description of the American church in an article that he wrote in 1939, shortly after his second and final visit to the States. Here there was no state-supported church, but a multitude of self-supporting denominations. Here there was little emphasis on confessional standards and theology, but an active and vigorous church life. Here there was a strict separation of church and state, yet the church was passionately concerned with the social, economic, and political affairs of the state. Here there was little strife among church communions, but a spirit of ecumenicity where cooperation and living together was the rule. Here there were few sharp and personal theological controversies, but an attitude of tolerance and openness toward dogmatic questions that seldom allowed intellectual differences to destroy personal fellowship.[18] Here students lived a life of togetherness in dormitories, which, as Bonhoeffer admits, "produces a strong spirit of comradeship, of mutual readiness to help."[19]

As would be expected, Bonhoeffer was not uncritical of the American church scene. He was particularly disturbed by the lax attitude toward the question of "truth," toward the striving after the right confession; equally disturbing was the superficial, untheological definition of the church and the generally inadequate scientific prep-

---

[18] Bonhoeffer remarks in his "Bericht über meinen Studienaufenthalt in Union Theological Seminary zu New York 1930/31" (GS I, p. 86) that the average American theological student does not feel at home in a dogmatics seminar. Although this must be generally admitted, it must be pointed out that the Continental and the Anglo-Saxon approaches to theological discussions are quite different, a fact that provides a constant source of misunderstanding, especially in ecumenical gatherings. The Continental theologian comes prepared for an *Auseinandersetzung*, in which each party states clearly and positively his personal, premeditated conviction and is willing to defend his position until it is obviously overcome by a more compelling one. On the contrary, an Anglo-Saxon generally understands himself as a part of a team that is to "work out" a solution through friendly co-operation and common consensus — with a generous use of the "royal we." The Continental does not mean to be hostile or unyielding, nor does the Anglo-Saxon intend to be unconcerned or accommodating. Rather, they represent two entirely different methodological approaches to the problem.

[19] *Op. cit.,* p. 85. As a rule Continental universities do not provide housing for students, and, with a few exceptions, students do not live together.

aration of the minister for his spiritual office. Yet his American experience made a deep impression on this European observer. In spite of its theological limitations, the American church life better embodied his own concept of the *sanctorum communio* than its Continental counterpart. The American democratic way disturbed his aristocratic presuppositions. The church's interest in matters of the state placed in question the deep-seated German tendency to divorce the affairs of the church from those of the state. The Anglo-Saxon mania for brevity and clarity suggested that some of the traditional, weighty German concepts might be linguistic subterfuge instead of tools for providing meaningful communication. This is not to suggest that Bonhoeffer was changed theologically by his American experience, for, while appreciative of its many good qualities, he remained basically critical of this "Protestantism without Reformation" to the end, but it is to assert that the year in America broadened his perspectives, whetted his ecumenical appetite, disturbed certain traditional attitudes, and perhaps even provides a clue to some of his later development.

Bonhoeffer returned to Germany in the summer of 1931, and in the fall he began lecturing at the University of Berlin.

B. Theological Exposition

What are Bonhoeffer's basic theological emphases during this formative period? There are two basic works to consider: *Sanctorum Communio* and *Act and Being,* and the leading ideas of both revolve around the concept of the church. *Sanctorum Communio* represents Bonhoeffer's independent contribution to the new theological movement that was struggling to overthrow the "consciousness theology" of the nineteenth century by a fresh understanding of the "Word of God."[20] In his subsequent investigation of *Act and Being,* on the

[20] Bonhoeffer raises the following objections to the idealistic philosophy and consciousness theology of the nineteenth century: (1) Idealism never penetrated to the social sphere, that is, to a proper understanding of person and fellowship. SC 22, 24, 27, 30, 47, 141 ff. (2) Idealism remains immanent, abstract, unhistorical thinking. SC 23, 25, 27, 35 f.; AS 18, 20, 22, 31. (3) Idealism identifies the Holy Spirit with the human spirit, that is, God and man. SC 120, 141 ff.; AS 28, 31. (4) Idealism has no adequate doctrine of sin. SC 27, 36, 155 f., 156 f. (5) Idealism ends with a concept of substance. AS 21, 37.

THEOLOGICAL FOUNDATION 27

other hand, Bonhoeffer not only continues his basic criticism of "liberal" theology, but also critically establishes his own position within the new theological movement itself, which by 1930 was already beginning to split up according to the individual interests of the theologians who had originally joined forces to battle a common foe.[21]

1. "Sanctorum Communio"

In *Sanctorum Communio*,[22] Bonhoeffer attempts an investigation of the social structure of the "fellowship of the saints," in which the insights of social philosophy, with its genetic interest in human sociality, and sociology, with its systematic interest in the structure of empirical communities, are made fruitful for Christian dogmatic thinking about the concept of the church. He is fully aware that the church is *more than* a mere religious fellowship that could be exhaustively interpreted by a phenomenological investigation of its structure, as takes place in sociology of religion, but at the same time he is convinced that Christian doctrines are completely understood only in relation to their social dimension. Thus the use of these two scientific disciplines can help to elucidate the *unique* structure of the church of Jesus Christ, which is known only through the revelation in Christ.

After emphasizing that man is never alone but always in community, the author defines the Christian concept of "person" and establishes the "I-Thou relation" as the basic ontic-ethical social relationship. "Person" presupposes "fellowship," and when this is recognized, one has also said something decisive concerning the concept of God, for the concepts of person, fellowship, and God are inextricably related. The concept of person, says Bonhoeffer, is only applicable to the fallen man, i.e., the man who no longer lives in

[21] In what follows, an endeavor has been made to condense Bonhoeffer's main ideas in these two difficult books. The writer is responsible for rendering the German into English, except for the direct quotations from *Sanctorum Communio*. The official translation of these passages has been furnished by the S.C.M. Press, Ltd., of London. The page references, however, refer to the German text, in keeping with references throughout the remainder of this work.

[22] Latin for "communion of saints" or "fellowship of the saints." Bonhoeffer defends this word order on p. 81, n. 1.

unbroken fellowship with God, but who has acquired the knowledge of good and evil. " Person " arises only when one meets a God-willed " barrier " (*Schranke*) in the concrete " moment " and is placed in the state of ethical responsibility, that is, of decision. The " other " then becomes a " thou," whose claim on me is valid only because the human thou is an image (*Abbild*) of the divine Thou. Bonhoeffer summarizes his thoughts as follows:

The person, with his concrete qualities of life, wholeness and uniqueness, is willed as an ultimate entity by God. The social relationships must thus be imagined as being built up purely interpersonally upon the unique and separate quality of each person. There is no overcoming of person by apersonal mind, no " unity " that might annul the multiplicity of persons. The basic social category is the I-Thou relation. The other man's Thou is the divine Thou. Thus the way to the human thou is the same as the way to the divine Thou, the way of recognition or rejection. In the " moment " the individual again and again becomes a person through the " other." The other man presents us with the same problem of cognition as does God himself. My real relation to the other man is orientated upon my relation to God. But since I first come to know God's " I " in the revelation of his love, so it is too with other men; it is on the basis of this conception that the idea of the church should be developed. Then it will become clear that the Christian person first achieves his true nature when God does not confront him as Thou, but enters into him as I. Hence, in some way the individual essentially and absolutely belongs together with the other, according to the will of God, even though, or even for the very reason that, each is completely separate from the other. (32 f.)

After establishing this basic relationship between person, God, and social being, Bonhoeffer completes the book in three chapters, which deal successively with the state of man before the Fall (the original unbroken society), the state of man in sin (the broken fellowship), and the state of man in the *sanctorum communio* (the Spirit-effected fellowship in the church of Jesus Christ).

The doctrine of man's state previous to his Fall, Bonhoeffer maintains, can give no new theological knowledge, but, like eschatology, belongs in the logic of the totality of dogmatics. It is essentially " hope projected backward " and has the double value of compelling a methodological elucidation of the structure of a complete dogmatics and of making concretely clear the real progress of things from unity through brokenness to unity. The author proceeds to analyze the condition of man in his original state from the viewpoint of social philosophy and sociology. The problem of social philosophy is the question of the relationship between human spirituality or intellectuality (*Geistigkeit*) [23] and sociality. An investigation of the fact that man as spirit is necessarily created in a community and that his general spirituality is bound in a net of sociality reveals a structural openness and a structural closedness of personal being. The openness is manifested by the fact that man knows himself as one who understands, expresses himself, and is understood. Only in reciprocal action with other spiritual persons is self-conscious thinking and willing possible and meaningful — a fact that is confirmed by the social phenomenon of speech and indicates that an " objective spirit " has become active in history.

This structural openness, which threatens to turn into the idea of an apersonal spirit (as in German idealistic philosophy, supremely in Hegel), demands closedness as a correlate. The closedness of personal being is documented by self-consciousness and self-determination as inward actions, separate from everything social. Here the basic synthesis of social and individual being comes to light: the individual personal spirit lives only by virtue of sociality, and the social spirit becomes real only in the individual form. Neither has priority over the other, but both must be held in equilibrium. This means that man is a single person and yet, as a member of a community, is also a collective person. Since an I-Thou relation is also possible between an individual person and a collective person, asserts Bonhoeffer, the positing of the latter in no way limits the basic form of social relationship. Before the eyes of God the structures of the collective person and the single person are the same. Bonhoeffer tells us what this means theologically in the following words:

Man is not conceived of by God as an isolated, individual being, but as a being in natural communication with other men. . . . God created

[23] *Geistigkeit*, which is often translated "spirituality," has to do primarily with man's mental or intellectual capabilities. It is to be differentiated from the word *Geistlichkeit*, which refers to spirituality in the religious sense.

man and woman, each designed for the other. God does not want a history of individual men, but the history of the human community. But neither does he want a community which absorbs the individual within itself — rather a community of individual human beings. In his sight the community and the individual are present at the same moment and rest upon the other. In his eyes the structures of the collective and the individual unit are the same. Upon these basic relationships rests the idea of the religious community and of the church. (52)

Having established that man has been created by God both as an individual and as a member of society, Bonhoeffer now approaches the original state of man from the viewpoint of sociology, which investigates the nature of social connections in general and classifies the concrete types of social volitional acts and social " structures." A social connection presupposes self-conscious, willful action. This means that human community is built on the separateness and diversity of persons and is constituted by the interaction of wills. It finds its unity in what is willed, but because in historical reality there is never total agreement concerning goals and aims, this unity is always a *relative* one. Indeed, even the formal unity of the empirical ecclesiastical community is materially only a relative unity. The inner opposition of individual wills simply must be recognized as a basic law of any community.

Volitional connections can be regarded either from the point of view of the determination of the *direction* of wills or from that of the relation of the *strength* of wills to one another. That is, persons can will with, next to, or against one another, but only the first is meaningful for building up a community. If persons will *with* one another, what is willed can be one of two things: an end in itself or a means to an end. Using Tönnies' terminology,[24] Bonhoeffer designates the result of the former a " fellowship " or " community " (*Gemeinschaft*) and the latter a " society " (*Gesellschaft*). A fellowship is essentially a " fellowship of life " (Scheler) and is usually entered by some concrete, living, unpolished action; it is even able to bear children in its midst as a part of the will of their parents, and it

---

[24] In *Gemeinschaft und Gesellschaft* (Eng. trans.: *Fundamental Concepts of Sociology*, 1940), Tönnies distinguishes between primary and secondary group relationships.

is characterized by an attitude of mutual interest and concern. In a society, on the other hand, persons band together for rational action. Here the union is entered by formal contract and is organized to achieve a definite end; it is in principle without tradition and does not admit immature children. A fellowship is capable of transcending time (*grenzzeitlich*) and, like history, finds its deepest meaning expressed by the formula "from God to God"; but a society is limited to time (*zeitbegrenzt*), and for it the end of history is not a boundary, but a real end.

With respect to the relative strength of wills, Bonhoeffer distinguishes between a relation of force (*Gewaltverhältnis*), in which the ruled will is set in motion mechanically by brute power, and a relation of rulership (*Herrschaftsverhältnis*), in which an understanding of the meaning of what is commanded is presupposed by the one who obeys. The former precludes any possibility of fellowship, whereas the latter may apply to either a fellowship or a society.

Now that he has stated the principles underlying his typology of social communities,[25] Bonhoeffer turns his attention to a difficult concept, which plays an important role throughout the remainder of the book: the "objective spirit." This concept, which is "a discovery of the qualitative thinking that broke through in Romanticism and Idealism" and is especially linked with the name of Hegel, implies that wherever wills unite there arises a "structure" (*Gefüge*), i.e., a third element not previously known, and this happens whether the uniting persons want it or not! This structure is the objective spirit of a community, which exerts an active will in relation to the members of the community, has its own form, leads an individual life beyond the members, and yet is only real through them. The more lively the individual persons, the more powerful the objective spirit. It is involved in reciprocal action with each person and with the community as a whole. In the ongoing life of a community it provides the dynamic point of continuity between past and present. That is, in the objective spirit there works an element that historically presses forward (its historicity) and at the same time an element that strives to extend itself (its sociality).

[25] The author recognizes several other types, such as "the masses," "co-operative societies," etc., but these are not directly relevant to his investigation.

An objective spirit exists in a society as well as in a fellowship, but a fundamental difference in these sociological types comes to light in the fact that a *personal* character can be ascribed to the objective spirit of a fellowship, but not to that of a society. The objective spirit of a society is considered a means to an end, whereas a person can never be a means to an end. Now we can see the importance of the concept of the objective spirit for Bonhoeffer, for it is integrally connected with his concept of the collective person. When a fellowship is viewed as a collective person, its center of action is its objective spirit. Thus the collective person is conceived to be metaphysically autonomous, even though genetically dependent on the individual persons. From this it follows that even in man's original state there was both *unity* and *fellowship:* one not excluding the other, one not identical with the other, but one demanding the other!

What happens when sin enters this picture? When "Adam" rebels and falls from God, he breaks not only the original fellowship between God and man but also that between man and man. In the world of Adam, the world of the old humanity, love is replaced by self-seeking, genuine morality and religion are replaced by legal ordinances and natural religion, the phenomenon of the human conscience arises, and ethical atomism enters history. With all fellowship broken, man is alone; but with the knowledge of his individual guilt before God there comes an insight into the qualitative character of sin, namely, that it has not only individual but also supra-individual significance. Indeed, sin must be considered an act of the individual and, at the same time, an act of the human race, which means that the knowledge of utter loneliness leads to a recognition of utmost solidarity with mankind in sin!

Bonhoeffer readily admits that this twin affirmation of the universality of sin and the guilt of every individual involves the Christian theologian in one of the most difficult logical problems of the whole of dogmatics. How is original sin to be understood? Everything depends, says the author, on finding in the *individual* sinful act the *total* sinful act, and he achieves this understanding by returning to the social philosophical concept of man as simultaneously a single person and a collective person. The concept of guilt must not rest on the biological concept of *genus*. Instead, just the opposite is true, and thereby one penetrates to the concept of an ethical collectivity of the race. The individual is thus established as a self-conscious and self-acting person, which is the presupposition for ethical relevance, and the race is understood as being made up of such persons. In other words, states Bonhoeffer, " in that he is an individual, man is race." When in a sinful action the individual rises up against God and thereby ascends to the ultimate height of spiritual individuality, he performs an action that is simultaneously the action of the human race in his person. With each sin the whole of humanity falls, and none of us is fundamentally different from Adam. Each is the " first " sinner.

The Adamic humanity is a collective person that has sinned as a whole, but as a collective person it can also be viewed as an ethical person, placed in the concrete situation of being addressed by the divine Thou. Here Bonhoeffer offers the illustration of Israel as the " people of God," with whom God acted as if the whole people were an individual. This people had a collective conscience, but when called to repent, not only the collective but also each individual conscience was aroused to decision. In truth the *entire* people never repented, just as the entire church never repents, but God can regard the situation " as if " all the people had repented. He can see the entire people in a few, just as he saw and reconciled the whole of humanity in one. The unique structure of the humanity of Adam is documented by the fact that it breaks up into *many* isolated individuals and yet is *one* humanity which has sinned as a whole. Bonhoeffer summarizes his thoughts in these words:

> The " mankind of sin " is one, even though it consists throughout of individuals; it is a collective person and yet subject to endless fragmentation; it is Adam, as every individual is both himself and Adam. This duality is its nature, annulled only by the unity of the new mankind in Christ. (80)

The entire development thus far has aimed toward the author's consideration of the *sanctorum communio*. In fact, it is only possible and meaningful when viewed from its standpoint, for the *peccatorum communio* (the fellowship of the sinners) lives on in the *sanctorum communio* and cannot be disregarded by the church, which is aware of the eschatological nature of its redemption through Christ. The various trains of thought are now united and ultimately transcended in the concept of the church. First, there were the thoughts about the basic ontic-personal relatedness of human beings to one another, next the discovery of the prevolitional sociality of the human spirit, and then an investigation of the forms of empirical community relationships, which always require *willful* social acts if they are to be called *personal* relationships. Finally, Bonhoeffer described the effect of sin upon relationships and empirical structures. In the concept of the church both the basic relationships and the concrete form of community must change, or better: be created anew.

At the outset of his development of the unique form of fellowship in the church, Bonhoeffer distinguishes two misunderstandings of the church. First, there is a *historicizing* misunderstanding, in which the church is confused with the religious community, and the reality of the new basic relationships, which are ordained by God and lie beyond all "religious motives " leading to empirical fellowship, is overlooked. Second, there is a *religious* misunderstanding, in which the church is confused with the Kingdom of God, and man's historical restriction is not taken seriously. That is, the historicity either becomes objectively divinized, as in Catholicism, or is simply looked upon as accidental, standing under the law of sin and death. Neither of these misunderstandings takes seriously the *reality* of the church, which is at the same time a historical fellowship and a God-established reality. When considering the church, either one can present a sociological morphology of an empirical phenomenon that is in principle not different from any other "religious fellowship," thereby making everything theological superfluous, or one can take seriously the claim of the church to be the church of God, thereby recognizing the fact that establishes it, namely, the fact of Christ, the Word of God. For Bonhoeffer, who emphatically chooses the latter course, the church is a *revelational reality* that must be accepted as such or denied. Before one can speak about the church, one must stand in the church, recognizing its reality and bowing to its claim. That is, only within the church can one find the criterion for judging the church!

What, then, is the church? Bonhoeffer states quite simply that it is "the new will of God with mankind." Since God's will is always directed toward concrete, historical men, the church has its beginning in history, but at the same time it is also consummated, for God's word is always act. Thus the church is already consummated in Christ, just as its beginning is established in him. He is the Cornerstone and the Foundation of the building, and yet the complete fullness of the church is his body. He is the first among many brothers, and yet all are one in him. Here a proper understanding of the preposition " in " becomes critical. We are reconciled *in* Christ, not just by him; the humanity of the new Adam is placed *in* him!

In order that the church, which is eternally realized in Christ, may be actualized in history, the will of God must be continually realized anew — no longer as fundamentally for all men, but in the personal appropriation by individuals. To accomplish this building up of the community of Christ in time, God reveals himself as Holy Spirit. The Holy Spirit is " the will of God which leads individuals into the Christian community, preserves it, and is only active in it," and only in the personal appropriation through the Holy Spirit, that is, in the standing in the actualized church, does one experience his election into the community that is established in Christ. The obstinacy of the concepts " realized church " and " actualized church," " revelation " and " time," " consummation " and " becoming," argues Bonhoeffer, cannot be logically overcome. Revelation not only apparently but *really* enters time, and exactly thereby it explodes the time-form. Bonhoeffer also stresses that the actualization through the Holy Spirit must not be contrasted with the *potentiality* in Christ, but rather with the *reality* in the revelation in Christ, which means that there is no " possibility " that the church, which is consummated and established in Christ, will not be actualized by the Holy Spirit! The eternally consummated church must *necessarily* be actualized in history, for Christ and the new humanity belong together.

The author continues his discussion of the church in four sections which deal with the *realization* of the church in and by Jesus Christ, the *actualization* of the real church through the work of the Holy Spirit, the *empirical form* of the church and the relation between *church and eschatology.*

First, the realization of the church: How does it happen and what are the results? It has already been established that man in sin is in utmost isolation and yet recognizes in his own guilt his bond with all of sinful humanity. This tension between isolation and togetherness, says Bonhoeffer, is abolished in Christ. He explains in these words:

> The thread between God and man, which the first Adam severed, is joined anew by God, and joined in such a way that he reveals his love in Christ. He no longer demands and summons, approaching mankind purely as Thou, but gives himself as an I, opening his heart. The church is grounded in the revelation of the heart of God. (97)

In Christ, mankind is really drawn into God's fellowship. In the one Adam there are many Adams, but there is only one Christ. The difference between Adam and Christ is best shown by their function as *representatives* (*Stellvertreter*).[26] Adam's action is not intended to be representative, but is utterly egocentric. In the Adamic humanity mankind falls anew with every man who becomes guilty, whereas in Christ, mankind is placed in the fellowship of God *once and for all* — a characteristic that belongs to the essence of *real* representation. Just as history is first constituted through death as the wages of sin (Rom. 6:23), so the continuity of temporal history is not empirically but *essentially* broken by the life of love. Death can still separate past and future for our eyes, of course, but no longer for the life of the love of Christ. For that reason the principle of representation or vicariousness becomes fundamental for the community of God in and through Christ. Not " solidarity," which is never possible between Christ and man, but " representation " is the life-principle of the new humanity. Because Christ now bears in himself the new life-principle of this community, he is at the same time established as the Lord of the community. That is, his relation to the church may be expressed in terms of " fellowship " and " lordship."

Bonhoeffer now asserts that because the whole new humanity is

[26] *Stellvertreter* may be translated " representative," " vicar," " deputy," or " substitute." When referring to the work of Christ, Bonhoeffer's meaning includes both representation (on our behalf) and substitution (in our place). In reference to Adam only the former would apply. Depending upon the context, all of the English translations are used in this work. This is also true of the cognate *Stellvertretung*, which is variously rendered as " representation," " vicariousness," " deputyship," and " substitution." No translation is totally satisfactory.

really placed (*gesetzt*) in Jesus Christ, in his historical life the total history of mankind is presented! The history of Jesus Christ, however, is closed to us without his word, and only by taking both together can we read off the past and future of mankind in it. Bonhoeffer now relates the history of Jesus to the realization of the church. This history is integrally connected with that of Israel. Jesus placed himself in the Israelitic community of God and thus under the law. The law had constituted this people whom God had chosen as a collective person, and complete obedience to the law was their proper calling (*Berufung*). However, because Israel perverted the meaning of the law by turning God's call for fulfillment into a claim of each individual on the calling God, the good and holy law became a power of wrath, which destroyed the community and isolated its members. Jesus does not declare himself in solidarity with this community, but in a vicarious and representative way he fulfills the law for all through love and thereby overcomes the Jewish view of the law and establishes a new community in his person. This does not mean, however, that Jesus founded the new community *during his lifetime*. To be sure, his call to repentance, bringing a consciousness of guilt and isolating individuals over against the law, destroyed the old community, and the knowledge of their inability to fulfill the law paved the way for the gift of Jesus: the good news that in love God had brought forth a new community out of this utmost isolation. Yet his love must become complete, and Jesus must fulfill the law even *unto death*. Of course, admits Bonhoeffer, we may look up the events of the Last Supper as the founding of the church, since Jesus then revealed his will to fellowship, but theologically the moment of the rise of the church is to be seen elsewhere.

In his death on the cross Jesus is abandoned by all his disciples and is utterly alone. This solitude, stresses Bonhoeffer, has special theological significance, because Jesus endures the judgment and wrath of God upon the *entire* self-seeking humanity that has perverted the law. He dies in solitude because he is made sin and cursed by the law for *all!* However, the " paradoxical reality of a community of the cross," which hides in itself the seeming contradiction of utmost solitude and the most intimate fellowship, becomes manifest for us in the glorious Easter message of Christ's resurrection, which reveals his death to be the *death of death!* With this event the boundary of history is abolished, the human body is turned into the resurrection body, the humanity of Adam becomes the church of Christ. But in the resurrection the church is realized, not actualized, for Christ has not yet ascended. The time between resurrection and ascension and the time after Pentecost are to be differentiated. In the first, the community lives in Christ as its Lord and life-principle; in the second, Christ lives in the community; in the first, Christ "represents" the community; in the second, the community possesses him as revelation, as Spirit. Therefore, claims Bonhoeffer, the founding day of the *actualized* church of Christ in history remains Pentecost. Just as human fellowship first arose when it became a spiritual (*geistige*) fellowship of wills, and just as the human spirit is active only in sociality, so the church springs up with the outpouring of the Spirit, and so the Holy Spirit is also the Spirit of the community of Christ.

It is Bonhoeffer's opinion that Jesus Christ was essentially as little the founder of the Christian religious fellowship as the founder of a religion. For both the glory belongs to the primitive community, to the apostles. This is why the question of whether or not Jesus founded a church is so ambiguous. Jesus Christ has brought, established, and proclaimed the reality of the new humanity. The primitive message was that God has placed the reality of the church, of the new humanity, in Jesus Christ; the picture of a new religion wooing adherents is from a later day! Not religion, but revelation! Not religious fellowship, but church! Nevertheless, maintains Bonhoeffer, there *is* a necessary connection between revelation and religion, between religious fellowship and church, and this is often misunderstood today. As pioneer (*Bahnbrecher*) and example (*Vorbild*) Jesus is also the founder of a religious fellowship during his earthly ministry, and after the resurrection he restores again the broken fellowship by his appearances to Peter and to the other disciples. For this reason Christ can truly be called the Foundation and the Cornerstone, the sole Ground on which the building of the church rests, the Reality on which the historical "total life" arose.

We are now aware that Bonhoeffer understands the relation of Jesus Christ to the church in a double sense: first, the church is consummated in him, thus time is abolished (*aufgehoben*); second, the church is to build up in time on him as its firm Foundation — he is the historical principle of the church. To Christ belongs, as it were, the vertical dimension or temporal determination of the church, whereas the spatial dimension falls within the province of the working of the Holy Spirit.

What is the principle on which the activity of Christ rests in relation to the new basic social conditions? The crucified and risen Christ is known by the church as the incarnate love of God to men, as the will of God for the renewal of the covenant, for instituting his reign, and therefore for fellowship. Two things still oppose him: time and the evil will. What has once happened (man's apostasy and evil will) remains as happened and cannot be looked upon by the true God as an " as if not," but must be really " undone," i.e., blotted out. This takes place, not through a reversal of time, but through divine punishment and a new creation of the good will. The guilt of man cannot simply be overlooked by God, for in this case the personality of man would not be taken seriously just in its guilt, and so there could be no new creation of person and fellowship. Thus in concrete time Jesus Christ takes on himself the guilt of all humanity and suffers the divine punishment for the sins of all men once and for all. The principle, then, of Christ's activity is that of vicarious representation. Bonhoeffer points out that many people today contest the punishment character of Jesus' suffering, but that Luther laid his greatest emphasis exactly on this aspect! He then gives this terse description of Christ's atoning work:

> Jesus, being himself innocent, takes the others' guilt and punishment upon himself, and as he himself dies as a criminal, he is accursed, for he bears the sins of the world and is punished for them; upon the felon's cross, however, vicarious love triumphs; obedience to God triumphs over guilt, and thereby guilt is in fact punished and overcome. (106)

Can this Christian view of vicarious and substitutionary action be held ethically? Must not the ethical person hold himself responsible for his actions before God and refuse to lay his guilt on another, while he goes free? Bonhoeffer sees the difficulty involved here and readily admits an ethical concept of heroic vicariousness in the human sphere, but he asserts that Christ's action for mankind is a *gift of God,* which rests on his love and is recognized only in the church. What Christ accomplishes for man *cannot* be accomplished by man; therefore God's offer should not be refused. Vicariousness is here no ethical possibility or norm, but alone the divine love for the church; it is not an ethical, but a *theological* concept! The new humanity is united and held by this principle.

Bonhoeffer summarizes the development of his thoughts concerning the realization of the church in these words:

Thus the Christian church is established in and through Christ in the three basic sociological relationships already known to us; his death isolates the individuals, each bears his own guilt, each has his own conscience; in the light of the resurrection the church (*Gemeinde*) of the cross is vindicated and sanctified as one in Christ. The new mankind is focused together in one point, in Jesus Christ; as, however, the love of God through Christ's vicarious action restores communion between God and man, so the human community too once again becomes a living reality in love. (107 f.)

The author now discusses the actualization of the church through the work of the Holy Spirit, and here again, he emphasizes, Jesus Christ must be in the center of things, for he is not someone who has simply made possible the church or who "represents" the church and can now be disregarded. On the contrary, he "is" the church! For God's eyes the church is present in Christ for eternity, so a temporal actualization of the church that did not involve this same Christ would be unthinkable. But how does this happen? Bonhoeffer answers: through the word of the crucified and risen Lord of the community that is promoted by the Spirit! The Spirit is able to work only through this word, which is the word of Christ himself. Christ is in the word; the Christ in whom the church is consummated woos the hearer's heart through the Spirit in order to bring him into his actualized community. Since there is fellowship with God only through Christ, and since Christ is present only in the word in his community, then it follows that there is fellowship with God only in the church. Every individualistic idea of the church shatters on this fact! Bonhoeffer sketches the relation between individual and church as follows:

THEOLOGICAL FOUNDATION 41

The Holy Spirit operates solely in the church as the communion of saints; thus each man who is apprehended by the Spirit must already be a part of that communion. No one, on the other hand, whom the Spirit has not yet apprehended can be in the communion; whence it then follows that the Spirit, by the same act whereby he moves the elect, who are called into the communion established by Christ, brings them into a particular church. Entry into the church forms the basis for faith, just as faith forms the basis for entry. (109)

The word of God is active in the congregation in three different ways. That is, the Holy Spirit works in the church in three differing forms, which are analogous to the three basic sociological relations that were recognized as valid in the church placed in Christ: as Spirit-multiplicity (*Geistvielheit*), Spirit-fellowship (*Geistgemeinschaft*) and Spirit-unity (*Geisteinheit*). We can now ascertain that these are also analogous to the basic sociological realities that were earlier recognized as forming the essential structure of every fellowship. Bonhoeffer emphasizes that both analogies are of greatest importance!

Multiplicity of Spirit in the church means that the Holy Spirit approaches each person as an individual and leads him into "solitude"; that is, he knows his own election and "possesses" all the benefits of Christ completely "for himself." This knowledge of the God-created individuality of the person, which is the point of departure for the predestinarian concept of the church (which in turn threatens to dissolve the church into an individualistic concept of the *numerus praedestinatorum!*) is correctly interpreted, states Bonhoeffer, only when the individual is understood to be elected as a *member of the community*. God sees the community of Christ and the individuals in *one* act of election. Therefore the predestinarian insistence on multiplicity is only a part of the total concept of the church and is meaningful and Christian only in connection with the whole.

Fellowship of Spirit in the church specifies that the Holy Spirit restores fellowship with God by bringing Christ into the heart of sinful man, thus creating faith and love. Faith in Christ, however, means also faith in the community in which he rules, and love means the gift of a new heart, a good will. Thus in the church the fellowship between man and man is also restored; the "other" is no longer essentially a demand but a gift, revelation of his love, and therewith the "thou" is for the "I" no longer law but gospel, and consequently an object of love. The *sanctorum communio,* then, is really a fellowship or community of love, and Bonhoeffer cites the following basic characteristics of Christian love. It is no human possibility, but is only possible out of faith in Christ and the working of the Holy Spirit, which is to say that love is grounded in obedience to the word of Christ. As a volitional act, it has a definite goal; its object is the *real* neighbor (not God *in* the "neighbor," but the *concrete* "thou"). Finally, love knows no boundaries.

Sociologically speaking, the Christian fellowship of love has a completely new kind of structure, in that it is simultaneously a *means to an end* and an *end in itself;* that is, it is organized for the purpose of attaining God's will and yet God's will is precisely this fellowship! Seen from another viewpoint, the *sanctorum communio* is a fellowship only by virtue of God's rulership in it, yet God himself gives man the will to obey his commands and an understanding of what is commanded! This paradoxical fact: that God rules, in that he serves, means that the church involves a relation of rulership rather than one of force. Bonhoeffer characterizes the concrete social actions that constitute the fellowship of love as, first, the God-established structural togetherness (*Miteinander*) of church and church member and, second, the daily ministration (*Füreinander*) of the members and the principle of vicariousness. The first means that the Christian community is so structured by God that it lives *one life;* where one of its members is, there is the whole church in its power, namely, in the power of Christ and the Holy Spirit. The second refers to the concrete acts of love that take place in the community, and Bonhoeffer lists three positive possibilities of how Christians may actualize their love for one another: self-denying, active work for one's neighbor, intercessory prayer, and mutual granting of the forgiveness of sins in the name of God.

Since this section on the *Geistgemeinschaft* is really the heart of the whole book, perhaps it is wise to present the author's summary of his thoughts:

THEOLOGICAL FOUNDATION

The basic ethical relationships, which were torn and severed in the *corpus peccati* (Bernard), are renewed by the Holy Spirit. The community is constituted by the complete self-forgetfulness of love. The relationship between I and Thou is no longer essentially a demanding but a giving one. Each reveals his heart to the other, as a heart subdued by the will of God, even though in actual fact the former basic ethical and social relationships between the I and Thou remain so long as conscience, law, and the wrath of God exist, so long, that is, as we walk by faith and not by sight. The Christian comes into being and exists only in the church. He is dependent upon it, which is as much as to say, dependent upon the other man. Each man sustains the other in active love, intercession, and forgiveness of sins through complete vicarious action, which is possible only in the church of Christ, resting as it does in its entirety upon the principle of vicarious action, that is, upon the love of God. But all are sustained by the church, which consists in this action for one another of its members. The church and its members are structurally together, and act vicariously for each other, by virtue of the church, and this is what constitutes the specific sociological character of the community based on love. In all this the singularity and aloneness of each member are not annulled. (139)

Unity of Spirit in the church means that God has sovereignly established a unity of the church and considers it as a collective person: " Christ existing as community " or " Christ existing as the church " (*Christus als Gemeinde existierend*). This God-willed original synthesis, which is not visible to the eye, should not be confused with harmony or agreement or affinity of souls or even equality. In fact, says Bonhoeffer, the unity is often strongest exactly where the conflict of wills is greatest, where dissimilarities are most pronounced! The decisive New Testament texts do not say: *one* theology and *one* rite, *one* opinion in all public and private matters and *one* standard of life, but: *one* body and *one* Spirit, *one* Lord, *one* faith, *one* baptism, *one* God and Father of us all; varieties of gifts, but *one* Spirit; varieties of service, but *one* Lord; varieties of workings, but *one* God! The unity of the church is established *in Christ,* which means it is a unity given from above, structured " before " all knowing and willing of the members — not ideal, but *real* unity, not " agreement in the Spirit," but " unity of the Spirit." However, this unity in which God looks on the multiplicity of persons as a collective person in no way abolishes the individuality and the fellowship of persons; on the contrary, unity, fellowship, and multiplicity of the Spirit belong together in the church.

Bonhoeffer next investigates the empirical form of the actualized church, which is "in the midst of us." Here he faces the problem of history and the community of the saints, and the problem of the *communio peccatorum* within the *sanctorum communio*. The empirical church is "the organized 'institution' of salvation, in the center of which stands the worship service with preaching and sacrament, or, sociologically expressed, the 'gathering' of the members." As the "historical result of the working of Jesus Christ" (Seeberg), it is the presentation of the *objective spirit* of the Christian community in its becoming and being, in inherited forms and structures, and in present aliveness and activity. The objective spirit, which was earlier recognized as a new spiritual (*geistige*) principle arising in every community, orders and links the volitional activity of the members, assumes definite form, exhibits a temporal and a spatial intention in accordance with its historical and social activity, bears the historical tradition, and repeatedly draws individuals into its activity. The presence of this sociological structure in the empirical church appears to justify its being observed and analyzed as any other religious fellowship, but such a procedure, insists Bonhoeffer, is based upon a complete misunderstanding. "Empirical church" is not at all identical with "religious fellowship," but, as a concrete, historical community in the relativity of its forms and in the imperfection and unpretentiousness of its appearance, it is the body of Christ, the presence of Christ on earth, because it has his word! Therefore, the objective spirit of the church, unlike any other, claims to be the bearer of the historical activity of Jesus Christ and the social activity of the Holy Spirit!

How, then, are we to understand the relation of the Christ-Spirit and the Holy Spirit of the *sanctorum communio* to the objective spirit of the empirical community? Because of the presence of human imperfection and sin in the latter, they clearly cannot be identified. On the other hand, if one interprets the empirical form of the church as simply sinful, or if, because of its imperfect character, one looks on it as a mere apparition of the ideal church of the future or as even unattainable in this world, then one has not reckoned seriously with its historical character. The first not, because Christ *entered history,* and so the church is his presence in history, which means that church history is the hidden center of world history; the second not, because the church is Christ existing as community, and regardless of the questionableness of the empirical form, it remains church as long as Christ is present in his word. Nevertheless, the fact that the church is the church of the word, that is, of faith, means that sin remains in the Christian community. Here we still walk in faith, which means we see only our sin and believe on our holiness! The fact that the *peccatorum communio* lives on in the *sanctorum communio,* the fact that the empirical church is stamped by the accidents of history and is thoroughly capable of error, the fact that there perhaps are many unpredestined individuals in the Christian community — all these facts forbid an identification of the objective spirit with the Christ-Spirit and Holy Spirit.

What, then, is the positive relationship? Bonhoeffer explains it in terms of *function.* Christ and the Holy Spirit *use* the historically given forms of the objective spiritual life in the upbuilding of the empirical church: the historical tendency of the Christ-Spirit works in the form of the objective spirit, and the Holy Spirit uses the objective spirit as the bearer of his social activity. But both confirm their presence to the church solely through the word, which means that the ever-changing, imperfect, sinful objective spirit of a human " religious fellowship " must *believe* that it is the church, " Christ existing as community," *sanctorum communio!* The identity cannot be confirmed historically and will remain invisible until the *eschata.* Yet a beginning has already been made, in that the Holy Spirit uses the objective spirit as the bearer of certain *visible* forms that he himself guarantees to be efficacious. These forms are preaching and the administration of the sacrament. However, the objective spirit does not bear these " as one carries a sack on his back," but it becomes sanctified by its own burden. That is, " it carries them in its heart! " Thus, the objective spirit is a means to an end and an end in itself, which accords with the previously given definition of the fellowship of love. It is the object of the Holy Spirit's work and the means of the same — a fact that again confirms the impossibility of their identification.

If this material distinction is to be held, however, is it possible to speak any longer of *one* church? Can the empirical church and the true (*wesentliche*) church logically and sociologically be forced under one concept? This question, says Bonhoeffer, sets the concept of the " true church " in its proper relation to the concept of the Kingdom of God. Both include, according to their essence, only those persons who are predestined, and both are concerned with the subjection of mankind to God's reigning and redeeming will. However, the Kingdom of God encompasses *all* the predestined and is from eternity to eternity, whereas the church involves only those elected in Christ as community and thus has its beginning in history. Consequently, Bonhoeffer prefers to call the church the " Kingdom of Christ." Since this is among us in a concrete, historical form, however, one must reckon with the presence of unpredestined " members " in the midst of the true church. That is, we must reckon the church as a " national " church (*Volkskirche*), not as a " voluntary " or " gathered " church (*Freiwilligkeitskirche*). But can a church, which according to its essence as a human fellowship is a fellowship of wills, be at the same time a national church? This, states Bonhoeffer, is the sociological formulation of the problem of the empirical church!

The solution to this problem is found in the nature of the " word " itself. In the first place, with the preaching of the word the *sanctorum communio* reaches out beyond itself and addresses all those who have the *possibility* of belonging to it. Furthermore, the existence of a national church underscores the impossibility of "separating the wheat from the tares " as long as we live " between the times." Nevertheless, a national church demands and repeatedly establishes a voluntary church, because the reaching out of the word continually calls forth the true church. That is, the proclamation of the word continually leads to the realization of the possible. Thus the logical and sociological unity of the national and the voluntary church, of the empirical and the true church, of the " visible " and the " invisible " church, is established by the word. However, stresses Bonhoeffer, there comes a time when the church may no longer be a national church, and this is when the church in its national form can no longer see the means of penetrating to a voluntary church. The decision in regard to such an emergency situation, however, is an ecclesiastical-political one and is not grounded dogmatically.

We have spoken of "the" empirical church, but is there such a phenomenon at all? Viewed historically, the church appears to be made up of countless individual congregations and the idea of "the empirical church" seems to be a static abstraction. The New Testament, which calls individual communities "body of Christ" and yet pictures all who are connected to Christ as one body with him, presents only the problem, not the answer. The answer to the problem, contends Bonhoeffer, is given by Zwingli in his concept of the "universal church" (*allgemeine Kirche*), which encompasses all individual churches. This accords with Bonhoeffer's own view that the many individual congregations do not stand atomistically next to one another, but are really united by God as a total community. In this total community, which is the "sum" of all the places where the gospel is proclaimed, there is one Spirit, one Word, one body, but real fellowship, *sanctorum communio*. The concept of the body of Christ in the New Testament, then, is not simply that of organic corporeality, where each individual congregation would only be a member of the body, i.e., of the universal church, but it refers to the presence of Christ and the working of the Spirit in his community. That is, the body of Christ is not a structural but a *functional* concept in relation to the working of Christ. Christ is completely in each individual and yet is only one; on the other hand, he is completely in no one and is possessed completely only by all together. Thus every individual congregation is Christ's body, and yet there is only one body; again, only the total community can actualize all the relationships in the body of Christ. This accords, of course, with the earlier established social-philosophical notion of the individual as a single person and a collective person at one and the same time.

Bonhoeffer next turns to the sociological forms and functions of the empirical church and discusses in sequence the assembly for worship, the *sanctorum communio* as the bearer of the "office," the sociological significance of cultic actions, and the sociological problem of the care of souls (*Seelsorge*).

A Christian community is held together by its gathering around the word. This means that the concrete function of the empirical church is the divine service of preaching and the administration of the sacraments. Preaching is an "office" (*Amt*) of the community and therefore *presupposes* an assembly. Preaching is a God-decreed activity of the community for the community, and the congregating of the community to hear the proclamation of the word of God is simply self-evident! Gathering for worship service, then, belongs to the essence of the church, for it is the will of God through which he realizes his will, which is to extend his reign over the social connections of men. Subjectively seen, individuals are moved to assemble for worship by the recognition that God wills to speak in the empirical church, that is, by the consciousness of belonging to the community that bears the preaching office and that hears the preached word. Thus the assembly is organically related to the life of the individual; indeed, says Bonhoeffer, "the assembly of the faithful remains our mother."

The word in the church is concretely present in the Bible and in the preached word, but *essentially in the latter*. That is, the Spirit has not bound himself substantially with the word of the Bible, whereas a definite promise of fruitfulness is attached to the word preached in the *sanctorum communio* (Isa. 55:11). Both the word of the Bible and the word of preaching remain the words of man, unless they are made God's word by the Holy Spirit. Preaching, which does not repeat past events but speaks to the present, is essentially a product of the objective spirit of the community, but precisely to this contingent, imperfect, sinful spirit is the promise given to be able to proclaim the word of God. On the basis of this promise, then, the Christian community is the bearer of an "office" of preaching and administration of sacraments, but the person who fills this office is completely independent of the community. This means that it is always possible for one who does not belong to the *sanctorum communio* and never will belong to it to preach! But because he uses the forms of the objective spirit, the Holy Spirit is also able to use him as an instrument of his activity. In the evangelical church there is no theurgy and no magic authority of the office or the individual holding it, which is simply another way of asserting the concept of the priesthood of all believers. The office rests on the community, and the fact that community, office, and assembly belong together indicates that "God wants to go through history with his holy people."

Preaching and the administration of the sacraments of Baptism and the Lord's Supper constitute the main "cultic" actions of the Christian community. A one-sided emphasis on any one of the three produces discernible sociological differences in the community concerned, although in the evangelical understanding of the church all three stand in necessary connection with the word, since the church is built on the word. Bonhoeffer delineates the differences in this way:

Whereas baptism characterizes the congregation's wish to spread God's Lordship as widely as possible (that is, it characterizes for us the fact of the national church), the congregation gathered for preaching is composed of those personally placed before the decision of accepting or rejecting the divine gift; it is both a national and a gathered church. At the Lord's Supper the church presents itself purely as a gathered church, as a confessing congregation, and is required and acknowledged as such by God. It does not, however, represent the pure *sanctorum communio;* it is the smallest of the three concentric, sociologically distinct circles, and is both the source of the church's effectiveness and equally on the other hand the focal point of all its life. This two-sidedness makes for its vitality, which is the vitality of the church in being at once the point at which God is aiming, and his instrument. (186)

For Bonhoeffer, evangelical baptism is infant baptism (*Kindertaufe*). Since children do not yet have faith (not even as *fides directa*) and yet the sacrament demands faith, the *objective spirit* of the community assumes the role of the subject of the faith and through baptism receives the child into itself. Thus baptism, which, on the one hand, is an efficacious divine action in the gift of grace by which the child is placed in the community of Christ, also involves the demand that the child *should remain* in the Christian community. Only then can the community carry its children "like a mother." The Lord's Supper is for Bonhoeffer a gift of God to each individual; further, however, it is a gift of God to the Christian community; and, finally, it is an obedient, symbolic human act before God. In the Lord's Supper lies the basic source for all that Bonhoeffer said earlier about the fellowship of love. Christ's spiritual presence is not only symbolized but is *really* given to the community, and with him are given all the priestly rights and duties that are the basis for brotherly love.

In the discussion of the sociological problem of the care of souls Bonhoeffer's strict differentiation between church and religious fellowship again becomes manifest. Every Christian brother is a "minister" with both a *priestly* and an *advisory* relationship to other members of the church. The concept of the advisory function brings forth a new problem. What meaning can the faith of another have for a Christian? What help is the "cloud of witnesses," example and model, the history of the church, tradition? An evangelical understanding must consider all of these ultimately as identical questions. Not only is Christ a gift and an example for men, but also one person is for another. Although a man standing before God must decide for himself what he has to do, it is likewise necessary that he seek the advice of another when faced with important decisions. This is a recognition of the concrete, historical relationship in which a person stands. It is simply a fact that man is surrounded by models, and he should use them, not to transfer the responsibility for his own action, but that he might see the open possibilities, on the ground of which he himself freely decides. It is God's will that man should use every possibility that can help him to a right decision.

This advisory function should not be slighted, but it likewise should not be confused with the Christian's priestly function, which is to pronounce the forgiveness of sins in the name of Jesus Christ. The priestly rights and duties indicate the *absolute* meaning of one for another as established by the idea of the church, whereas the advisory function accords with the *relative* meaning of one for another as established by the historicity of man. An overlooking of this difference, warns the author, results in a misunderstanding of the whole evangelical concept of the church.

In a section on authority and freedom in the empirical church Bonhoeffer distinguishes between the *absolute* authority of the *word of God,* which demands absolute obedience, i.e., absolute freedom, and the *relative* authority of the *church,* which demands relative obedience, i.e., relative freedom. The concept of the relative authority of the church is annoying to many Protestants, who protest that it endangers the freedom of conscience, but Bonhoeffer points out that exactly in the recognition of the necessity of this concept lies the boundary of the Reformation gospel over against all enthusiastic "sects." The church must not only preach, but it must also speak authoritatively on matters that serve to maintain the purity of its word and on important current events. It has the right to demand a relative obedience of its members, a *sacrificium intellectus,* and perhaps even in certain cases a *sacrificium conscientiae.* Only God can tell an individual the moment when the absolute authority of the word compels him to rebel against the relative authority of the church, and such a rebellion can never be an arbitrary action, but only an act of obedience that is executed in the deepest attachment to the church and to the word living in it.

Bonhoeffer has now reached the point of trying to classify the church as a sociological type. Like a society, the church is a means to an end, namely, the attainment of God's will. Like a fellowship, the church is an end in itself, i.e., just this fellowship is the fulfillment of the will of God. But unlike both, the church is a fellowship of the Spirit, that is, the Spirit-founded and Spirit-effected fellowship and community of God, " Christ existing as community," the presence of Christ. The fact of the Spirit introduces an inner antinomian factor into the structure of the church, simultaneously expressing its transcendent foundation and characterizing it as a community that is ruled rather than coerced. The church, then, is both a means to an end and an end in itself, and its uniqueness exists in the fact that these elements are united by God, in that he gives himself as the means to his purpose and thereby creates a fellowship existing in Spirit-effected love. This means, however, that its uniqueness can only be comprehended theologically, never morphologically-sociologically. The fellowship of the Spirit, with its life-principle of love, is a form of fellowship *sui generis;* it exists in faith in the word of God, which means that its structure is grounded in the Christian notion of revelation.

Since the *sanctorum communio* is bound to nothing but the word of God and is found wherever the word is preached, according to the promise of Isa. 55:11, Bonhoeffer concludes that the Weber-Troeltsch distinction between church and sect is completely untenable, that no genetic explanation of the church is adequate, and that even in the sociologically peculiar Roman Catholic Church (an institution in which the Spirit is bound to the "office," not to the community) the presence of the *sanctorum communio* is to be believed by virtue of the activity of God's word.

In a discussion of the relation between faith in the *sanctorum communio* and the "experience of the church," the author attempts to justify the scientific method of his investigation, to clarify decisively the problem of "church and religious fellowship," to warn against the all-too-great statements being issued at that time about the "experience of the church," and to call for dogmatic reflection. The mere fact, asserts Bonhoeffer, that we have been able to form a concept of the church over against that of the religious fellowship indicates that a specifically Christian sociology is not grounded in faith as experience, but in faith in so far as it grasps realities. The method is justified, then, because church can only be substantially understood as a *divine act,* and that means in the confession of faith, and only on the ground of this as "experience." The church is not "made" by the experience of fellowship, but is established by God in Christ before all experiencing.

Referring specifically to statements being made by people connected with the German Youth Movement at that time, Bonhoeffer says that there is too much talk of "will to church" and "experience of the church," too many uninformed utterances that confuse a romantic idea of fellowship with the communion of the saints. "Our time is not poor in experiences," remarks Bonhoeffer, "but in faith." However, "to believe on the church" does not mean to believe on an invisible church or the Kingdom of God in the church as a *coetus electorum,* but it means to believe that God has made the concrete, empirical church, in which the word is preached and the sacrament is administered, into his own community, that it is the body of Christ, the presence of Christ in the world, and that, according to promise, God's Spirit is active in it. Bonhoeffer expresses what he means in terms of the classical statement concerning the church in the Apostles' Creed:

We believe in the church as *una,* for it is " Christ existing as community " and Christ is the one Lord over those who are all one in him; as *sancta,* since the Holy Spirit is at work in it; and as *catholica,* since as the church of God it has its call over the whole world, and is present wherever God's word is preached in the world. We believe in the church not as an unattainable ideal, or one which has still to be attained, but as a present reality. (210 f.)

The author ends his investigation with a section on "church and eschatology," and here he emphasizes that in the church we walk by faith, not by sight. This means that history cannot bring the final solution to things; not even the end of history can do that. The meaning of history is not that it progressively develops, but that "each epoch is directly related to God" (Ranke). The course of church history, claims Bonhoeffer, teaches fundamentally no more concerning eschatological meaning than any presently understood moment. There are two basic strivings that oppose each other in history and will continue with ever-increasing power: the endeavor of the *sanctorum communio* to penetrate all human community life and the resistance to this penetration. It would not be correct to characterize these opposing forces as the "empirical church" and the "world," for the cleft runs right through the middle of the church. Instead, the final antagonists in history will remain the *sanctorum communio* and the *antichrist.*

Christian eschatology, says Bonhoeffer, is essentially *community eschatology.* It is concerned with the consummation of the church and the individuals in it, and it separates into thoughts about *judgment* and *eternal life.* The question is: what happens to a human fellowship in the judgment? Judgment takes place on persons — not just on individual persons, but also on collective persons. Both "fellowships" and "societies" are judged, but only fellowships are judged as collective persons; societies, which are limited to time, do not continue beyond history, so their members are judged only as individuals. How God can reject a collective person and yet accept individual persons out of it, and vice versa, remains a mystery to us, but that fellowships are judged as collective persons is known in the New Testament. Here Bonhoeffer cites such cases as Chorazin, Bethsaida, Capernaum, Matt. 11:21 ff., and the words to the churches in Rev., chs. 2 and 3, especially 3:10 and 3:16. In the Last Judgment every person comes before God's judgment, some perhaps for the first time, and confronted with God's holiness and their own guilt, each one becomes "alone." Nevertheless, there is a loneliness before the *grace* of God and a loneliness before the *wrath* of God. It is eternal death to exist in the loneliness of the wrath of God, cut off from ethical communication with man and God, and at the same time conscious of one's guilt and of what one is missing. In the judgment of wrath God recognizes as free the wills that resist to the end. The one who wants only himself has his wish granted, but at the same time he experiences the fact that he has thereby died spiritually, for man *lives* only in fellowship with other men and with God. On the other hand, the loneliness of the judgment of grace signifies the judgment of faith in the eternal community, the final decision. The meaning of this moment is that the loneliness would be completely overcome in the community, that there would be individual personality only in the reality of the community. In the moment in which man must in solitude live through the unspeakable distress of painful repentance before the eyes of God, he steps completely into the community of Christ, which is bearing him.

It is Bonhoeffer's opinion that the deepest meaning of the idea of the resurrection of the body does not lie in the necessity of all men, Christian and godless, to stand in the Last Judgment, but lies rather in the Christian concepts of person and fellowship. In the Christian person body and soul are bound together in indissolvable unity, and concrete fellowship is only possible by virtue of man's corporeality. Thus the new spiritual body of the resurrection is the surety and the condition for the eternal fellowship of personal spirits.

Although he must speak of eternal life and eternal death, Bonhoeffer says that he is unable to avoid the idea of apocatastasis or universal salvation. Every man is conscious of his contribution to the guilt of the whole of humanity, and "there is no justification or sanctification of man thinkable if he may not be certain that God would also draw to himself all those in whose guilt he is guilty." Yet Bonhoeffer admits that this sort of talk remains here only hope and can never enter the system.

In eternal life with God there is fellowship of the Spirit, which demands a communion of whole persons in spiritual corporeality. Thus all mystical notions of a final melting into the All-Person of

God are stymied from the beginning. Creator and creature remain separated persons, just as the creatures remain separate from one another; yet all together they form the mighty unity of the community of God, which is grounded and kindled in mutual love. The I and Thou are no longer foreign, but now reveal their hearts to each other. Now the objective spirit of the community has really become the Holy Spirit, the experience of the "religious" community is really the experience of the church, and the collective person of the church is really "Christ existing as community." Out of the Kingdom of Christ has come the Kingdom of God, and the *ministerium Christi,* of the Holy Spirit and of the word, is now at an end. Christ himself delivers over his community to the Father, and God is all in all. Not *ecclesia triumphans,* but Kingdom of God; no longer repentance and faith, but serving and beholding! The victory is won, the Kingdom has become God's. That, concludes Bonhoeffer, is the hope of today's church, of the *sanctorum communio!*

2. "Act and Being"

Act and Being (*Akt und Sein*) represents Bonhoeffer's attempt to elucidate the unique character of the Christian way to knowledge by relating it to the two opposing philosophical solutions that have influenced the understanding of revelation in recent theology: the transcendental, which emphasizes "act," and the ontological, which emphasizes "being." The problem with which modern theology is struggling, namely, the problem of whether revelation is to be interpreted in terms of act or in terms of being, is a problem bequeathed by Kant and idealism. It involves the formation of pure theological concepts, the "objectivity" of the idea of God, an adequate theory of cognition, and a determination of the relation between "God's being" and the intellectual act comprehending this. It should be theologically interpreted what "God's being in the revelation" means and how it is known, how faith as act and revelation as being are related and whether revelation is given to man only in the execution of an act (*Aktvollzug*) or if there is a "being" in the revelation for him. In short, whether one begins with a concept of act or a concept of being makes a decisive difference in one's entire theology; it affects the doctrines of the knowledge of God, of man, and of sin and grace. Bonhoeffer's avowed purpose is " to bring the concern of pure transcendentalism and the concern of pure ontology into unity in ' churchly thinking.' "

The placing together of act and being is not identical with that of consciousness and being, because the latter concepts do not exclude one another. Even to consciousness (*Bewusst-sein*) belongs a predicate of being, just in being conscious. Act should be thought of as pure intentionality, completely foreign to being. Act denotes relationship, confinement to consciousness, discontinuity, whereas being suggests remaining in itself, transcendence of consciousness, continuity. Because act takes place consciously, it is necessary to differentiate between direct consciousness (*actus directus*) and consciousness of reflection (*actus reflexus*). In the former, consciousness is " directed toward " something external to itself; in the latter, it is able to be objectively conscious of itself by reflection on itself. It is not that act offers no material for reflection, but only that act, with its intrinsic intentionality, is always already broken by reflection. For this reason, act can never be " found " by reflection. This difference, states Bonhoeffer, is of decisive importance for theology. Being as *being*-conscious is also not fundamentally exhausted in being-*conscious*.[27] When taking place in consciousness, act is a temporal, psychic happening, but act is as little understood when it is " explained " as a happening in time, as being is understood when it is defined as an " extant." [28] Act can never be " explained," only " understood " (Dilthey), just as being can never be " proved," only " exhibited."

The author's investigation of the act-being problem is divided into three parts. The first is an inquiry into the possibility of using previously reported solutions of the problem in the Christian concept of God and of revelation. These are tested on the self-understanding of man underlying each solution, and it is on this accompanying

---

[27] Here the play on words is difficult to convey in English. The German equivalent of " consciousness " is *Bewusstsein*, which Bonhoeffer hyphenates to emphasize his point, i.e., Bewusst-*sein* is not exhausted in *Bewusst*-sein.

[28] The term Bonhoeffer uses here is *Seiendes*, which means literally " that which is " or " the extant." It is differentiated from *Sein*, which is consistently translated " being," as the true is from truth or the real is from reality. There are many things that are true, but the truth is the same in one and all. There are many things that *are*, but the category of " being " applies to one and all.

self-understanding that the possibility of using a pure transcendental or a pure ontological supposition in theology is wrecked, for in both cases the understanding proves to be that of the autonomous ego, which understands itself out of itself and empowers itself. The contingent character of revelation precludes the possibility of the self's understanding itself outside of its relation to revelation, and for this reason revelation must yield its own theory of knowledge. In the second part Bonhoeffer shows that, because neither an interpretation according to act nor an interpretation according to being can do full justice to the whole of revelation, the concept of revelation must be thought in the concretion of the concept of the church, that is, in sociological categories, in which the act-interpretation and the being-interpretation encounter each other and are drawn into one. The dialectic of act and being is known theologically as the dialectic of faith and church — one not to be thought without the other, one "sustained" (*aufgehoben*) [29] in the other. The theological concepts of "object" and "knowledge" turn out to be determined by the sociological category of "person" and must be transformed accordingly. The sphere of "*a* being," of "there is" (*es gibt*), of hardened concepts of being, is brought into movement through the sociological category. Concepts of being, to the extent that they are won from the revelation, remain determined by the concepts of sin and grace, "Adam" and Christ. In theology, says Bonhoeffer, there are no primarily creational, ontological categories that are separate from these. This idea of "being" (of sin and of man in sin, of grace and of man in grace) is carried through by the author in the final part in a further concretion of the concept of the church. The investigation ends with an interpretation of "being in Christ" as determined by past and future, reflection and intentionality. The past is "pre-

[29] The verb *aufheben* is very difficult to translate. Its basic meaning is "to raise," "to lift up," or "to elevate," but this can assume either a positive or a negative interpretation. Positively, it can mean "to preserve," "to sustain," "to maintain," "to support," "to nourish." Negatively, it can mean "to abolish," "to destroy," "to negate," "to annul." In Hegel's philosophy the word denotes both a negation and a preservation in a higher synthesis. As a general rule, one should begin with the basic meaning and then ask whether a positive or negative connotation is involved. In *Akt und Sein*, Bonhoeffer usually uses *aufheben* in its positive meaning, e.g., "thinking is *preserved* in being" or "faith is *sustained* in the church" (never act without being, never being without act!).

served" in the future; the reflection is "preserved" in the intentionality. The man of conscience becomes a child.

At the beginning of his investigation of the transcendental solution to the epistemological problem and the ensuing self-understanding of man, the author distinguishes between a pure transcendental philosophy, as Kant endeavored to develop it, and the transcendentalistic philosophy that emerged in post-Kantian idealism.[30] The two have in common the fundamental belief that the ego can attain self-understanding by reflecting upon itself, but a marked difference arises in their attitude toward the transcendent, i.e., the object of thinking.

For pure transcendentalism, thinking is always "between" and "in relation to" transcendence. The object of thought must be posited as transcendent of thinking, i.e., as a "thing in itself" that does not come into the power of the thinking ego. Knowledge of an external reality is only possible through a synthesis that is grounded and executed in the unity of the transcendental apperception, a synthesis that logically *precedes* the empirical and must be thought a priori. Knowledge is valid, then, not through some thought agreement of the knowledge with the object of knowledge, but through the necessity of the synthesis a priori. Thus the question of being, that is, the question of the reality of the object of thought external to the ego, is never raised, for being exists only in the *act* of being *thought*. With this, Kant has gone beyond the "dogmatism" of the question of being by resolving the concept of being into the concept of act. Truth is only in pure act. Being "is" only "in relation to" knowing, and knowing is "in relation to" transcendence.

For Kant, then, an understanding of human existence is a kind of knowing oneself "in relation to." The self can never come to itself, because then it would no longer be "in relation to" a transcendent and therefore no longer pure act. The self cannot be thought, because it is the condition of thinking. It is never an object, but synthesis a priori, i.e., before the object. Here, asserts Bonhoeffer, a deep

---

[30] Bonhoeffer is fully aware that his interpretation of Kant and idealism is stylized. The historical Kant was never a *pure* transcendental philosopher, although Bonhoeffer believes that this is what he *wanted* to be. But systematic questions are under discussion here, not historical ones. Cf. p. 13, n. 1; 16, n. 6.

THEOLOGICAL FOUNDATION 59

contradiction is revealed. The self, as the condition of thinking, is logically *prior to* thinking, but because all knowledge concerning the self is wrought by thought, *thinking is prior to the self*. This means that thinking drives to the boundary of the "nonobjective," without which there is nothing objective, simply because it is the condition of the conditioned. It is the boundary of existence out of which man lives, since the unconditioned (his existence) is at any given time before him, but just always already past when he tries to understand it.

A double attitude is possible toward this "drive to the boundary" in the concept of the self and of thinking. One is for the self, which is attempting to think about itself, to see itself as its limitation, to recognize itself as the *boundary point* of philosophizing, and Bonhoeffer believes that this accords with Kant's intention. The other possibility is for thinking to ignore its limitation, raise itself to a position of lordship over the nonobjective, and make the thinking self the *point of departure* for philosophizing. This, says Bonhoeffer, is the turn from Kant's transcendentalism to post-Kantian idealism, and its consequence is the loss of both reality and transcendence, the one through the other! The transcendent is drawn into the thinking self, so that now there is a pure monism, a system of pure transcendence or of pure immanence, which are really the same thing.

That the objects of my knowledge (the outside world) are "in relation to me" is a transcendental judgment; that they are "through me" is idealism. Whereas the "in relation to" of pure transcendentalism recognized a transcendent to which the aspect of being still adhered and which really stood opposite the thinking self, the substitution of "through" in idealism expresses the authority of reason over transcendence and asserts that there is no being independent of the self. Thus the concept of being is *completely* resolved into the concept of act. The ego now creates its own world. Human existence is contemplation, the home-coming of the eternal ego to itself. Spirit is understood out of spirit, and so man, who is spirit, can understand himself out of himself — one may even say "out of God," as long as God is in me, as long as God is the unconditioned personality that I am! All concepts of being have apparently been destroyed, and a purified concept of act rules epistemology and anthropology. With this apparent radicalization of the transcendental supposition, however, something surprising happens. The spirit, which never comes into the embarrassing situation of being " in relation to " a transcendent, remains alone, by itself. It is substance, that is, absolute being. In idealism, especially in Hegel, a viewing together of act and being that would satisfy the demands of the problem appears to have been reached — if, adds Bonhoeffer, the philosopher himself did not shatter on the reality of his own existence. Hegel wrote a philosophy of the angels, but not of human existence! The concrete man is simply not in full possession of the Spirit. The idea that he can find God simply by thinking on himself can only lead to the bitterly disappointing discovery of his aloneness.

In idealism, then, the world is " through " the ego, which means that the ego and God the Creator exchange roles, and God is somehow placed in unity with the ego itself. God " is " only so long as I think. In transcendentalism the ego and God remain limit-concepts " in relation to " which thinking (human existence) always " is." God can never be objectively knowable. But if this is so, then what is the nature of the transcendent, i.e., God? How can the reason define its boundary over against an *unknown?* Even if it is the free decision of the practical reason, it remains the self-chosen boundary of the reason. It is this innermost obscurity which leads to the recognition that even in transcendentalism the reason remains alone! In the final analysis, the reason does not understand itself " in relation to " the transcendent, but " in relation to " itself. Therefore, in both transcendentalism and idealism the ego remains imprisoned in itself. This, says the author, is what the early Protestant theologians meant by the " corruption of the reason." It is the self's ontic inversion into itself, the *cor curvum in se* (Luther). Thus, neither out of transcendentalism nor idealism can man win an understanding of himself, nor can he find God. Transcendentalism ends with a nonobjective, unknowable God, while idealism ultimately identifies God and man. Neither of these solutions satisfies the demands of the Christian notion of revelation and therefore neither can provide a Christian theory of cognition.

Bonhoeffer now turns to the ontological attempt to solve the act-being problem. It is the concern of a pure ontology to show the priority of being over consciousness and to disclose this being. Ontology wants to say that there is something real existing outside of consciousness, outside of the logical sphere and the limits of reason. The real problem of ontology, says Bonhoeffer, lies in its conception. In the uniting of *logos* (reason) and *on* (being), two equally strong claims encounter each other. Ontology can be a science only by one, here the logos, abandoning its claim or by one moving into the other. But that can take place only in a thought-movement (*Denkbewegung*), so that the thought-movement itself must somehow actually belong to being. Here, states the author, the step in modern philosophy from Husserl-Scheler to Heidegger is sketched.

If the logos really abandons its claim, then it abandons its system of immanence. The question is only whether this is an executable possibility for it per se. The logos has a way of apparently relinquishing itself, in order to recover itself all the more powerfully! The attempt to think of thinking itself as being remains the final crisis in which transcendentalism, idealism, and ontology separate. The first thinks of thinking " in relation to " transcendence, idealism takes transcendent being into thinking, and ontology leaves being in full freedom from thinking, gives it priority over thinking. Pure ontology must therefore remain a *critical* science that does not turn being into a givenness (*Gegebenheit*), because being transcends the given (*a* being). Thinking must again and again be " sustained " (*aufgehoben*) in being. Here the logos must renounce the usurpation of creative power. Out of pure spontaneity must come, for the sake of the freedom of being, receptivity. That is, out of creative thinking comes the beholding, the pure intuition. From here, however, it is only a step to *systematic* ontology, which opens up being itself to the beholding. But here there is clearly a retreat behind the transcendental and idealistic formulation of the question. In the final analysis, thinking is able to behold the " eternal essences," i.e., being, in *a* being.

Bonhoeffer now analyzes successively the ontological solutions of Husserl, Scheler, Heidegger, and Thomism, represented specifically by Przywara, and he concludes that none of these is able to solve the act-being problem in a way that does justice to the Christian concept of revelation. Husserl's phenomenology, which " brackets " existence from the outset, ultimately understands the event of knowledge as creative, as somehow "begetting" the object of knowledge. Being as *existentia* is resolved into *essentia,* and therewith is sealed the step to idealism. Scheler, who took up Husserl's supposition in order to purify it from the taint of idealism and to lead to its application in the fields of ethics and philosophy of religion, clearly gives the *on* priority over the logos, but he ends by allowing the beholding ego to receive into itself the whole world and even God in the "feeling of value" (*Wertfühlen*). Being is given into the hand of man — not that he produces it, but that it is accessible to him. Heidegger takes ontology itself as the object of his phenomenological investigation and proceeds to an existentialistic analysis of man's peculiar mode of being as *Dasein,* that is, as concrete *human* existence in time, as man's "being *there,*" in the world. Thinking does not produce its own world, but as *Dasein* it finds itself always already in the world. Heidegger succeeds in forcing act and being together in the concept of *Dasein,* since *Dasein* is neither a discontinuous series of individual acts nor the continuity of a time-transcendent being, but a continual deciding and yet already having been decided. Nevertheless, asserts Bonhoeffer, his consciously atheistic philosophy of finiteness is, by its very nature, a *closed* finiteness that leaves no room for revelation. With the knowledge in the revelation that finiteness is creatureliness, i.e., open for God, all concepts of being must be formed anew.

In Catholic-Thomistic philosophy, which presupposes the priority of being over thinking, man, whose *essentia* is related to but different from his *esse,* stands in a relation of similarity to God, in whom *essentia* and *esse* coincide. Thus the relationship between man and God is neither one of exclusiveness nor of identity, but one of similarity, as "becoming" is similar to "being." This Thomistic principle of *analogia entis* (analogy of being), which is championed by Przywara, appears to secure the opening of the concept of being to the transcendent, but the question remains whether the transcendence of the "Is" of God really adequately expresses the Christian understanding of the transcendence of God, who not simply "is," but "is" the Righteous, "is" the Holy, "is" Love. Ultimately, Thomism turns the contingency of the revelation of God in law and gospel into a general doctrine of being, an immanent metaphysics.

THEOLOGICAL FOUNDATION 63

In the final analysis, concludes Bonhoeffer, every ontological supposition is as unusable theologically as a transcendental supposition. If pure transcendentalism set free a being that is transcendent of consciousness, " in relation to which " human existence is thought, and if pure ontology intends to think of being as an a priori of thinking, so that thinking is sustained in being, then it is unavoidable that in the first case the limits of the reason are established by itself and that in the second case being somehow comes into the power of the thinking ego. Consequently, in both cases the ego understands itself out of itself in a closed system. A philosophy, asserts Bonhoeffer, can per se leave no room for revelation. It would know the revelation and would acknowledge itself as a Christian philosophy only in the recognition that the space that it wanted to usurp is *already* occupied by another, namely, by Christ.

The offense that Christian thinking takes at every autonomous self-understanding is that it thinks it can place itself in the truth. But for Christian theology " truth " signifies that relationship to God which first becomes possible with the *word* of God, which is spoken about man and to man in the revelation of the law and gospel. This means that the knowledge of oneself and of God " in truth " is already a " being in . . ." — be it now Adam or Christ. The fact of " not being able to give oneself the truth," however, is never knowledge that is accessible to a systematic metaphysics (not even to a " critical philosophy "!), because this knowledge would mean that one had already placed himself in the truth. Thinking, stresses Bonhoeffer, is as little capable of liberating the *cor curvum in se* from man as good works. Only a thinking that " is " from the truth, bound in obedience to Christ, is able to stand in the truth. Therefore, we are directed toward the revelation itself and yet cannot understand even this step as a last possible one, but as one that must already have been taken in order that we can take it.

The author begins the second part of his investigation by indicating the consequences that follow from a pure act-interpretation and a pure being-interpretation of revelation. When revelation is interpreted according to act, man's knowledge of God and of self is thought to be dependent upon the sovereign and free revealing act of God himself. The contingent character of the act means that this "knowledge" remains inaccessible to man's reflection and can only "happen" from time to time in "direct consciousness." This sort of thinking, which Bonhoeffer finds at that time in the "dialectical theology" of Karl Barth,[31] presupposes a purely *formal* understanding of the freedom of God, and it follows that theological thinking must remain fundamentally profane thinking. God remains free from every grasp of the knowing ego and thus moves into the nonobjective sphere; that is, God always remains Subject and shuns every attempt of man to know him as an object. Thus man can speak of God only indirectly, which is to say, dialectically. Furthermore, human existence must be thought of in terms of God-effected decisions, and it becomes problematic how the human being is to be thought of in continuity. In Bonhoeffer's opinion this thinking, which resolves the God-man relation into pure acts, conceals a transcendental supposition. This raises the question of whether this formal-actualistic understanding of the freedom and contingency of God in his revelation should underlie theological thinking. After all, declares Bonhoeffer, in the revelation it is not so much a question of the freedom of God beyond it, i.e., of God's eternal remaining-with-himself and aseity, but rather of God's coming forth out of himself in the revelation, of his *given* word, of his covenant, of his freedom, which finds its strongest proof just in his freely binding himself to historical man, in his placing himself at man's disposal. God is not free from man, but *for* man! Christ is the Word of the freedom of God. God *is* there; that means, not in the eternal nonobjectivity, but, expressed with all provisionality, "haveable," apprehensible, in his word in the church. Thus Bonhoeffer places a "material" understanding of God's freedom over against the "formal."

On the other hand, if revelation is interpreted according to being, the concern is directed toward an understanding of the continuity of the revelation and of man. It must be true of the revelation that God "is" in the revelation; it must be true of man that he "is" and acts only out of this being. The being of the revelation is fundamentally

[31] Bonhoeffer cites specifically Barth's statements in his first prolegomena to dogmatics, *Die christliche Dogmatik im Entwurf* (1927), and in an article on "Schicksal und Idee in der Theologie," published in *Zwischen den Zeiten*, Heft 4, 1929. It is noteworthy that Barth himself was dissatisfied with his first attempt at dogmatics and began anew in 1932 with *Die kirchliche Dogmatik*.

THEOLOGICAL FOUNDATION 65

transcendent of consciousness, and "objective." As a "givenness," it is there, accessible, extant. It is independent of act and does not come under its power. Bonhoeffer discusses three possibilities for interpreting the revelation according to being. In the first, revelation is understood as *doctrine,* but this binds God to a human "system," which man can accept or reject. The second possibility is to understand revelation as a *psychical experience,* but God is then found and understood and classified in a human system of religious experiences, which can in principle always be reproduced. Unlike these two, which ultimately give revelation into the power of the human subject, the third attempts to establish the being of the revelation trans-subjectively by understanding it as an institution of God, and to this possibility belong the Roman Catholic Church and the verbally inspired Bible of Protestant Orthodoxy. God "is" in the institution in direct connection with and at the disposal of man. However, objects the author, an institution is unable to touch the existence of man as absolutely sinful and cannot stand opposite man as an "object" in the pure sense, for this is only possible in an encounter with another *person.* That Roman Catholicism directs its being-interpretation of the revelation toward the concept of the church is a valid insight, says Bonhoeffer, but the church is not to be conceived institutionally, but personally.

The excellence of the ontological interpretation is that for it the being of the old and new man, as well as the being of the revelation, is a reality that is transcendent of consciousness and does not depend on the act of faith. This agrees with the Christian faith, which affirms that the reality of its "object" exists in itself, whether it is believed or not. However, this interpretation lacks precisely the object of *faith,* since it identifies the being of the revelation with doctrine or experience or an institution, and thus turns God's self-manifestation into an extant, into *a* being, something creaturely. But *no* extant is able to touch and turn the existence of man, not even the "claim of the Thou," which Grisebach and Gogarten want to place opposite the autonomous ego, for even here the ego can assert itself, since it "bears" the claim of the neighbor. Likewise, Bultmann's attempt to gain the basis for theological concepts from Heidegger's ontology, which takes actuality into the concept of being as a "potentiality of being" (*Seinkönnen*), that is, as potential being, must also fail, for the being of the revelation and of the new man is for him a possibility that is found in man from the outset. It does not mean a fundamentally new *being* of man, but only a new "self-understanding." In the final analysis, all of these attempts deliver the revelation into human hands and end with an autonomous understanding of being.

It is Bonhoeffer's conviction, however, that these attempts do not present a *pure* ontology, in which thinking does not overcome being, but is "preserved" in being, in which revelation is not identified with an extant, but remains "objective" and capable of being beheld just *in* the extant. For ontological thinking, it is *proper* that being, which is capable of being exhibited, should also be "existing" being, for first through the transcending of the extant can being be brought to a pure givenness, i.e., can it be purely exhibited. For a pure ontological interpretation, therefore, it is just as wrong to anchor the revelation to an extant as to volatilize it as something nonextant. A pure ontology demands a concept of knowledge that touches man's existence but does not persist in pure actualism, and an object of knowledge that is so "opposed" to the ego that it limits and threatens the ego's way of existence and is fundamentally free. This means that the knowing is grounded and sustained in a being-known.

Thus far Bonhoeffer has attempted to show that neither an autonomous actualism nor an autonomous ontologism can offer a solution to the act-being problem that satisfies the Christian understanding of revelation, although he has indicated that a *pure* ontology points in the right direction. An adequate solution, however, demands a specifically *theological* ontology, and this is found in the concept of the *church* as a theological-sociological category. In this concept the concerns of both the act-interpretation and the being-interpretation are preserved and drawn together. Man's mode of being in the church is as a person in fellowship. As a being of a real, continuous relationship, it is more than a mere actuality from time to time, and yet it establishes an actuality of the person, which again is directed toward the being in fellowship.

The author now discusses the being of the revelation in the Christian community. Revelation can only be thought in relation to the church, which is constituted by the present proclamation of Christ's death and resurrection. This proclamation must be "present" in order to assure the contingency character of the revelation. In the proclamation the revelation "comes to" (future!) man in the church and thus a past happening is brought into the present. This determining of the present by the future, i.e., by the proclamation of the once-for-all event of the cross and resurrection, must take place in the church, for it is the presence of Christ, "Christ existing as community." In the proclamation of the community for the community Christ is the common "subject" of the proclamation and of the community, so that neither can be understood apart from the other. The evangelical notion of the church, then, is thought of in terms of person; God reveals himself in the church as person. Here Christ has given himself to his new humanity, so that in his person are included all those whom he has acquired. "Church" is a community created by Christ and established in him, a community in which Christ reveals himself as the New Man, or better: as the new humanity itself.

This understanding of revelation changes the character of the act-being problem. In Christ, God gives himself to his community and to each member in such a way that the acting subject in the community, both proclaiming and believing, is Christ! Only in this community of persons can the gospel be really proclaimed and believed, so that here the gospel is somehow held fast. That is, the freedom of God has become bound to the community of persons, and just this turns out to be God's freedom: that he binds himself to man! Thus the church *really* has at its disposal the word of forgiveness, so that in the community it can not only be existentially spoken: I am forgiven, but as the Christian church it may also proclaim in preaching and sacrament: you are forgiven, and every church member may and should "become a Christ" to the other by such proclaiming of the gospel!

Revelation, then, takes place in the Christian community, and it demands its own sociology. Up until now, says Bonhoeffer, the whole act-being problem has been individualistically oriented, and it is just for that reason that the transcendental and ontological solutions miscarry. The being of the revelation neither lies in a past event, a controllable extant that does not touch man's existence, nor can it be conceived as a continually free, pure, nonobjective act that strikes man's existence from time to time. It "is" rather the being of the fellowship of persons that is constituted and terminated by the person of Christ, and in which the individual person always already finds himself in his new way of existence. With this solution Bonhoeffer has guaranteed three things: the being of the revelation can be thought of in continuity, the existence of man is really touched, and the being of the revelation can be conceived neither as something extant and objective nor as something nonextant and nonobjective.

First, the continuity of the revelation, which means its continual presence (in the sense of "what is future"), is assured, because the church preaches Christ, his death and resurrection. If only the individual heard the preaching, the continuity would be endangered, but the church itself hears the word of the church, even if an individual from time to time does not hear it. Preaching is always heard! Thus the continuity is not situated in man, but is guaranteed suprapersonally by a fellowship of persons. Second, that man's existence is really affected is assured by his being drawn into the fellowship of the church, in which he always finds himself already placed in the truth of his old and new existence. This is grounded, however, in the personal character of the community, whose subject is the Christ, for only through his person can the existence of man be touched, placed in truth, and transferred into a new way of existence. First through Christ's person does another become a "person" for us, and this person in turn "becomes a Christ" for us in demand and promise, in existential limitation from without, and as such also becomes the guarantee of the continuity of revelation. Third, within the church the mode of being is that of the "person" and the "fellowship," and this mode of being neither ties down the revelation to an extant that remains in the past and existentially irrelevant, nor volatilizes the revelation into a nonobjectivity that destroys the continuity. Still, it satisfies the demands of both, for the possibility of an existential contact is connected with something concretely objective, yet something that opposes the ego as the absolute "outside" and that can never be drawn into the control of man. Of course, stresses Bonhoeffer, all this is understandable only to faith, that is, to the one who is placed in the truth and for whom another has become a genuine person through the person of Christ.

The author next discusses man's mode of existence in the church, which he describes in terms of *pati*, Luther's term for characterizing man's being in the community of Christ. *Pati* is a Latin term that means "bearing" or "suffering" or "enduring"; man bears the new humanity by believing, praying, and proclaiming, and yet he still knows himself borne in all his doings by the community, by Christ. Bonhoeffer expresses what happens in the church in these words:

I hear another man really proclaim the gospel to me. He extends to me the sacrament: you are forgiven. He and the community pray for me, and I hear the gospel, join the prayer, and know myself in the word, sacrament, and prayer of the community of Christ to be bound with the new humanity, be it now here or elsewhere, borne by it, bearing it. Here I, the historically whole man, individual and humanity, am touched. I believe, that is, I know myself borne. I am borne (*pati*), therefore I am (*esse*), therefore I believe (*agere*). Here the circle is closed, for even the *agere* is here *pati*. However, the ego is always the historical one, only in faith a new one. (99)

Therefore, a man's existence is really touched and placed into a new way of existence through being a person in the community, and yet this being, in which the believer in the community shares, is not dependent on the act of faith that is directed toward it. On the other hand, only in faith does man know the being of the revelation and his own being in the church of Christ as independent of faith! Here the concerns of a pure actualism and a pure ontology are satisfied and drawn together.

Faith is "in relation to" being (church); only in faith does being become accessible, i.e., only in faith "is" being. But faith knows this being as independent of itself, knows itself as a way of being of the same. Being transcends the extant; it is the extant's, as well as the ego's, own ground of being. Thus act comes out of being, just as it goes into being. On the other hand, being is in relation to act and yet free. The being of the revelation, as trembling in the balance between something objective and something nonobjective, is "person," God's revealed person and the personal fellowship which is founded through it. (100)

The author now investigates the concept of knowledge that accords with the act-being unity in the church. On the one hand, he wants to avoid dissolving man's knowledge into a not-knowing, which requires a dialectical type of thinking that is a priori uncertain, and, on the other hand, he wants to avoid turning revelation into an extant, which delivers it completely into the hands of man and precludes its being a revelation *of God*. Being a person in Christ's fellowship involves a new kind of knowledge that must be expressed in social categories. In order to explain it, Bonhoeffer differentiates three different kinds of knowledge that correspond to three sociologically different functions of the church: believing knowledge, preaching knowledge, and theological knowledge. The first could be called " existential knowledge," the latter two " churchly knowledge."

Believing knowledge is knowing oneself overcome and forgiven by the person of Christ through the preached word. In faith, which is a God-given *reality,* man knows Christ as a person who confronts him — knowable, yet free, completely " outside " the ego. Through the person of Christ, who is simultaneously the Creator of man's new being as person and the Lord " in relation to " whom the person is created, man's neighbor first moves out of the world of things into the social sphere of persons. This new understanding of the concept of person, namely, that a person " is " only in the act of giving himself, but " is " nevertheless free from the one to whom he gives himself, unites the transcendental and ontological suppositions. Since this knowledge is gained through the Christ-Person, it is valid only for the fellowship of persons in the Christian church. Christ, who is preached in the congregation, gives himself to the church member, but because Christ himself creates faith by bestowing the Holy Spirit, the member knows him as the free Lord over his existence. Christ " is " only " in the believing," but nevertheless " is " Lord over the believing. Faith, as a concrete being-grasped by Christ, is an *actus directus* that is not accessible to reflection. For reflection there remains only the past spoken word of Christ as a general proposition. Word and person have stepped apart, and this is the situation of preaching and of theological knowledge.

Preaching knowledge is what the preacher, as bearer of the preaching office of the congregation, "knows" about what he preaches: Jesus Christ the Crucified. In the power of Christ, i.e., in the power of the congregation, the preacher has the full authority to proclaim the gospel to those who listen, to forgive sins in preaching and sacrament. Here there can be no uncertainty, for in the preaching of the given word of God, Christ himself may be proclaimed as "subject" of the speaking. Nevertheless, the preacher must reflect on the "what" of the revelation, and he finds for his reflection mere words, propositions, remembrances about a divine event, not the living, creative word of Christ himself. However, to the preaching, as an office of the congregation, the promise is given that when the preacher says the "words" and "propositions" rightly (*recte docetur!*), the living Christ testifies to himself in them. But, asks Bonhoeffer, how can the preacher speak "rightly," when he can still say only "propositions"? Here the problem of theological knowledge is expressed, and with it the further question: how is a theological science possible?

Theological knowledge is churchly knowledge that has as its object the happening that is preserved in the memory of the Christian community, in the Bible, in preaching and sacrament, prayer, confession, in the words of the Christ-Person. Theology, states Bonhoeffer, is a function of the church; there is no church without preaching and no preaching without remembrance, and theology is the remembrance of the church. As such it serves to inform the church about the presuppositions of Christian preaching; that is, it strives toward the formation of dogma. Theology is a science that has as its object its own presuppositions, which means that it stands between past and future preaching. Theology should relate past preaching to the real person of Christ and should place dogmas before future preaching, on the basis of which the preacher can preach "correctly." Consequently, dogma is logically not the goal but the presupposition of preaching. It would appear from what has been said about theology as a science that reflects on its object that theological thinking could not be differentiated in principle from profane thinking. However, there is a difference, and this lies not in the theological method, but in the *obedience* of theological thinking. The dialectical method of the "critical reservation," for instance, is no more humble or existential than any honest systematic thinking. What differentiates theology from profane thinking is alone the fact that it is committed to the church. Theological thinking knows its limitations and humbly submits itself to the judgment of the Christian community, which alone knows that the word that theology has as its object is spoken always anew beyond theology, and that theology is only the preserved, ordered remembrance of this word. As such, however, it is grounded in the very structure of the church.

For the preaching it follows that the preacher must be a theologian, although preaching knowledge is differentiated from theological knowledge by the qualified situation in which the preacher must speak the word to a concrete, historical congregation that is now assembled. The object of his knowing is no longer the already-spoken word, but the word that must be spoken just now to this particular congregation. This word is spoken neither as an existential confession nor as theologically pure doctrine, but in the power of Christ and his community (everything depends on his office!) the preacher proclaims the gospel of forgiveness to the congregation, because the congregation wants to hear it. From a sociological point of view, the preacher is essentially in the community and secondarily an individual, whereas the theologian is essentially an individual and secondarily in the community. The believer, however, is just as essentially an individual as "in the community."

Bonhoeffer summarizes his thoughts as follows:

In the knowledge of faith there is absolutely no reflection. The question about the possibility of faith can only be answered by its reality. But because this reality shuns being exhibited as an extant, every reflection proves to be destructive. Faith does not look on itself, but alone to Christ. Whether faith is faith is not confirmable, not even believable, but believing faith *is* faith. That such faith takes place in "direct consciousness" is just as certain as that it, in its qualified actual reality, is not reproducible by reflection. Consequently, it can never be said: Here and there I have believed. If the object of the knowledge of faith is the living word of Christ, then that of theological knowledge is the spoken word and that of preaching knowledge is the word of proclamation to be spoken just now to the congregation. As an act of an individual, preaching knowledge is reflective, just as theological knowledge. In the office of the congregation, to which he has to proclaim forgiveness of sins, the preacher sees his knowledge as knowledge of the congregation and thereby qualified for its upbuilding. (112 f.)

Bonhoeffer now returns to the beginning of his investigation and the problem of a theological doctrine of the self-understanding of man in connection with his " being placed in the truth " by revelation. " In faith " man understands himself to be in the church of Christ in his new being, a way of existence that was not present in man's own possibilities. He sees his existence established solely by the word of the Christ-Person. Being is being in Christ, and here alone is unity and wholeness of life. Therefore man recognizes his old mode of being as being in Adam. There is, emphasizes Bonhoeffer, no formal, metaphysical, psychological determination of the being of man that is not grounded in the proposition: he is " in Christ " or " in Adam." Man is " in relation to " truth because he " is " in the truth (a given, revealed truth!); he is " in relation to " Christ because he is " in Christ " (a given relationship, *iustitia passiva!*). In other words, in that God knows man, man knows God, but to be known by God means to become a new man! God recognizes the righteous man and the sinner in one. Of course, states Bonhoeffer, the mediator of this truth remains the " understanding " (*Sinn*), the " clear " word, but it is not because God's word makes sense that it touches the existence of man, but because it is *God's* word, the word of the Creator, Reconciler, and Redeemer. All of this, which is understood in faith, remains preserved for the theologian only in the " remembrance." Therefore, says Bonhoeffer, every theologian's anthropology, even what he himself has here developed, remains doctrine, system, autonomous self-understanding. *Only in the church,* where Christ's word is " thought " and the living Christ himself works, is it understood that a theology that wants to serve the concrete church also serves in reality, as autonomous thinking, the law of Christ. A theological understanding of the self, then, no longer means " to understand oneself placed in the truth " (it is that in faith), but, " reflective thinking placed in the service of the church." Therefore, Bonhoeffer suggests that this alteration of Luther's words is valid for theologians: *reflecte fortiter, sed fortius fide et gaude in Christo.* (Reflect boldly, but believe and rejoice in Christ more boldly.)

In the third and final part of his investigation, Bonhoeffer considers the act-being problem in the concrete doctrine of man " in Adam " and " in Christ." " Being in Adam," which the author thinks is a sharper ontological, Biblically grounded definition for being a sinner, is known by man only through revelation. Otherwise it would be no existential determination of a human being, and the possibility of man's ability to place himself in the truth by withdrawing from his sinful being to some deeper sinless being, would inevitably lead to Semi-Pelagianism or, ontologically speaking, to the doctrine of *causae secundae*. Through faith in God's word, man knows that being " in Adam " means being in untruth, being the creator and lord of one's own world. This means, however, that the sinner remains alone in the lie of self-glorification. Ontologically, it means that sin is the overpowering of the *Da-sein* by the *Wie-sein*. That is, man's being " there " as a creature is distorted by man's own interpretation of the " how " of his being, since he understands himself, not as creature, but as creator. The ensuing loneliness and the burden of being the creator and bearer of his own world produces in sinful man an inner anxiety, and since he is his own judge, he raises an accusation against himself in the language of his conscience and drives himself to active repentance. But the conscience and repentance of the man in Adam represent his final grasp after himself, a confirmation and justification of his autocratic being-alone. In a misunderstanding of his situation, man " seeks himself in himself " (Luther), still hoping to save his sinful existence by repentance (*contritio actival*), but his conscience belongs to the devil. Salvation comes only when Christ breaks into man's aloneness and kills this conscience and places man in the truth.

Is sin to be thought as act or being? If it is thought to be a free and conscious act that takes place from time to time, then its continuity is not understandable. The fact that man *is* a sinner and not simply one who *commits* sins is not expressed. On the other hand, if sin is thought in terms of static being, as man's " substance," then its individual guilt and act-character is eliminated. Bonhoeffer finds the solution to this dilemma in the New Testament concept of " being in Adam," where Adam is both " I " and humanity. He describes the relationship as follows:

In the judgment which the death of Christ brings over me I see myself dying completely, for I as a whole am guilty as the doer of my life. The decisions of my life were always self-seeking. I have decided wrongly, and therefore Christ is my death; and because I alone wanted to be lord, I am also alone in death. But the death of Christ kills my entire being as a man, kills in me humanity, because I am myself and mankind in one. In my fall from God humanity fell. Thus the burden of the ego before the cross grows unbearable; it is itself Adam, it is itself the first who has done and always does anew that incomprehensible deed — sin as act. But in this act, with which I completely and repeatedly charge myself, I find myself always already in the humanity of Adam, or better, I see the humanity in me necessarily accomplishing this, my own free act. As a man the self stands captivated in this old humanity which fell through me. It is not as an individual, but always already in humanity. And exactly because the deed of the individual is at the same time the deed of humanity, man must know himself responsible for the total guilt of mankind. (123 f.)

Thus in the concept of "Adam," Bonhoeffer finds the key to an interpretation that maintains both the contingency of the act of sin and the continuity of the being in sin. Man is a sinner, in that he stands in the fellowship of fallen humanity; in that he commits sin, he finds himself already in sinful humanity; but he stands as a sinner in the fallen humanity precisely as one who time and again commits the act of sin.

The author ends the section on "being in Adam" with a discussion of sinful man's everyday life, knowledge of the conscience, and temptation (*Anfechtung*).[82] The day-to-day life of man "in Adam" is one of guilt, a decision for being-alone that continually falls because it has already fallen. It is life in flight from oneself and from death, but since at least in death man must finally face the judgment of Christ, his flight is hopeless and leads only to despair. Although man's conscience tries to justify his being-alone by in-

[82] *Anfechtung* is another difficult word to translate into English. The basic meaning of the verb *anfechten* is "to combat" or "to assail" or "to attack." Thus *Anfechtung* denotes a temptation in which man is sorely beset and disturbed by an attack from without, genuine spiritual tribulation.

terpreting it merely as a general awareness of being left alone, his aloneness is revealed as guilt through the temptation in which Christ combats man through the law. In this temptation man's flight is arrested, he is forced to recognize his guilt and he dies to Christ, to the law. But in the spiritual death of the sinner predestination takes place. God can let man die in the knowledge of his sin, or he can convey him through this death into his church. If the latter, then he turns man's view away from man himself and directs it toward Christ, the crucified and resurrected Conqueror of the temptation unto death.

"Seek yourself only in Christ and not in yourself; then you will find yourself eternally in him" (Luther). With this quotation Bonhoeffer begins his discussion of "being in Christ." It is the gift of faith that man no longer looks toward himself, but solely to the salvation that has come to him from without. He finds himself in Christ, because he is already in him in that he seeks himself there. To be in Christ means to be released from the power of one's own ego and to come under the power of Christ, where for the first time one knows himself as a creature of God. Viewed ontologically, the *Da-sein* is released from the power of the *Wie-sein* and is placed under the power of Christ, wherein it finds its primary freedom as a creature of God. Only "in Christ" does man know himself as a creature of God; "in Adam" he was both creator and creature at the same time. To know oneself as a creature of God means to know in faith that the old man is dead and the new man is risen from the dead. It means to know God as Creator and Lord over one's being a person. Being in Christ is being directed toward Christ, which is only possible by already being in the community of Christ. Thus the transcendental and the ontological suppositions again are brought together.

Bonhoeffer next turns from the formal to the historical determination of being in Christ, which is defined by the past and future. Determination by the past involves the conscience, which is found not only in Adam but also in the church of Christ. Conscience is found only where sin is present, but since man in Christ is no longer ruled by sin, conscience is a determination by the past in Adam. It does not belong to the "future things"; it is man's reflection on himself and is primarily man's own voice, not God's voice. If being in Christ is being directed toward him, then man obviously falls out of this being when he reflects on himself. Herein lies the problem of the Christian conscience.

For a solution Bonhoeffer differentiates between two forms of conscience that pertain to the man in Christ. First, there is the form of conscience that places itself between Christ and the believer, points to his sin, accuses him, and rejects him from communion with Christ. This is real temptation and rebellion against Christ, because it is a disregarding of the grace offered in Christ. In this temptation even the man in the church stands in real danger of losing Christ, if Christ himself does not come and kill the conscience and renew man's faith. But in faith man finds himself already again in the church! This temptation belongs entirely to the righteousness of the flesh, and this conscience is itself apostasy from Christ. The second form of conscience is included in the intention toward Christ. It is the "perceiving of sin" in faith. Whoever seeks himself in Christ sees himself always in sin, but this sin is now no longer able to pervert the view toward Christ. Man sees his sin in the light of Christ's forgiveness, so that now repentance is no longer man's final grasp after himself, but repentance in faith in the forgiveness (*contritio passiva!*). Daily repentance, stresses the author, does not mean losing oneself in oneself, but finding oneself in Christ! Reflection now means a daily dying of the old man in faith, for only in faith do we know Christ's death for us and our dying this death in baptism. The harder this daily death attacks us, the stronger is the power of the past over us.

The determination of the being in Christ by the past is borne by the determination by the future, where man is completely led away from himself in his pure view toward Christ — not a self-negating, mystical view, to be sure, but a direct act of faith in which man no longer sees sin or death or even himself or his faith, but only Christ as his Lord and God. This *fides directa,* which is an act of faith executed by man's consciousness but not accessible to reflection, rests on the objectivity of the event of revelation in word and sacrament. To see Christ in word and sacrament, declares Bonhoeffer, means to see the crucified and resurrected Christ in the neighbor and in the creation in one act. Only here is revealed a future that in faith determines the present.

Bonhoeffer understands this being determined by the future as the eschatological possibility of the child. The child sees himself in the power of the thrust toward the "future," and only for that reason can he live for the present, whereas the mature man, who wants to be determined by the present, falls into the past, into himself, into death and guilt. The present can be lived only out of the future. Here the child becomes a theological problem: *actus directus* or *actus reflexus,* infant baptism or religiosity? *Actus directus,* as an act that is directed solely from and to Christ, and infant baptism, as a paradoxical event of revelation without the reflected answer of the consciousness, which Bonhoeffer finds united in Old Protestant Dogmatics,[33] designate the eschatological prolepsis (*Auftakt*) under which the life is placed. Both are to be understood, says Bonhoeffer, only in connection with the "Last Things." Baptism is the calling of man to become a child, which is to be understood only eschatologically. Infant baptism can be meaningfully discussed only among members of the Christian community, because only the man with the faith that is preserved in the presence of revelation understands that the child is near the "Eschata" and can hold fast to baptism as the inviolable word of God, as the eschatological foundation of his life. Bonhoeffer summarizes his thoughts with these words:

Because baptism lies temporally in the past and yet is an eschatological happening, my entire past life assumes seriousness and temporal continuity. It lies between eternity and eternity, established by God's word and "in relation to" God's word. Thus my past, as well as that of the Christian community in general, is grounded, determined, and "judged" by the future. (138)

The author admits that all of this talk about the *actus directus,* which is never apprehended in reflection, about infant baptism, and about faith, which "eliminates" itself, appears to leave open the possibility of the eschatology of the apocatastasis, but he concludes that this can be no more than the sighing of theology when it must speak of belief and unbelief, election and reprobation.

In the pure being-directed toward Christ, concludes Bonhoeffer, the *Da-sein* and the *Wie-sein* are set in proper relationship, the

---

[33] See p. 136, n. 29, where he cites Hollaz: *Examen. Cap. de gratia regenerante* and refers to Delitzsch's *Biblische Psychologie.*

tormenting knowledge of the inner strife of the self finds the " happy conscience," the slave becomes free, the one who became a man in loneliness and misery becomes a child in the community of Christ. This is the new creation of the new man of the future, who no longer looks back on himself, but only away from himself to the revelation of God in Christ; who is brought forth out of the narrowness of the world into the breadth of the heavens; who becomes what he was or yet never was: a creature of God, a child.

Chapter II

Theological Application

Bonhoeffer said to the church: Your theme is the world! (Eberhard Bethge.)

A. BIOGRAPHICAL INTRODUCTION (1932–1939)

The Germany to which Dietrich Bonhoeffer returned in 1931 was already pregnant with revolutionary forces that required only the masterful midwifery of Adolf Hitler to give birth to the engrossing phenomenon of National Socialism. The humiliation of defeat in World War I, the resentment kindled by the enforced confession of sole guilt for the war at the Treaty of Versailles, and the subsequent stringent economic strictures imposed by the Allies had produced a profound psychological reaction in the proud German people, which made them unusually receptive to the new gospel promising emancipation and extolling the virtues of the German race, blood, and soil.[1] Hitler had long since proclaimed his intentions in *Mein Kampf* (Vol. I, 1925; Vol. II, 1927); Alfred Rosenberg had provided the party philosophy in *The Myth of the Twentieth Century (Der Mythus des 20. Jahrhunderts)* (1930); and poverty, unemployment, and social unrest, together with the constant menace of Russian Bolshevism, afforded fertile ground for the rise of the new party that preached *"Deutschland über alles!"* After the 1930 elections the seats held by National Socialists in the Reichstag jumped from 12 to 107, and the star of a new Fuehrer began to rise in the German sky.

[1] In a sermon preached at a youth conference in America during his student days at Union Theological Seminary, Bonhoeffer describes the terrible effects of the war upon his country and renounces the myth of Germany's sole guilt for the conflict. See GS I, pp. 66 ff.

As yet, however, the new political developments had not radically affected the normal pattern of life in Germany, so Bonhoeffer fitted readily into the routine of his church and university assignments. Before he commenced teaching in the fall, however, he had two significant experiences. The first was a three-week visit in July to Bonn, where he met and listened to Prof. Karl Barth. In letters to his friend Erwin Sutz, of Zürich, the young theologian tells in detail the extraordinary impression made by Barth's open and vigorous personality and his gifted ability as a theologian and teacher. " I believe," writes Bonhoeffer, " I have seldom regretted an omission in my theological past so much as not having come [to hear Barth] earlier." [2] This meeting proved to be the beginning of a friendly and stimulating acquaintanceship, which continued through occasional correspondence and personal encounters throughout the remainder of Bonhoeffer's life.[3] The second experience was his participation, at the behest of his church, in the conference of the World Alliance for Promoting International Friendship Through the Churches, which met September 1–5 in Cambridge, England. This marked the beginning of Bonhoeffer's work in the so-called ecumenical movement; and at the affiliated International Youth Conference he was elected International Youth Secretary for Germany and Central Europe, which made him an official leader of the youth division of the World Alliance. His theological profundity, linguistic ability, and natural friendliness soon marked him as one of the best known and most respected German figures in ecumenical circles.

In the fall of 1931, Bonhoeffer not only assumed his teaching duties at the University of Berlin, where he offered a course on " The History of the Systematic Theology of the Twentieth Century " (" Die Geschichte der systematischen Theologie des 20. Jahrhunderts ") and a seminar on " The Idea of Philosophy and Protestant Theology " (" Die Idee der Philosophie und die protestantische Theologie "), but he also became student pastor at the Technical College (Technische Hochschule) in the Charlottenburg district of Berlin, where his preaching services were crowded. In addition, he soon agreed to

[2] GS I, p. 19.
[3] See their exchange of letters in MW I, pp. 106–121, and Bonhoeffer's references to Barth in PFG.

take over an "impossible" confirmation class of fifty boys in the poverty-stricken North Berlin district of Wedding, a class that was so unruly that Bonhoeffer's predecessor had given it up for lost. It is a tribute to Bonhoeffer's pastoral ability that he soon had the boys studying the teachings of the church with enthusiasm, and it is characteristic of his earnestness that he moved into the district on New Year's Day of 1932 and lived among his young "parishioners," inviting groups of them to his room in the evenings to eat and to play games, and finally to read the Bible and to receive catechetical instruction. Moreover, he resolutely visited the home of each boy, an eye-opening experience that made him question whether the church, which was again learning how to preach, was also learning how to carry out its pastoral duties![4] In March the members of the class were confirmed in the church, and although his official relationship was now at an end, Bonhoeffer remained in fellowship with many of the boys for years.

During the summer semester of 1932,[5] Bonhoeffer lectured on "The Nature of the Church" ("Das Wesen der Kirche") and conducted a seminar on the provocative subject "Is There a Christian Ethic?" ("Gibt es eine christliche Ethik?"). Otherwise he was busily engaged in his ecumenical responsibilities: a meeting of the International Youth Secretaries in London (April 4); the French-English Regional Youth Conference at Epsom (April 5–8); the Theological Conference for Ecumenical Youth Work at Berlin (April 29–30), where Bonhoeffer vigorously objected to General Superintendent Wilhelm Zöllner's uncritical concept of the unity of the church and developed his concept of orders of preservation (*Erhaltungsordnungen*) in opposition to Prof. Wilhelm Stählin's and Pastor Peter's [6] concept of orders of creation (*Schöpfungsordnungen*); the German-French Regional Youth Conference at Westerberg (beginning of July); a Youth Peace Conference organized by the Central Council of the Czechoslovakian Church and held at

[4] GS I, p. 29.

[5] German universities generally have two semesters each year: a winter semester, which runs from October until March, and a summer semester, which runs from April through July.

[6] Peter later became the German Christian Bishop in Magdeburg! For an account of this important conference, see GS I, pp. 121 ff.

Cernohorske Kupele (July 20-30), where Bonhoeffer presented a paper entitled "Concerning the Theological Foundation of the Work of the World Alliance" ("Zur theologischen Begründung der Weltbundarbeit"); a meeting of the Management Committee of the World Alliance at Geneva (August 18); the International Youth Conference at Gland, Switzerland (August 24-31), where Bonhoeffer delivered an address beginning with the tantalizing words: "The church is dead" ("*Die Kirche ist tot*"). This year of activity as International Youth Secretary for Germany and Central Europe was time-consuming and often exasperating for the theologically minded young teacher, but at the same time it immensely broadened his ecumenical contacts, provoked much deep thought about the attitude of the church toward war, and disclosed the enormous cleavage between the Continental and the Anglo-Saxon approach to the problems of the day.[7]

In the fall of 1932, Bonhoeffer began his winter semester lectures on "Creation and Sin: Theological Exegesis of Genesis 1-3" ("Schöpfung und Sünde: Theologische Exegese von Genesis 1-3"), which, at the request of his students, were later published in book form as *Creation and Fall* (*Schöpfung und Fall*), and he conducted a seminar on "The Latest Theology: A Discussion of New Systematic-theological Publications" ("Jüngste Theologie: Besprechung systematisch-theologischer Neuerscheinungen"). He also wrote an illuminating essay on "The Social Gospel" ("Das Social Gospel"), in which he traces the historical development of this American movement, discusses its leading concepts, and appraises its positive contributions and its theological weaknesses. In November he delivered an address on "Thy Kingdom Come! The Prayer of the Church for God's Kingdom on Earth" ("Dein Reich komme! Das Gebet der Gemeinde um Gottes Reich auf Erden"),[8] in which he explained the relationship between church and state.

By now, however, the time for normalcy in German church and

[7] Bonhoeffer's own reports on the various ecumenical conferences in which he participated may be found in GS I.

[8] Published by the Furche Verlag in 1933 as Heft 78 in the series *Stimmen aus der deutschen christlichen Studentenbewegung;* republished in 1957, together with an exposition of the first three commandments, which Bonhoeffer wrote in prison, and an epilogue by Eberhard Bethge, as Furche-Bücherei number 146.

educational affairs was fast drawing to a close, for the political teapot of National Socialism, with its proclamation of the "Fuehrer-principle" and its accompanying demand for a "co-ordination" (*Gleichschaltung*)[9] in all areas of German life, was beginning to boil over even into ecclesiastical circles. In the 1932 elections the Nazis captured 230 seats in the Reichstag and became the strongest party in the Government, and in the same year pastors belonging to the German Christian Faith Movement, a movement within the German Evangelical Church that avowedly tried to combine Christianity with the principles of National Socialism, won a third of the seats in the November election of the Church of the Old Prussian Union. Germany was riding the crest of a pseudoreligious awakening of extreme nationalism, the "Horst Wessel Song" was fast becoming the new national anthem, and *"Juden 'raus!"* ("Out with the Jews!") the most popular propaganda slogan. Even in the church there were only a few men at this critical time who had enough vision to see through the perpetrated confusion between the gospel of Christ and the gospel of Hitler, and to declare in no uncertain terms the inherent opposition of the one to the other. Dietrich Bonhoeffer was one of these men.

On January 30, 1933, Adolf Hitler was installed as Chancellor of the Third German Reich. On February 1, Bonhoeffer delivered a radio address in Berlin on "Changes in the Conception of the Leader in the Young Generation" ("Wandlungen des Führerbegriffes in der jungen Generation"), in which he pointed out the dangers of the seductive new leader-concept that was bound to the "person" instead of the "office." This, he said, could only lead to idolatry. The broadcast was broken off by the authorities before he had finished, and Dietrich Bonhoeffer was branded from the outset as an opponent of the Nazi regime.

The year 1933 brought an apparent victory to the German Christians within the German Evangelical Church, what with the enactment of a new church constitution incorporating the "Fuehrer-

---

[9] G. C. Richards, the translator of Anders Nygren's *The Church Controversy in Germany*, translates *Gleichschaltung* as "a switching over into uniformity," thereby approximating the common meaning of the term in the German electrical vocabulary. See p. 11.

principle" in the form of a Reichsbishop; the German Christian triumph in the General Church Election (July 23); the election of Hitler's friend and adviser in church affairs, Army Chaplain Ludwig Müller, as Bishop of Prussia; the introduction of the "Aryan Paragraph," which prohibited anyone of Jewish blood or anyone married to a Jew to hold an office in the church, at the Prussian General Synod (September 5); and, finally, the election of Müller as Reichsbishop at the National Synod at Wittenberg (September 27). At the same time, however, an opposition movement began to grow within the church, marked by such events as the Altona Pastors' Confession, inspired by Hans Asmussen (January 11), Otto Dibelius' letter of warning to his pastors (March 8), Karl Barth's publication of *Theological Existence Today!* (June 25), the clear statement of the Marburg Theological Faculty concerning the "Aryan Paragraph" (September 20), and the formation of the "Pastors' Emergency League" (*Pfarrernotbund*) under the leadership of Martin Niemoeller (September 21). Bonhoeffer aligned himself solidly with this evangelical opposition. At the request of Theodor Heuss, he expanded his radio address into a lecture on "The Leader and the Individual in the Young Generation" ("Der Führer und der Einzelne in der jungen Generation") and delivered it in March at the German School for Politics. In addition, he warned the church of its political responsibility in an essay, "What Is Church?" ("Was ist Kirche?"); clarified the attitude of the church toward the Jewish question in another essay, "The Church Before the Question of the Jews" ("Die Kirche vor der Judenfrage"); and was one of the theologians who helped draft the so-called "Bethel Confession," which was outlined in August and published under the editorship of Martin Niemoeller in November as "The Confession of the Fathers and the Confessing Congregation" ("Das Bekenntnis der Väter und die bekennende Gemeinde").[10]

Bonhoeffer's lecture at the university during the summer semester of 1933 was on "Christology" ("Christologie"), and this proved to be his last teaching assignment for some time, for in October he took a leave of absence and went to London to become pastor of two

---

[10] Bonhoeffer actually withdrew his support from the final edition, because he did not think the confession was strong enough.

German-speaking congregations, St. Paul's and Sydenham. Bonhoeffer's reasons for leaving Germany at this critical time were varied. First, his departure dramatized his complete break with the German Christians, who had gained control of the Evangelical Church. Second, the work in England offered an opportunity to establish important ecumenical contacts for the rising Confessing Church. Third, Bonhoeffer had a genuine yearning for the pastoral ministry, and his conscience forbade his accepting a parish in his own Prussian Church, where he would now have to subscribe to the " Aryan Paragraph." Fourth, he had become less and less satisfied with the situation at the University of Berlin, for his theology was now suspect because of his association with Karl Barth; he had no colleagues with whom he was theologically congenial; and he had come to regard a university as a poor environment in which to train ministerial candidates. Finally, Bonhoeffer's own theological thinking was in a state of flux. His emphasis was shifting from dogmatics to simple Biblical exegesis, and he was becoming more and more concerned with the ethical demands of the Sermon on the Mount and what it means to be a disciple of Christ.

While in London, Bonhoeffer not only preached regularly and carried out his many pastoral duties but also kept in close contact with the German Church Struggle, flying back from time to time for important conferences with the leaders of the evangelical opposition. Furthermore, he established firm contacts with English ecumenical church leaders, such as George Bell, Bishop of Chichester, and he soon was recognized as one of the most reliable interpreters of the German Church Struggle to the outside world.

In August of 1934, Bonhoeffer attended the joint meeting of the World Alliance and the Universal Christian Council for Life and Work at Fanö, Denmark, where he led the German youth delegation of the World Alliance and delivered an address on " The Church and the Peoples of the World," in which he urged that " a radical call to peace " be sent to all the nations of the world " in the name of Christ! " The meeting at Fanö was a critical one for the Universal Christian Council, for it could not simply ignore the church struggle that was raging in Germany. The official delegation from the German Evangelical Church was composed mainly of German Christians under the leadership of Bishop Theodor Heckel, head of the Foreign Affairs Office of the church. No representative of the Confessing Church was officially there, although Bonhoeffer and a few other members were present as delegates to the meeting of the World Alliance. In spite of the presence and opposition of the German Christians, however, the Council boldly denounced the National Socialist church rule as "incompatible with the true nature of the Christian church" and declared its sympathy with the Confessing Church by electing Dr. Karl Koch, president of the Confessional Synod, and Dietrich Bonhoeffer, "co-opted" members of the Council, and by passing the following resolution by a large majority: "The Council desires to assure its brethren in the Confessional Synod of the German Evangelical Church of its prayers and heartfelt sympathy in their witness to the principles of the gospel, and of its resolve to maintain close fellowship with them."[11]

Through his acquaintance with C. F. Andrews, Gandhi's friend and biographer, whom he first met at the Gland Youth Conference, Bonhoeffer became interested in going to India to meet Gandhi and to study his nonviolence method of pacifism, but before he could make the journey, he received a call from the Confessing Church to return to his homeland and take over the leadership of an "illegal" seminary for training vicars of the Confessing Church in Pomerania.[12] An acquaintance at that time says this about his decision: "I shall always remember him pacing up and down our lounge trying to decide whether to remain here or to give up his church here and return to the persecuted church in Germany; longing to visit Gandhi and India and feeling a premonition that unless he seized that moment he would never go. I knew, being himself, how he must eventually decide."[13] In a typically unselfish way the twenty-nine-

[11] Quoted in A. S. Duncan-Jones's *The Struggle for Religious Freedom in Germany* (Victor Gollancz, Ltd., London, 1938), p. 248. Also see G. K. A. Bell's *The Church and Humanity (1939-1946)* (Longmans, Green & Co., Inc., London, 1946), pp. 183 f. Quotations from the Bell book are used by permission of Longmans, Green & Co., Inc.

[12] This was a so-called *Predigerseminar,* where ministerial candidates who have completed their formal, academic education and have served as an assistant minister (*Vikar*) in a congregation for six months or a year receive a final period of intensive instruction in a seminary of the church.

[13] Reported by Franz Hildebrandt in the *Bonhoeffer Gedenkheft,* p. 14.

year-old pastor dropped his Indian plans, left the London ministry, which he had enjoyed for a year and a half, and went back to a difficult, dangerous, disintegrating situation in Germany.

On April 26, 1935, he met his first class of twenty-five vicars at Zingst on the Baltic Sea, where he was to set up his seminary in some straw-thatched cottages.[14] Soon thereafter, however, he moved the seminary to a large old house at Finkenwalde near Stettin, and there he introduced a kind of theological education that was startlingly new in Germany: a communal life in which Jesus Christ's call to discipleship was taken seriously; a life that strove for a proper balance between work and worship, the academic and the practical, discipline and freedom; a life in which he shared with his students his personal possessions, material and spiritual, his time and his plans. Here vicars were not only to hear lectures and to study books (mostly from Bonhoeffer's own library!), but were also to learn to live together, to pray, to meditate on the words of Scripture, to confess their sins, to forgive sins in the name of Christ, and to make door-to-door pastoral calls at the homes in the village. And, of course, there were times devoted to pure fun, evenings when the group gathered around the piano and sang familiar songs (and unfamiliar ones, such as the Negro spirituals that Bonhoeffer had learned in America!), as well as times of physical labor, washing and drying dishes, and cleaning house. Those who experienced this fellowship in the so-called "Brother-house" of Finkenwalde affirm that the atmosphere was neither ascetic nor pietistic, but one of real joy and freedom under the Word of God.

In spite of his many tasks as leader of the seminary, Bonhoeffer found time during the summer of 1935 to deliver addresses on "Christ in the Psalms" ("Christus in den Psalmen") and "The Making Present of New Testament Texts" ("Vergegenwärtigung neutestamentlicher Texte"). Drawing on his extensive ecumenical experience, he also wrote a discerning essay on "The Confessing Church and the Oikoumene" ("Die Bekennende Kirche und die Oekumene"), in which he indicates the mutual significance of the

---

[14] One of these vicars was Eberhard Bethge, who later became his assistant and closest friend, and who married his niece in 1943. Bethge is the friend to whom Bonhoeffer wrote his letters from prison, and it is Bethge who has edited all of his posthumous works.

encounter between the German Confessing Church and the ecumenical movement. Finally, Eberhard Bethge reports that Bonhoeffer made regular trips from Finkenwalde to Berlin during 1935 and 1936 in order to resume his teaching at the University of Berlin, that is, until August 5, 1936, when his authority to teach at the university as a *Privatdozent* was withdrawn. After a year of bearing the total responsibility of leadership in Finkenwalde, Bonhoeffer realized that this not only was unwise and impractical for the enterprise, but also presented a dangerous temptation to him personally, so he arranged for several of the members of the seminary's first class to leave their church assignments and to live in the house and share the work with him.[15]

At the official invitation of the Swedish Ecumenical Council, Bonhoeffer, together with Inspector of Studies Wilhelm Rott, took the vicars of his Finkenwalde seminary on a study tour of Denmark and Sweden from February 29 until March 11, 1936. The entire trip was an unforgettable ecumenical experience, for the Danish and Swedish church officials, who were in sympathy with the German Confessing Church, did their utmost to make the guests feel at home and to acquaint them with the church and university life in their countries. They visited Copenhagen, Lund, Stockholm, Uppsala, and many small towns; they were taken on conducted tours through some of the best-known universities, cathedrals, churches, shrines, and church institutions; they heard lectures by many of Scandinavia's renowned theologians and churchmen; they attended receptions given by the highest church officials; and, most important, they were given opportunity to tell about the German Church Struggle and to gain support for the evangelical resistance movement. On several occasions Bonhoeffer gave an address on the theme "Visible and Invisible Church," and this usually brought forth a lively discussion. All in all, such a tour at this particular time was quite unusual, and the invitation was undoubtedly dependent upon Bonhoeffer's good name in the ecumenical movement.[16]

August of 1936 was a particularly busy month for Dietrich Bon-

---

[15] "Dietrich Bonhoeffer: An Account of His Life," by Eberhard Bethge, in *The Plough*, Vol. III, No. 2, p. 35.

[16] A detailed report of the trip is given in *Junge Kirche*, 4. Jahrg. H. 9, May 2, 1936, pp. 420–426.

hoeffer. The Olympic Games were being held in Berlin, and since they had attracted many visitors to Hitler's Reich, the Confessing Church took this opportunity to inform as many outsiders as possible about the true situation of the church in Germany. A series of daily lectures by prominent leaders of the Confessing Church was held at the Apostle Paul Church. Bonhoeffer was one of those chosen for this service, and he spoke on "The Inner Life of the Evangelical Church in Germany" ("Das innere Leben der evangelischen Kirche in Deutschland"). Later in the month he was a member of the Confessing Church's delegation, which was led by President Koch and Hans Böhm, to the meeting of the Universal Christian Council for Life and Work at Chamby, Switzerland (August 20–26).[17] This meeting, which was preparatory for the World Conference on Church, Community, and State at Oxford in 1937, was peculiar in having two German delegations: besides that of the Confessing Church, there was an "official" delegation from the Reich Church, headed by General Superintendent Zöllner and Bishop Heckel. Both delegations were subsequently invited to the Oxford Conference, but, as it turned out, the Nazi Government allowed neither to attend. Nevertheless, both groups contributed preliminary studies of the theme, the Reich Church's being the book *Church, People, and State* (*Kirche, Volk, und Staat*), edited by Dr. Eugen Gerstenmaier, while the Confessing Church sent a short report mainly composed by Hans Böhm and Bonhoeffer. As one commentator has pointed out, a comparison of these two documents reveals the immense difference of spirit between the two groups.[18]

Except for a series of Bible studies on "King David" ("König David") and "The Reconstruction of Jerusalem According to Ezra and Nehemiah" ("Der Wiederaufbau Jerusalems nach Esra und Nehemia"), all of Bonhoeffer's writings in 1936 dealt with the church

[17] Bethge accompanied Bonhoeffer to Chamby, and afterward the two proceeded to Italy, traveling as far south as Rome, then returned to Germany by way of Zürich, where they visited Bonhoeffer's friend Erwin Sutz. Bonhoeffer mentions this trip often in his letters from prison.

[18] Hans Böhm's article on "Bekennende Kirche und Oekumene" in *Bekennende Kirche: Martin Niemöller zum 60. Geburtstag* (Chr. Kaiser Verlag, Munich, 1952), p. 193. See also Karl Kupisch, *Zwischen Idealismus und Massendemokratie* (Lettner Verlag, Berlin, 1955), pp. 252 f.; *Junge Kirche*, Sept. 5, 1936, p. 826.

struggle. His sharp statement that "whoever knowingly separates himself from the Confessing Church in Germany separates himself from salvation," which was published in an essay entitled "Concerning the Question of Church Communion" ("Zur Frage nach der Kirchengemeinschaft"), created a storm of controversy and called forth Helmut Gollwitzer's mildly critical "Pointers and Considerations" ("Hinweise und Bedenken"), which Bonhoeffer answered with his "Questions" ("Fragen").[19] In June he circulated among the pastors of the Pomeranian Council of Brethren a mimeographed article with the title "False Doctrine in the Confessing Church?" ("Irrlehre in der Bekennenden Kirche?"), in which he stanchly defended the decision of the Oeynhausen Synod[20] to refuse to cooperate with the new "church committees" that had been established by Hanns Kerrl, the notorious Minister for Church Affairs whom Hitler had appointed in 1935 to supplant the ineffective Reichsbishop Müller. "Whoever has said 'Yes' to the fundamental declaration of Barmen," asserts Bonhoeffer, "must also say 'Yes' to the fundamental declaration of Oeynhausen." He then proceeded to prove, on the basis of Scripture and the Lutheran Confessional Writings, that those "Lutherans" who objected to the Oeynhausen Synod's declaration concerning the *order* of the church were performing a poor service to Lutheranism!

In 1937, Bonhoeffer published the book that made him famous in Germany: *The Cost of Discipleship (Nachfolge)*. This work, which he had begun in 1935, was a profound interpretation of the Sermon on the Mount and what it means to follow Jesus Christ. A small Bible study on *Temptation (Versuchung)* also stems from this year, although the manuscript was first published posthumously in 1953.

[19] All these articles appeared in the journal *Evangelische Theologie*.
[20] The opposition of the Confessing Church to the state-supported German Christion Reich Church took form at four great Confessional Synods, which bear the names of the cities in which the assembly took place: Barmen (May 29-31, 1934), Dahlem (September 19-20, 1934), Augsburg (June 4-6, 1935), and Oeynhausen (February 17-22, 1936). The original unity of the Lutheran, Reformed, and United Churches, which joined in the Confessional Synods, was considerably shaken after Oeynhausen, when the bishops of the so-called "intact" Lutheran Churches (Marahrens of Hannover, Meiser of Bavaria, Wurm of Württemberg) moved to set up a Lutheran Council as an independent agency to negotiate with the governing authorities.

During the week of April 12–17, 1937, there was a reunion at Finkenwalde of the "first class," those pastors who, with Bonhoeffer, had established the seminary two years earlier, and Bonhoeffer introduced each day with this Bible study. At a conference at Finkenwalde in May he delivered an address on "Propositions Concerning the Power of the Keys and Church Discipline in the New Testament" ("Sätze über Schlüsselgewalt und Gemeindezucht im Neuen Testament"). In October of 1937 the Finkenwalde seminary was disbanded by the order of Heinrich Himmler, the infamous leader of the Nazi S.S. (Hitler's Black Guards) and head of the Secret Police. The same work, however, was begun again in the winter semester with two groups of ministerial candidates (*Sammelvikariaten*) who periodically met together for instruction. Approximately ten vicars gathered in Köslin, another eight to ten in the village Gross-Schlönwitz bei Schlawe, each group being under the protection of the respective Church Superintendents. Bonhoeffer lived in Schlawe, but spent half a week teaching at each location, i.e., in Köslin and Gross-Schlönwitz. Eberhard Bethge lived in the village Gross-Schlönwitz and assumed the leadership of that section of the "seminary."

In 1938, Bonhoeffer addressed his fellow pastors of Pomerania on the subject "Our Way According to the Testimony of Scripture" ("Unser Weg nach dem Zeugnis der Schrift"), and warned them against the growing temptation to quit the Confessing Church. He powerfully defends the decisions made by the Confessional Synods of Barmen and Dahlem from the standpoint of the New Testament doctrine of the church. In 1939 he published *Life Together* (*Gemeinsames Leben*), a small but extremely influential work that embodies the fruit of the two-year experience of communal life at the Brotherhouse of Finkenwalde. Mention should also be made here of the many sermons that Bonhoeffer preached during these years when he was preparing young men for the ministry. Many of these were mimeographed and circulated among the "graduates" of his "school," and they are exceptional expositions of Scripture from the heart and mind of a man for whom preaching was an integral part of life.

By 1939 the dark clouds of war were on the horizon. Hitler's army had marched into Czechoslovakia in March, just one year after the "annexation" of Austria to the Third Reich, and an attack on Poland was just a matter of time. On March 12, 1939, Bonhoeffer, accompanied by his friend Bethge, went to England to visit his former congregations, and while in London he renewed his ecumenical contacts with Bishop Bell of Chichester and Leonard Hodgson, and met Visser 't Hooft for the first time.[21] He was also in correspondence with Reinhold Niebuhr, who was in Scotland at the time giving the Gifford Lectures. For many reasons it seemed wise to Bonhoeffer's Anglo-Saxon friends that he should leave Germany. First of all, he was due for military service in July, and they knew that he would refuse to serve and feared what might happen to him. When asked by a Swede at the Fanö meeting of the Universal Christian Council, "What will you do if war comes?", Bonhoeffer had replied, "I shall pray to Christ to give me the power not to take up arms." Second, because Bonhoeffer virtually embodied the spirit of the church struggle, it was felt that he could play a valuable role in acquainting the outside world with the true nature of the German situation. Third, for the sake of the isolated Confessing Church it was of utmost importance that its ecumenical contacts be kept open and secure. Finally, there was a quite natural desire to save the life of this unusually gifted man for the work of the church after the war. In order for Bonhoeffer to obtain permission from the Nazis to leave Germany for a considerable length of time, however, there had to be some rather formidable reason, and it was Niebuhr who suggested that he could get him an official invitation to lecture and teach in America.

Bonhoeffer returned to Germany the middle of April and conferred with the Council of Brethren about the possibility of obtaining a leave of absence from his teaching duties in order to go to America, and he pledged to return to Germany and resume his work in the Confessing Church in about a year, unless some unforeseen development changed the whole situation. At first the Council was reluctant to let him go because of the shortage of teachers, but in view of the importance of ecumenical contact between their church and the

[21] Visser 't Hooft tells of this encounter in *Das Zeugnis eines Boten* (Geneva, 1945), pp. 6f.

church in America (Bonhoeffer's personal difficulties came in only as a secondary consideration), they agreed. Through Niebuhr's efforts Bonhoeffer then received a formal invitation to come to America under the general auspices of the Central Bureau of Interchurch Aid and Union Theological Seminary of New York City. His duties were to be "a combination of pastoral service, preaching, and lecturing," he was to begin by the middle of June, and the term of service was not fixed, but would occupy him "for at least the next two or three years."[22] With this document Bonhoeffer was able to obtain permission to leave Germany, but before he departed, he left a small note on his table for his successor in the seminary work. In it he expressed the hope that he would continue the present course of study, assured him that he was taking over one of the best jobs in the Confessing Church, and, last but not least, exhorted him to take frequent walks with the brethren in the nearby woods!

Bonhoeffer flew to London on June 4, 1939, sailed from Southampton on the seventh, and arrived in New York on the twelfth. From the outset, however, his anxiety for his brothers in Germany weighed upon his mind, and his own departure from the scene of battle to the security and comfort of America troubled his conscience. Because of his unusual qualifications, the American Christian Committee proposed that Bonhoeffer work as a pastor for the German refugees who were flowing into New York City, but soon after his arrival he wrote a letter to the man who had sent the official invitation, Dr. Henry Leiper, explaining that he could make no permanent commitments, for he had to be free to return to Germany in case the situation worsened. Also, he did not wish to take such a job away from a refugee pastor who *could* not return to Germany. Soon afterward he received word from home that war was almost certain to break out by September, and he unhesitatingly decided to return to his homeland. At that time he wrote Niebuhr a letter somewhat to this effect: "Sitting here in Dr. Coffin's garden [he was visiting the President of Union Theological Seminary at his country home in Connecticut], I have had the time to think and to pray about my situation and that of my nation and to have God's will for me clarified. I have come to the conclusion that I have made a mistake in

[22] See this preparatory correspondence in GS I, pp. 287 ff.

coming to America. I must live through this difficult period of our national history with the Christian people of Germany. I will have no right to participate in the reconstruction of Christian life in Germany after the war if I do not share the trials of this time with my people. My brothers in the Confessional Synod wanted me to go. They may have been right in urging me to do so; but I was wrong in going. Such a decision each man must make for himself. Christians in Germany will face the terrible alternative either of willing the defeat of their nation in order that Christian civilization may survive, or willing the victory of their nation and thereby destroying our civilization. I know which of these alternatives I must choose; but I cannot make that choice in security." [23]

Bonhoeffer had originally planned to visit his friend Paul Lehmann, who was at that time a professor at Elmhurst College in Illinois, but in view of his altered plans he wrote Lehmann urging him to come to New York. This Lehmann did, and during their last days together, he tried to persuade him to remain in America. Bonhoeffer had made up his mind, however, and there was nothing left for Lehmann but to accompany him to the pier, where he boarded a German ship on July 7 and sailed for England. He arrived in London July 15 and proceeded to Germany on July 25. While he was in America, Bonhoeffer had written in his diary: "I do not understand why I am here. . . . The short prayer in which we thought of our German brothers almost overwhelmed me. . . . If matters become more uncertain, I shall certainly return to Germany. . . . In the event of war I shall not stay in America. . . ." While crossing the Atlantic, he wrote: "Since coming on board ship my inner disruption about the future has disappeared." [24]

B. Theological Exposition

How did Bonhoeffer carry over his basic idea of the church into his life and work and theology during the hectic period of the *Kirchenkampf* in Germany? To answer this question we must ex-

---

[23] Quoted by Reinhold Neibuhr in "The Death of a Martyr," in *Christianity and Crisis*, Vol. V, No. II, p. 6.

[24] Quotations are taken from Bethge's foreword to PFG, pp. 8 f. Also see GS I, pp. 291 ff.

amine almost a decade of theological writings, most of which are short essays and many of which were never published during his lifetime. In what follows these have been grouped into three categories: those concerned with the ecumenical movement, with the German church controversy, and with the theological exposition of Holy Scripture.[25] It should be noted that during this period, which cannot be understood apart from the politico-ecclesiastical events in Germany, Bonhoeffer's interest turns more and more to the question of ethics, his theological contribution increasingly takes the form of Biblical exegesis, and his style of writing becomes ever more simple and direct.

1. The Ecumenical Movement

Dietrich Bonhoeffer was extraordinarily qualified to represent the German Evangelical Church in the ecumenical movement. He was not only gifted with an incisive mind and natural linguistic ability, but also possessed a cosmopolitan spirit. Quite early in his career he lived for considerable periods of time in Spain, the United States, and England, and he had traveled in North Africa, Mexico, and most of the European countries. More important, he had struggled with the theological problem of the church and had arrived at a position from which he could make a positive contribution to ecumenical discussions.

Three things should be remembered concerning Bonhoeffer's relation to the Oikoumene. First, his direct participation, which began in 1931, was during a comparatively early phase of the movement. At this time he was one of the few German churchmen who were interested in and understood this twentieth-century phenomenon. Second, he worked initially among the youth and represented, more or less, the viewpoint of the rising generation. This meant, on the one hand, that he was sometimes impatient with the older views, and, on the other hand, that he was often irked by the theological immaturity of his youthful associates. Third, he was involved most intimately with that part of the ecumenical movement which dealt

[25] The material examined is not exhaustive, but includes most of the important items. Official English translations have been used and cited where possible; otherwise the writer is again responsible for translating and condensing the German texts.

with "practical Christianity": the World Alliance for Promoting International Friendship Through the Churches, and the Universal Christian Council for Life and Work. This suited his desire to correlate faith and action, but his belief that practice must be grounded theologically made him critical of those who sought only pragmatic solutions to the practical problems of the church.

What, now, was Dietrich Bonhoeffer's theological contribution to the ecumenical movement? His understanding of the work of the movement is most comprehensively expressed in an address delivered in Czechoslovakia entitled "Concerning the Theological Foundation of the Work of the World Alliance" (1932).[26] Theology, says Bonhoeffer, is the information of the church concerning its own nature on the basis of its understanding of the revelation of God in Christ. Whenever the church comes to a new understanding of itself, it brings forth a theology congruous with this new self-understanding. As yet, he points out, there is no theology of the ecumenical movement, and yet, if the movement truly represents a new turning point in the church's understanding of itself, then it must *necessarily* produce a theology. Thus far the churches have come together with a concern only for common Christian action and have disregarded theological differences, and first when they are in the midst of the ocean do they notice that the ice on which they stand is full of cracks! It would do no good for them to act before the world and before one another *as if* they knew the Christian truth, when in fact they do not; no good could come from hiding behind pious resolutions and so-called Christian principles. The questions: What is Christianity? and How does the work of the ecumenical movement appear in the light of the truth of the gospel? must be answered for the sake of movement itself.

Bonhoeffer now attempts to answer these questions in terms of the part of the Oikoumene with which he is associated, namely, the World Alliance for Promoting International Friendship Through the Churches. Whether it is conscious of it or not, he says, the work of the World Alliance is based upon a certain understanding of the church, which may be formulated in this statement: As the one congregation of the Lord Jesus Christ, who is Lord of the world,

[26] GS I, pp. 140–158.

the church has the commission to speak his word to the whole world. It is this claim of Christ on the *whole world* that unifies the churches and defines their task. But in what authority does the church speak when it announces the claim of Christ on the world? In the authority, asserts Bonhoeffer, in which the church alone can speak, namely, in the authority of the present, living Christ. The church is the *Christus praesens,* and the word of the church has authority because it is the word of the present Christ. This word is *both gospel and commandment:* not commandment alone, for that would be a retreat to the synagogue; and not gospel alone, for that would be a fall into fanaticism. If it is to be authoritative, the word of the church to the world must strike the world in its total reality here and now, must stem from the most profound understanding of the world itself. That is, the church must speak a *concrete* word; otherwise its word will be powerless. Therefore, the church cannot proclaim eternally valid principles, but only commandments that are true today, because what " always " is true is just " today " not true. God is for us " always " precisely God " today "!

But how can the gospel and how can the commandment be proclaimed with authority, i.e., with complete concreteness? Here we face a problem of unusual difficulty and range. Can the church proclaim the commandment of God with the same assurance that it proclaims his gospel? Can it say, " We need a socialist economic order " or " Do not wage war," as well as, " Your sins are forgiven "? Neither gospel nor commandment is proclaimed with full power unless spoken concretely, but wherein lies the principle of concretion with the gospel and wherein with the commandment? Bonhoeffer's answer: the gospel becomes concrete with the hearer, the commandment becomes concrete through the proclaimer! As a statement spoken to the congregation in the proclamation, in the preaching, or at the Lord's Supper, the assertion, " Your sins are forgiven! " is of such a nature that it encounters the hearer in fullest concretion. On the contrary, the commandment needs to be filled with concrete content by the proclaimer; the commandment, " You shall love your neighbor! " is as such so general that it needs to be made explicitly concrete if I am to perceive what it means for me here and now. And only as this concrete word, emphasizes Bonhoeffer, is it God's word.

This means that the proclaimer must know the actual situation to which he speaks so well that the commandment strikes home. For instance, in the case of a decision for or against war, the church must not only be able to say, "There should really be no war; but there are also necessary wars," and now leave it to each individual to apply this principle, but it should be able to say concretely, "Go to war" or "Do not go to war." Or in the social question, the final word of the church should not be to say, "It is wrong that one has an abundance when another hungers; but property is willed by God and may not be touched," and now again leave the application to the individual. No, says Bonhoeffer, when the church really has a commandment of God, then it must proclaim it in the most concrete form out of the fullest knowledge of the matter at hand and must call for obedience. A commandment must be concrete or it is no commandment. God's commandment demands something quite definite from us now, and the church should proclaim this to the congregation.

Just here, however, an immense difficulty arises. If the church must know the facts of any case down to the minutest details, then it always runs the risk of overlooking or even underestimating this or that fact, or this or that point of view, and this again would make it uncertain about its commandment. There are two positions that can be taken in regard to this dilemma: first, the difficulty may be evaded by a retreat to the level of principles, which is the way the churches have almost always gone; or second, the difficulty may be faced squarely, and in spite of all dangers, something may be ventured. Either the church risks the deliberate and qualified silence of a not-knowing, or it risks the concrete, exclusive, radical commandment. In this case the church dares to speak this commandment as God's own commandment, clearly recognizing that it may thereby blaspheme God's name, that it errs and sins, but knowing that it may utter the commandment in faith in the word of the forgiveness of sins, which is also valid for it. Thus the proclamation of the commandment is grounded in the proclamation of the forgiveness of sins! The church cannot command unless it itself has faith in the forgiveness of sins and unless it points all those whom it commands to this its proclamation of the forgiveness of sins.

The validity of the proclamation of the commandment, then, is safeguarded by the proclamation of the forgiveness of sins, but what certifies the validity of the proclamation of forgiveness? Bonhoeffer answers: *the sacrament!* In the sacrament the general statement, " Your sins are forgiven! " is bound to water, wine, and bread; here it reaches the concretion peculiar to it, which, as a concrete here and now of the word of God, is understood alone by the believing hearer. What the sacrament is for the proclamation of the gospel, *the knowledge of the concrete reality* is for the proclamation of the commandment. The *reality,* namely, what really obtains in the factual situation, is the sacrament of the commandment! As the sacraments of Baptism and the Lord's Supper are the only forms of the reality of the first creation in this aeon, and as they are sacraments by virtue of their origin in creation, so the " ethical sacrament " of the reality is to be designated as a sacrament only in so far as this reality itself is wholly grounded in its relation to the reality of creation. Therefore, just as the fallen world and fallen reality continue solely through their relation to the created world and created reality, so the commandment rests upon the forgiveness of sins.

Bonhoeffer now asks from whence the church knows what God's commandment is for a particular time, since this is certainly not self-evident. On the contrary, the knowledge of God's commandment is an act of God's revelation. Where does the church perceive this revelation? Various answers can be given. Some say the Biblical law, the Sermon on the Mount, is the absolute norm for our action, and all we have to do is to take it seriously and obey. But, says Bonhoeffer, even the Sermon on the Mount may not become for us a legal statute. It is in its commandments an illustration of what God's commandment can be, but not what it is precisely today and precisely for us. The commandment is not there once for all, but it is given ever anew. Only thereby are we free from the law, which places itself between us and God, and able to listen to God alone. Others want to find the commandment of God in the orders of creation. Because certain orders were given in accordance with creation, one should not rebel against them, but should humbly accept them. Also here God's commandment is thought to be once for all there, capable of being found at any time. This, emphasizes Bonhoeffer, is an especially dangerous view, for by identifying the *status quo* with the will of God established in creation, one can justify almost anything: the segregation of peoples, national strife, war, the struggle between classes, the subjugation of the weak to the strong, life-and-death economic competition. The fallacy of this view is that it does not take seriously the fact that the world is fallen and is ruled by sin, that creation and sin are now so interwoven that no human eye can separate them and that every human order is an order of the fallen world and not an order of creation. The so-called "orders of creation" are now veiled and invisible and can furnish no basis for the recognition of God's commandment.

Both of these answers must be rejected, continues Bonhoeffer, because the commandment of God can come only from where the promise and fulfillment come, namely, from Jesus Christ. What we should do must be known from Christ alone, not, however, from him as the preaching prophet of the Sermon on the Mount, but from him as that one who gives us life and forgiveness, who has fulfilled the commandment of God in our stead, who brings and promises the new world. We can perceive the commandment only at the point where the law is fulfilled, and so we are directed exclusively to Jesus Christ. But therewith we also perceive that the world order of the fallen creation is directed solely toward Christ, toward the new creation. What was previously dark and hidden from our vision now moves into a new light, for we see that all these worldly orders exist only because they are directed toward Christ. They stand under the preservation of God so long as they remain open for Christ. That is, they are "orders of preservation," not "orders of creation."

Preservation is God's action with the fallen world whereby he guarantees the possibility of the new creation; orders of preservation are forms of the purposive structure against sin in the direction of the gospel. Every order or institution, even the oldest and most sacred, can and must be shattered if it becomes closed and hardened and no longer permits the proclamation of the revelation. It is from this standpoint that the church of Christ has to judge the orders of the world, and it is from here that it must hear the commandment of God. In the historical change of the orders of the world the church has only to ask this question: Which orders are able to check most speedily this radical falling of the world into death and sin and to hold open the way for the gospel? Thus the commandment, which the church hears solely from Christ and perceives in the orders of preservation, is the absolutely critical and radical commandment that is limited by nothing — not even so-called " orders of creation." The church's risking and deciding for or against an order of preservation would be impossible if it did not happen in faith in the God who in Christ also forgives the church its sins. But in this faith the church *must* venture and decide!

Bonhoeffer now applies this theological criterion to the World Alliance's concrete problem of peace. Up until this time the Alliance, under the overpowering influence of the Anglo-Saxon theological thinking, has absolutized the ideal of peace by considering it as a reality of the gospel, as a piece of the Kingdom of God on earth, and therefore not as an order of preservation, but as an order of consummation valid in itself. External peace is as such a " very good " condition; it is consequently an order of creation and of the Kingdom of God, and thus it is to be unconditionally preserved. This view, asserts Bonhoeffer, must be rejected as fanatic and unevangelical. International peace is neither a reality of the gospel nor a piece of the Kingdom of God, but a commandment of the wrathful God, an order of the preservation of the world for the sake of Christ. It is therefore no absolute ideal condition, but an order that is directed toward something else and is not worthy in itself. As an order of preservation, it can receive the stamp of absolute urgency, not for its own sake, but solely for the sake of the hearing of the revelation.

The broken character of the order of peace finds expression in the fact that the peace commanded by God has two limits: truth and justice. A fellowship of peace can only exist when it rests neither on lies nor on injustice, but on the forgiveness of sins. For Anglo-Saxon thinking, truth and justice always remain subordinated to the ideal of peace. Indeed, the very presence of peace is the proof that truth and justice are preserved. Precisely because an order of peace is a reality of the gospel and of the Kingdom of God, truth and justice can never be opposed to it. It has become clear, however, that this view is illusory. Neither the external order of peace nor the peace that derives from the battle for truth and justice on behalf of peace, but alone the *peace of God* that produces the forgiveness of sins is the reality of the gospel in which truth and justice are preserved. Neither a static concept of peace nor a static concept of truth can lead to the evangelical understanding of peace in its relation to the concepts of truth and righteousness. Because an external order of peace may completely violate truth and justice and thereby threaten to make impossible the hearing of the revelation in Christ, struggle is a fundamental possibility of action in view of Christ. It is not an order of creation, but may be an order of preservation toward the new creation. That is, struggle may in certain cases better preserve the openness for the revelation in Christ than external peace, if in fact it shatters an order that is hardened and closed in itself. However, Bonhoeffer quickly adds, this justification of *struggle* does not at all mean a justification of *war*. Modern warfare is simply not comparable to what was called " war " in the past. The war of today can no longer fall under the concept of struggle because it means the certain self-destruction of both participants. Therefore, it can no longer be designated as an order of preservation for the sake of the gospel just because it is absolutely destructive. Because war can in no way be understood as an order of preservation, but would actually *prevent* the view to revelation, the church must understand God's *present* commandment to be the *outlawing of war*. This in no way excludes struggle as such from the world, but it excludes a definite *means* of struggle, which today stands under the prohibition of God. It has nothing to do with the fanatic lifting up of one commandment — perhaps the fifth — above others, but concerns our obedience to the commandment of God that meets us today, the commandment that there should no longer be war because it robs man of his view to revelation.

Until now the World Alliance has believed that peace could be assured by achieving an " understanding " among nations, an understanding that the Anglo-Saxons in particular have believed would come about through *personal acquaintance*. While this is a necessary first step, asserts Bonhoeffer, it is by no means the most important. What the ecumenical movement needs more than anything else is *one, great, common proclamation* that would lead people together, and this can come only *via a theology,* so we end where we started!

Bonhoeffer concludes his address with two brief questions: "To whom does the church speak?" and "Who is this church which speaks?" He gives this answer to the first: the church speaks to *Christendom,* saying that it should hear its word as the commandment of God deriving from the forgiveness of sins, and it also speaks to the *world,* saying that it should change conditions, for not only the will of man but also conditions can be " good " when they relate to the new creation through Christ. Of course, the world or state cannot hear the true, authoritative word of the church, but the church can become a noteworthy critic of the world's action and can indicate the critical limits of the world's possibilities. And who is this church? Bonhoeffer answers: the church that proclaims the gospel according to the truth. Now the really distressing question that separates the various churches arises: the question of truth. Bonhoeffer knows no answer to this most urgent problem of the ecumenical movement. He can only point to this: that where the church recognizes the guilt of its shredded knowledge of the truth and yet believes that under the commandment of God it still must speak, the forgiveness of sins is promised to the humble! To be sure, this indication can be no human solution of our distress, but solely the expression for the waiting of the whole church on the redemption. That the church in its trouble should remain humble and should live from the forgiveness alone — that, concludes Bonhoeffer, is the last information that can be given here.

In his address to the International Youth Conference at Gland, Switzerland (1932), which begins with the words " The church is dead . . . ,"[27] Bonhoeffer asserts that the World Alliance is not simply a useful organization but a definite form of the church. Those who come together are seeking to hear Christ, and they hear him in the voice of their brother. They hear God's commandment of peace, and yet they stand in fear before a world that is torn by conflict and seems to be possessed by demons. What the church must know when facing this situation is that all of its education toward understanding, all of its talk of good will and setting up of organizations, will be of no avail unless the Lord himself comes and drives out the demons. Jesus Christ, who on the cross has made peace with God and man-

[27] GS I, pp. 162–170.

kind, must be present in the preaching and Sacrament if the demons and the gods of the world are to be exorcised, for they tremble alone before the cross! Christ himself is the church's peace, and his cross is not in some faraway realm, but stands right in the midst of the world, calling forth wrath and judgment over the world of hate and proclaiming peace. With its proclamation of peace the church gives to the world the message of the new humanity, the sacred brotherhood in Christ, a brotherhood of those who are bound together in listening to the word of the Lord, who repent and confess their guilt for not hearing his commandment as they should, who know that their action, while indispensable, is nevertheless provisional, and finally, who look forward to the return of the Lord, who will judge the old world and set up the new. In this world, concludes Bonhoeffer, there is peace only in the struggle for truth and justice, but in the new world there will be the eternal peace of the love of God. That is the new heaven and the new earth, which God himself will create.

In an address on " The Church and the People of the World " at Fanö (1934),[28] Bonhoeffer urges the Universal Christian Council to send out to the churches and to the world a *radical* call for peace in the name of Christ. Christians who take up arms against one another, he declares, take up arms against Christ himself! How can peace be attained? Through political treaties, investment of international capital in various countries, universal peaceful rearmament? No, for in all these schemes peace is confused with safety. Peace is something that must be dared; it is a great venture! Peace is in fact the opposite of security. It means to submit oneself entirely to the law of God, wanting no security, but in faith and obedience placing the destiny of nations in the hand of Almighty God. Who of us, asks Bonhoeffer, can say that he knows what it might mean for the world if one nation should meet the attack of an aggressor, not with weapons in hand, but praying, defenseless — and for that very reason protected by " a Bulwark never failing "?

In his essay on " The Confessing Church and the Oikoumene " (1935),[29] Bonhoeffer was chiefly concerned with the relation of the Oikoumene to the church's confession of faith and to the question

[28] GS I, pp. 447–449.   [29] GS I, pp. 240–261.

of truth. Here he argues that the Oikoumene can speak and act with authority only if it claims to be church, and there is church only as a *confessing* church. A confessionless or confession-free " church " is not church, but a kind of fanaticism which makes itself lord over the Bible and the word of God. The creed or confession, explains Bonhoeffer, is simply the formulated answer of the church, spoken in its own words, to the word of God in Holy Scripture; and unity of confession belongs to the true unity of the church. If this is true, however, then how can the Oikoumene, with its many churches having different confessional bases, be the *one* church and speak a common, authoritative word? The majority of those in the ecumenical movement solve the problem with this line of reasoning: According to Scripture there is one, holy, catholic church, and each of the existing churches is a special form of this one church. As the branches of a tree stem from a common root and trunk and yet only all together make up the whole tree, or as all the members of a body must be present in order to make up the whole body, so the fellowship of all the churches of the world first makes up the one, holy, catholic church. The meaning of the ecumenical movement, then, is to display the rich diversity and harmony of Christendom. No one church demands sole recognition; each brings its special gift and performs its special service for the whole. First in the unity lies the truth.

Bonhoeffer asserts that this argumentation, which has become the dogma of the ecumenical movement, must be destroyed by the German Confessing Church! The proposition that only in unity is there truth may be correct and Biblical, but just as correct and Biblical is the opposite: that only in the truth is unity possible. Truth has a separating power, and there are situations, such as the church struggle between the Confessing Church and the German Christians, in which the truth completely divides the true church from an anti-Christian " church." Here all conversation between the two must definitely be broken off. Of course, continues the author, it would be doctrinaire to deduce from this that the Confessing Church could not come together with other churches simply because the confessional basis is not the same. Such an attitude would fail to grasp the difference between a *living confession* and a confession that is understood as a total system of doctrine, with which one can rationally and schematically measure other churches. A living confession does not mean to pit one dogmatic thesis against another, but rather indicates a confession which concerns the life and death of the church. Naturally it should be a clearly formulated, theologically grounded confession, but here theology is placed completely at the service of the living, struggling church. It is this sort of living confession which divides, and which *must* divide, the Confessing Church from the German Christians. On the other hand, concludes Bonhoeffer, the confession that provides a basis for the Confessing Church's participation with the other churches in the ecumenical movement is the common *confession of sin,* which recognizes the guilt of each in the torn condition of Christendom and knows that the whole church lives solely by the grace of God in Jesus Christ!

2. The German Church Struggle

The struggle of the Confessing Church against the Hitler-inspired and state-dominated Reich Church of the German Christians was at bottom a conflict over the proper relationship between church and state. This question became a burning issue in 1933, and during this year Bonhoeffer published three essays that reveal his attitude toward the problem.

In " Thy Kingdom Come! The Prayer of the Church for God's Kingdom on Earth," the young theologian describes church and state as the two forms of the Kingdom of God on earth and explains their necessary, mutual relatedness. He cites three facts about our world which form the background of his discussion. First, God created the earth, formed man from its soil, and pronounced his blessing of " very good " upon his creation. Second, because of man's disobedience and fall, God cursed the earth, so that now it bears thorns and thistles, God's face is hidden from his creature, and man is enslaved by the powers of dying, loneliness, and thirst. Third, Jesus Christ, God's own Son, came to this cursed earth, bore the flesh taken from its soil, was crucified on the " tree of the curse " planted deep into the earth, and in the midst of this dying, divided, thirsting world, broke through the curse by his resurrection! In this miracle of the resurrection, whereby God says a profound " Yes! " to the world, the Kingdom of God has come on earth. The coming of the Kingdom of God, emphasizes Bonhoeffer, means nothing else than the coming of God himself, and his coming in Christ signifies not only a break-through and destruction of the curse, but at the same time an affirmation of the earth, an entrance into its orders, its communities, its history.

Thus the Kingdom of God on earth assumes this twofold form: first, the final Kingdom of the resurrection miracle, which breaks through the curse of death, solitude, and thirst and brings to nought all man's earthly kingdoms; second, the Kingdom of order, which affirms and preserves the earth with its laws, communities, and history. The former we call "church," the latter "state." Each is integrally related to the other; neither can stand alone. The Kingdom of God assumes form in the church in so far as the church witnesses to the miracle of God's new creation; the Kingdom of God assumes form in the state in so far as the state preserves the order of the old creation. Thus the church witnesses to the overcoming of the power of death by the miracle of the resurrection; the state upholds the order of the preservation of life. In the church the power of loneliness is overcome by the miracle of confession and forgiveness and the creation of a new community; in the state the given orders of society, marriage, family, people, are preserved in the world of the curse. In the church the thirst of egocentric man for his own self is overcome by the proclamation of the cross and resurrection of Christ and is transfigured into a loving thirst for the other, namely, for God and the brother; in the state the thirst of man, which may bode good or evil for others, is ordered and restrained by responsible authority. From this it becomes clear, therefore, that the church limits the state and the state limits the church. Both of them must remain cognizant of this mutual limitation and bear the strain of existing side by side without overstepping the boundary between them. That is, the church may never become state, and the state may never become church. All of this, of course, remains pure theory until we introduce the people into the picture. Because they are called to the Kingdom of God, the people stand in both church and state; they must live obediently in both, yet take seriously the limit of each. That the church has its office alone in the miracle and that the state has its office solely in the order, and that between church and state the people of God, Christendom, should now live obediently — that, concludes Bonhoeffer, is the prayer for the Kingdom of God on earth!

In an essay entitled "What Is Church?" Bonhoeffer elaborates somewhat the church's responsibility in respect to the state. Since the preaching of the church proclaims the break-through of the limits of human possibility and thus the destruction of the laws of the world, it is necessarily "political." Precisely as "political," however, it sets from the beginning the critical limit of all political action. The church is the end of politics, says Bonhoeffer, and therefore political and apolitical at the same time! It has the possibility of speaking two "political words." The first word of the church to politics is the call to the recognition of its own limitation, which the church calls "sin" and the state calls "reality," but which both might call "finitude." The first word is not "Christianization of politics," but "politics within a finite context," and this releases the church from party politics and places it in the genuine political sphere free from party allegiance. But what about the church's second word? Beyond the sober indication of the limitation, can the church perceive a commandment of God that would involve it *directly* in the political affairs of the state, even in certain circumstances to the formation of its own party? In principle, states Bonhoeffer, this possibility cannot be excluded, yet here the church must be extremely cautious. In the first place, the commandment would have to be completely concrete and not simply the carrying out of some program based on a "Christian" political ideology. Further, the church would have to ask itself quite seriously if it had *really* received this commandment, and if so, whether it demanded direct political action *as a party* or if it would not be wiser to work through existing parties. Finally, the church would have to consider whether the speaking of this second word was worth jeopardizing its first word. However, concludes Bonhoeffer, in the end, the speaking of the second word must remain an ultimate possibility for the church.

The question of the treatment of the Jews in Hitler's Third Reich evoked a third essay in 1933 involving the church-state relationship: "The Church Before the Jewish Question." Here Bonhoeffer says that so long as the state acts to maintain justice and order, the church as such may not engage in direct political action against it. This does not mean, of course, that the church takes no interest in political affairs, for it is the responsibility of the church to ask the state again and again whether it is fulfilling its duties *as a state,* that is, whether it is acting to produce law and order. The church must protest both when there is *too little order,* i.e., when the state allows a group of its citizens to live beyond the law, and when there is *too much order,* i.e., when the state represses the proclamation of the Christian gospel or suppresses the Christian faith. The latter situation would be grotesque indeed, because the state that endangers the Christian proclamation negates its own self, contravenes its *raison d'être!*

The author now sets out what he considers to be the church's three possibilities of action over against the state: first, the church may question the state concerning the legitimacy of its actions and ask the state to fulfill its proper obligations; second, the church may help the victims of improper state action, and this it should do regardless of whether the injured are church members or not; third, the church may not only dress the wounds of those who have been run over by the " wheel of state," but may throw its own self into the spokes of the wheel! This last action, of course, would involve *direct* political action by the church and is only possible when the church sees the state refusing to be the state, refusing to carry out its function of maintaining law and order and thereby endangering the church's own function, that is, when the state is able to realize arbitrarily and unrestrainedly " too little " or " too much " order. In this case the church would be *in statu confessionis,* and the state would be in the situation of self-negation. In the end, however, this third possibility, which leads the church into conflict with the existing state, is only the paradoxical expression for its final recognition of the state! Here the church recognizes the necessity of the state and acts to restore the proper functions of its divine office. With regard to the Jewish question at that time, Bonhoeffer concludes that for the church the first two possibilities are obligatory demands of the hour, but the third could only be decided by an " evangelical council " and could never be casuistically constructed beforehand.

The incidents that provoked these early statements of Bonhoeffer concerning the relationship of church and state merely foreshadowed the struggle that was yet to come. Until now the boundary between church and state seemed clearly defined, and one had only to guard the boundary and explain the duties of each in respect to the other. But all at once the situation changed, and the church found its clear view vis-à-vis the state clouded by treason within its own borders! The German Christians, who professed to be church but who were consciously or unconsciously manipulated by the diabolic cunning of the Nazi state, were able to confuse the issues to such an extent that the church struggle appeared to be an inner-church instead of a church-state affair. Nevertheless, the German Evangelical Church was not without leaders of vision who saw through the disguise of this " wolf in sheep's clothing " and recognized the German Christians as tools of a pagan state and not church at all. Bonhoeffer's " third possibility " was now at hand, and the victim of the irresponsibly driven " vehicle of state " was none other than the church itself! As a result, an " evangelical council " was soon summoned and political action against the state that was denying its true statehood became a bitter reality. At the Barmen Confessional Synod the false doctrines of the German Christians were declared to be incongruous with the church of Christ, and at Dahlem the Confessing Church set up its own church government and declared itself to be the true church of Christ in Germany. Although Bonhoeffer was in London at the time of these Confessional Synods, he agreed thoroughly with the action taken at both and was one of the stanchest supporters of the Confessing Church's position.

Because the German Church Struggle was carried out under the guise of an inner cleavage between the Confessors and the German Christians, instead of a clear-cut church-state conflict, the question of fellowship between the two groups became exceedingly important. It was to this problem that Bonhoeffer addressed his controversial essay " Concerning the Question of Church Communion " (1936). He begins by asserting that the true church can never wish to draw its own boundary, for God alone knows the real members of his church. To attempt to define the nature of the church from a determination of its boundary, as in Roman Catholicism, is to interpret God's call to salvation in a legalistic way. Contrary to this, the Reformers disengaged the question, "What is the church?" from the question, "Who belongs to the church?" and simply proclaimed to the world, "Here is the true church!" Come here and hear the true gospel and receive the true sacrament! That is, says the author, the church does not set its own limits, but *encounters* a boundary that is drawn by the outside world when it refuses the church's gospel. The boundary of the church, then, is fixed when the church has a concrete encounter with unbelief and is thereby forced to make a living decision in a completely objective situation.

Although the church has no theoretical standards that can be used with legal precision in making this decision, it is not without definite guides. For instance, *baptism* gives the church a *general* determination of its bounds. On the one hand, however, baptism is not broad enough, since it does not include those who *desire* but for some reason are unable to receive baptism and those who undergo "blood baptism"; and, on the other hand, it is not limited enough, since among the baptized there are false teachers and dead members who cannot belong to the church. Using the criterion of baptism, then, the church knows a relative external limit and, at the same time, an inner limit that does not encompass all of the baptized. Now how does the church determine this innermost limit? By *doctrine* and *confession,* asserts Bonhoeffer! The confession of the church is constitutive for church communion. But now the question arises as to what confession is to be used: the ancient symbols, the Reformation confessional writings, some modern ecumenical formula? What authority do the differentiating doctrines of the individual churches have? Bonhoeffer here points out that often two church groups will hold many confessional articles in common, but will divide over one particular doctrine. For instance, the Reformation Church broke with the Roman Church over the single doctrine of justification, and later it was the doctrine of the Lord's Supper that prevented communion between the Lutheran and Reformed Churches. What does this mean? First, it is a recognition and confirmation of the church confession as such; there is really only one true confession, but one group has falsely understood a part of that confession and has to that extent separated itself from the truth. Secondly, it means that church fellowship is always something qualitatively total; there can be fellowship only when a *given, total, a priori unity* is recognized by an ecclesiastical decision of faith, and on the basis of this prior unity a confession can be formulated which does not allow theological differences to be church-splitting oppositions. That is, the confessional unity of a church is an act of ecclesiastical decision as a decision of faith, not an act of theological formulation. Thirdly, it means that the establishment of the point on which a dissension becomes a church-splitting antithesis is itself an act of church decision, and not something that can be legalistically determined beforehand. The decision arises when the church sees the invasion of the adversary in a special way at one particular place, and the place is by no means always the same. Fourthly, it means that a clear difference is seen between the task of dogmatics and that of the confession; the confession is not a combination of dogmatic propositions, from which now all the consequences are to be drawn. Otherwise, every doctrinal difference would necessarily lead to a division of the church. Instead, it is the *decision* concerning the church's limits which is executed by the church *on the basis of its theology.*

It follows, continues Bonhoeffer, that none of the confessions or creeds at hand is suitable to determine definitively the extent of the church. The boundary between the oppositions that split theological schools of thought and those which split churches is fundamentally not to be established. The boundary of the church does not stand at its own disposal, but must always be confirmed in the decision, and only in this final openness of decision is the possibility maintained that " school " oppositions grow from church-splitting oppositions, and vice versa.

Since the limit of the church is fixed from without, it may take as many forms as there is enmity against the gospel. It is a different matter whether the line is drawn by the world or by an anti-Christian " church " or by " another church." The difference between the latter two, both of which may teach false doctrine, is a matter of church decision and depends on whether the false doctrine is used against the true church in order to destroy it. The struggle of the true church with an anti-Christian church is a matter of life and death and excludes any possibility of fellowship between the two. On the other hand, " another church " may also teach false doctrine, yet because it is not bent on destruction but stands in a common confession of guilt for the brokenness of the body of Christ, communion with this church is possible. This, in fact, is the basis of the meeting of the churches in the ecumenical movement.

If it is clear that the question of church communion can be answered solely by a church decision, says Bonhoeffer, then it must now be said that this decision may in no case be avoided, but will accompany the struggle of the church each step of the way. Nevertheless, it will always remain the "strange work" of the church, a work that must be done in order that the church can carry out its "proper work." In the end, then, the decision about its limits is a merciful act of the church, both for its members and for those on the outside, because it is the final, "strange" possibility to make distinct its call to salvation.

Bonhoeffer now considers the concrete struggle of the Confessing Church against the German Christians. The Barmen Confessional Synod declared the doctrine of the German Christians to be false at several decisive points. The Dahlem Confessional Synod took upon itself the responsibility of asserting that the government of the Reich Church had by its doctrine and actions *excluded itself* from the true church of Christ. Moreover, the Confessing Church had decided to establish its own administrative body and to declare that it was the true church of Christ in Germany. These are historical facts, but what do they mean? First of all, asserts Bonhoeffer, these living, synodical decisions must be looked upon as the will of God! The Reich Church government is anti-Christian and has expelled itself from the true church, and all further communion and discussion between the Confessing Church and the German Christians of the Reich Church (even in the Oikoumene!) is at an end. We can no more go behind Barmen and Dahlem, precisely because we can no more go behind God's word! Furthermore, the fact that the Lutheran and Reformed Churches have come together as equals and have made these joint declarations denotes a decisive departure from the Augsburg Confession. There are only two possible attitudes toward these synods: either one rejects them completely on the basis of the *Augustana,* or one humbly accepts them and leaves it to God to make of them what he pleases. Finally, these decisions signify an ultimate affirmation of Cyprian's famous dictum: *Extra ecclesiam nulla salus,* outside the church there is no salvation! The limits of the church are the limits of salvation, so that whoever knowingly separates himself from the Confessing Church in Germany separates himself from salvation! However, warns Bonhoeffer, this can never be a theoretical truth or speculative proposition, but only an existential confession of faith of the true church.

Thus, the decision of the church concerning its limits is never an attempt to bind God's freedom and omnipotence, never a speculation over the saved and the damned, but is always an act of obedience consonant with the church's mission to proclaim the gospel: " Here is the true church! " It should not be a source of temptation for the church, he concludes, but should only serve to strengthen the assurance of salvation for the faithful.

After the Oeynhausen Confessional Synod, which refused to recognize the state-appointed " church committees " as proper administrators of church affairs and declared that " the church bound to the word of God is alone called to judge and decide in matters of doctrine and order," many Lutherans who were tempted to co-operate with the committees began to accuse the Confessing Church (in the name of " Lutheranism "!) of succumbing to Reformed doctrine in regard to the order of the church. They claimed that it was contrary to Lutheran doctrine to give the order of the church such legal weight; that the various churches must be free to choose their own order so long as this does not contradict God's word; that the church can never demand unconditional obedience in matters of order, that is, in matters of administration, constitution, etc. Consequently, these Lutherans began to imply that " false doctrine " had penetrated into the Confessing Church itself!

Bonhoeffer combats this notion in an article entitled " False Doctrine in the Confessing Church? " (1936), in which he shows that the Oeynhausen Declaration accords both with Scripture and with the Lutheran Confessional Writings themselves. Here he establishes three points. First, it is Lutheran doctrine that all church order stands in the service of the proclamation; it is not an end in itself, but a means to an end, so it can assume various forms. It is an adiaphoron, a matter of indifference. Therefore, there is a decisive difference between church confession and church order. Second, it is Lutheran doctrine that all offices and orders of the church must accord with the confession of the church. Therefore, church confession and church order cannot be separated. Third, it is Lutheran doctrine that the congregation is free to structure its order in the service of the proclamation, but that *in statu confessionis,* that is, when the church is attacked from without, even the orders belong to the confessional stand of the church and, for the sake of the gospel, may not be yielded. Thus, what is an adiaphoron within the church is toward the outside not an adiaphoron, but an integral part of the confession. Therefore, *in statu confessionis,* church confession and church order are one. Lutheran doctrine, then, is in complete agreement with the Reformed view on this point, the only difference between the two being that for Reformed doctrine church order is no adiaphoron even *within* the church.

Four years after Barmen and Dahlem, under the pressure of persecution and the demand that pastors take a personal oath to Hitler, many pastors and congregations were seriously questioning the resolutions of these Synods and were greatly tempted to leave the Confessing Church and join the so-called " neutrals " or place themselves under the state-proffered church consistory. At this time Dietrich Bonhoeffer again came to the defense of the " Barmen-Dahlem way " with an address to his brother pastors in Pomerania on " Our Way According to the Testimony of Scripture " (1938). After explaining that Scriptural proof can be given only for the truth of a doctrine (to be sure, when it is grounded both in individual texts and in the *whole* of Scripture!) and never for the rightness of a way (Scriptural proof does not relieve us from faith but leads us into the venture of faith and obedience to God's word!), Bonhoeffer gives evidence from the Bible supporting these six propositions which found expression in the Dahlem Declarations: (*a*) We are the one church. (*b*) The church requires a church administration. (*c*) The church administration can be appointed only by the church itself; it serves only the proclamation of the gospel and the proper congregational life. (*d*) The proclamation in the church is bound to the church's commission. (*e*) Obedience to a heretical church government is disobedience to Christ. (*f*) The church leaves the concern for the future to its Lord.

Bonhoeffer brings forth little that is theologically new in this address, but he pleads persuasively for recognition of these two facts: first, that the Declarations of Barmen and Dahlem are fundamentally true and integrally connected; second, that many in the Confessing Church have incurred guilt by not remaining faithful to the concern of Barmen and Dahlem, namely, the concern for the right proclamation of the gospel and the right building up of the congregation. That is, they have neglected the church's real mission by becoming too interested in the question of church government! This is the beginning of the criticism that Bonhoeffer expresses in his letters from prison, viz., the charge that the Confessing Church became too busy defending its own existence and thereby neglected its proper function of " being there for the other."

In a late memorandum concerning the " Conclusion of the Church Struggle " (probably 1942), Bonhoeffer outlines what he believes must take place for a successful ending of the church struggle. In general he calls for a lifting of all the oppressive measures taken by the state against the German Evangelical Church and a restoration of its complete independence. He expects little resistance from the German Christians and suggests that they be allowed to continue as a " free church," but that they be denied any opportunity for political activity or activity that would endanger church unity. He also calls for a new ordering of the German Evangelical Church under the leadership of the Confessing Church, with an immediate appointment of a provisional church administration, which within six months would hold church elections and work out a new constitution. In reordering the church, warns Bonhoeffer, it must by all means be avoided that the leadership should again come into the hands of the reactionary circles of the former General Superintendents and of the authoritarian church bureaucracy. This would be for both church and state a retrogressive solution of the church problem! A solution that will place the relation of church and state on a new basis, concludes Bonhoeffer, must come from the young generation of pastors and laymen who have been tested and proved in the church struggle itself.

In conclusion, it must be pointed out that Dietrich Bonhoeffer's involvement in the resistance movement that led to the unsuccessful attempt on Hitler's life on July 20, 1944, and to Bonhoeffer's own imprisonment and execution, is in a very real sense an unofficial and indirect continuation of his personal struggle on behalf of the church in Germany. Someone had to risk throwing himself into the spokes of an insanely driven " wheel of state," not only for the sake of the church, but for all the people of a war-torn world.

We might summarize Bonhoeffer's attitude during the German Church Struggle in the following statements:

a. The Kingdom of God on earth assumes form in the church and in the state.

b. Church and state are separate, in that each performs a different function within the divine economy, but are necessarily interrelated, in that one cannot properly exist without the other.

c. The German Church Struggle arose when the Nazi state attempted to " co-ordinate " the Evangelical Church; therefore, it was not essentially directed against the Nazi state as such, but against the state's interference in the life of the church.

d. By interfering with the life and work of the church, the state is denying its own essence as a state, for the state has the God-given task of preserving order, so that the church may proclaim the gospel.

e. The church can have but one Lord; therefore, the German Christians, who have accepted the lordship of the Nazi state, have expelled themselves from the church and have thereby relinquished all fellowship.

f. The attack on the church from the outside has led to a state of confession in which church order is no longer adiaphorous, but a matter of confession. Therefore, there can be no obedience to or relationship with any church organs established by the state, but only with the organs established by the church itself.

g. The church must never become so preoccupied with its " strange work " of deciding its limits and fighting about church order that it neglects its " proper work " of proclaiming the gospel and building up the Christian community.

h. The church struggle can end only when the state ceases its interference in the life of the church, i.e., when the state carries out its proper function as state and thus allows the church to be the church.

3. Theological Interpretation of Scripture

During the 1930's, Dietrich Bonhoeffer's interest in systematic theology diminished, and he turned more and more to the realm of practical theology and the theological exposition of the Bible. It would be false to imagine that his interest in theology as such had decreased, for in truth he simply found another way of expressing this interest, a way that seemed to him at this time more suitable and perhaps even necessary. By "theological interpretation of the Bible," Bonhoeffer meant an interpretation that accepts the Bible as the book of the church and makes this the presupposition of its methodology. Its method, then, is a continual referring from the text, which is to be ascertained with all the methods of philological and historical research, back to this presupposition. Only thus can it claim to be scientific.[30]

In what follows, an attempt is made to present Bonhoeffer's main theological insights in the various works of this period which interpret Holy Scripture as "the book of the church."

a. "Creation and Fall"

Creation and Fall (*Schöpfung und Fall*) stems from Bonhoeffer's lectures at the University of Berlin during the winter semester of 1932–1933. His theological interpretation of Gen., chs. 1 to 3, was so popular with his students that they requested him to make it available in published form. In the book Bonhoeffer systematically works through the verses of the first three chapters of Genesis, beginning each section with the quotation of a verse or group of verses (generally from the Luther translation) and following with his exposition. In the following condensation the verses are usually not written out or cited, but one can generally correlate interpretation and verse (or verses) by a consecutive following of the Genesis text.

Man, begins Bonhoeffer, stands in the middle between a lost beginning and a lost end and can now know of the beginning only by hearing the word of God, who is himself the Creator and thus the beginning. "Beginning" is no temporal designation, but an absolutely unrepeatable, unique, free happening; it is, in short, creation.

[30] See SchF, pp. 6 ff.

The Creator creates the creature, and the connection between the two is conditioned solely by freedom, that is, it is unconditioned! There is no cause and effect relation, for between the two stands only *das Nichts,* nothingness. Freedom takes place in and out of nothingness (there are no necessities in God!), and creation comes out of this nothingness. *Das Nichts* is not the " nothingness " of philosophical thinking, which ultimately is nothing else than the ground of being; not the final attempt to explain the creation of what exists; not the " stuff " out of which the world paradoxically arises; not a " something " at all, not even a negative " something "; not some primal possibility, the ground of God himself. No, the nothingness that lies between God's freedom and the creation " is " " nothing " at all, but rather happens in God's act itself, and it happens always as that which is already negated, i.e., no longer as the happening, but as the always already happened. Nothingness is not something " between " God and creation; God affirms the nothingness only in so far as he has already overcome it.

The world stands in the nothingness, i.e., in the beginning, and that means in the freedom of God. But, says Bonhoeffer, this also means that the God of the Creation, of the absolute beginning, is the God of the resurrection. The world stands from the beginning under the sign of the resurrection of Christ from the dead! In fact, only because we know about the resurrection do we know about God's creation in the beginning, about God's creating out of nothingness. Between the dead and the resurrected Christ there was absolutely no continuum other than the freedom of God. One might even say, that with the death of Christ on the cross *das Nichts* is taken into God himself, but he who is in the beginning lives, destroys the nothingness, and produces the new creation in his resurrection! That God lets us who stand in the middle know that he is at the beginning and will be at the end, and that he is free over the world, is sheer mercy, grace, forgiveness, and consolation!

The earth as it is brought forth from the hands of God is without form and void, but as such it stands in silent worship and praise of the Creator. But what is the darkness that was upon the face of the deep? The darkness and the chaos, stresses Bonhoeffer, is God's work, and the fact that it lies far below him in the depths indicates the exaltation of God above his creation. That is, it is simply a sign of God's glory. Just as we look down giddily from a high mountaintop into the shadowy abyss of the valleys below, so is the earth under God's feet — far, strange, dark, deep, but his work. Nevertheless, this "darkness upon the face of the deep" is the first allusion to the power of darkness, to the passion of Jesus Christ. The darkness, the *tehom,* includes in itself strength and power, which now serve to glorify the Creator, but when once torn loose from the origin, from the beginning, become refractory and rebellious. Yet God is Lord over the deep, and the brooding of the Spirit over the face of the waters is merely that moment of hesitation between *Da-sein* and *So-sein,* the moment of God's planning and thinking between the creation of what is formless and chaotic power and its assumption of form. God gives his work form and thus its own being, but this being has no other function than to serve and to glorify him.

In contrast to all myths of creation, Bonhoeffer points out, the God of the Bible speaks — and it is so! This emphasizes that God remains Creator and creation remains his creature; the sole continuity between God and his work is his word, and if this word were not there, the world would fall to pieces! God's word is not his nature or even his essence, but his commandment. God speaks, and this means he *freely* creates and remains free vis-à-vis his creation. God is in the world as word because he is the absolute Other beyond the world, and he is the absolute Other because he is in the world *in the word!* For this reason, we do not know the Creator "out of" his works, as if the substance or nature or essence of the work is somehow ultimately identical with the nature of God, as if there were some kind of continuum (cause and effect!), but only because God acknowledges these works through his word and because *we believe* this word about these works.

Word, continues Bonhoeffer, means *spoken* word, not symbol, significance, or idea. Furthermore, that God creates by speaking means that thought and name and work are one in God. The word of command and its execution, which in us are hopelessly separated, are for God indissolubly one. With God the imperative is the indicative, and the fact that this is impossible for us indicates that we no longer live in the unity of God's active word, but have fallen.

"And God said, 'Let there be light'; and there was light." As formless night takes on form through the light of morning, so the formless chaos takes on form through the creation of that primitive light. And as that word about the abysmal darkness is the first indication of the Passion of Jesus Christ, so the freeing of the subjugated, formless deep to its own being by the light is an indication of the "light which shines in the darkness." "And God saw that the light was good." This approving look of God means that God loves his work and wants to preserve it. Creating and preserving are two sides of the one act of God. That God's work is good does not mean that the world is the best of all thinkable worlds, but that it lives completely before God, that it lives from him and toward him and that he is its Lord. Here is meant a "good" that is undifferentiated from evil, a good that exists simply in the fact that it is under the Lordship of God.

Bonhoeffer now points out the difference between *creatio continua* and preservation. The idea of continuous creation means that the world is repeatedly snatched from nothingness, and this idea of a discontinuous continuity robs God's creativeness of its absolute freedom and uniqueness, and ignores the reality of the fallen world, which is not a forever newly created but a *preserved* world. Creation means snatching away from nonbeing; preservation means affirming the being. Creation is real *beginning*, always "before" my knowledge and before the preservation. Preservation is always *in relation* to creation; creation is in itself. Creation and preservation are here still one, both related to the original good work of God; but, says Bonhoeffer, there is a difference between the preservation of the original and the preservation of the fallen creation.

The successive creation of day, the firmament, the dry land, the heavenly bodies, and the living creatures leads up to God's creation of man in his own image. Everything created until now has not been in God's image, but has taken the form of his commandment. It has come out of freedom, yet is itself not in a free but in a *conditioned* state. Only the truly free could be an image of God and fully proclaim the wonder of his creativeness. "Then God said, 'Let us make man in our image, after our likeness.'" The plural in the Hebrew, says Bonhoeffer, designates the significance and sublimity of this act, but it should also be noted that, unlike the previous creation, God does not simply call forth man from nonbeing, but that we ourselves, as it were, are drawn into God's own plans and thereby are shown that something completely new and peculiar is about to happen. This, of course, does not mean to deny man's connection with the animal world, but merely underscores the distinctive relationship between God and man.

That God creates his image on earth in man means that man is similar to God in that he is free. To be sure, he is free alone through the creation of God, through God's word, and he is only free *for* the praise of the Creator. Freedom in the language of the Bible is not something that man has for himself, but something that he has for the other! No man is free *an sich*. Freedom is not a quality of man, no possession, nothing objective; it is rather a relation between two! To be free means " to be free for the other " because the other has bound me to himself. It is not an attribute that is at man's disposal, but is simply a happening, something that happens to one through another. And how do we know this? Only through the fact that this is the message of the gospel itself, namely, that God's freedom has been given to us, that God does not want to be free for himself, but for man! Because God in Christ is free for man and does not keep his freedom for himself, there is for us a concept of freedom only as a " freedom for." That God is free for us means that we are free for God!

The paradox of created freedom remains irremovable. In fact, asserts Bonhoeffer, this point needs to be sharpened. " Created freedom " means here — and this is what goes beyond all of God's previous action — that God himself enters into that which he has created. Now he not only commands and his word happens, but he also enters into the created and thereby creates freedom! It is this which differentiates man from the rest of creation. This is what the old dogmaticians meant when they spoke of the indwelling of the Trinity in Adam. In the free creature the Holy Spirit adores the Creator; in the created freedom the uncreated freedom praises itself. The creature loves the Creator because the Creator loves the creature. Created *freedom* is freedom in the Holy Spirit, but as *created* freedom it is the freedom of man himself.

How is the freedom of the Creator differentiated from the freedom of the creature? How is man free? In the fact, answers Bonhoeffer, that the creature is related to the other creature; man is free for man! "Male and female he created them." Man is not alone, but exists in duality, and in this *being dependent upon the other* rests his creatureliness. Man's creatureliness, like his freedom, is not a quality or a possession or something existing in itself, but can only be defined as man's being opposite another, with another, dependent on another. Consequently, the "image which is after the likeness of God" is no *analogia entis* (analogy of being), whereby man in his being-in-and-for-himself would be similar to the being of God. There is no such analogy between man and God, because God, who alone exists in-and-for-himself in his aseity, still at the same time must be thought as existing for his creature, giving his freedom to man, giving himself, and therefore not existing alone, in so far as he is the God who in Christ testifies to his "being for man." The similarity of man to God is not an *analogia entis,* but an *analogia relationis* (analogy of relation), but this means that even the *relatio* is not a capability or possibility of man, not a structure of his being, but a given, established relationship, *justitia passiva,* and in this given relationship freedom is also given. Therefore, the *analogia* is not a likeness that man has in his possession or at his disposal, but is a similarity that derives entirely from the prototype and thus always refers us to the original itself and is "similar" solely in this reference. *Analogia relationis,* then, is the relationship established by God himself and is *analogia* only in this relationship established by God. The relationship of creature to creature is a God-given relationship because it exists in freedom, and freedom comes from God.

Man in his similarity to God, in his duality as male and female, is created into the world of nature and living things, and just as his freedom in respect to another man exists in his being free *for* him, his freedom in respect to the rest of the created world exists in his being free *from* it. That is, man can control it and rule it as its lord, and precisely this is the other aspect of man's likeness to God. Man is to rule over God's creation as one who has received the commission and power from God himself. Thus man's freedom from the created world is not some ideal freedom of the spirit from nature, but the freedom to rule includes an integral connection with that which is ruled. In my creatureliness, states Bonhoeffer, I belong entirely to the world, but my freedom from it exists in the fact that this world, to which I am bound as a master to his servant or a farmer to his soil, is subjugated precisely in order that I should *rule* over it! It is my earth, and the stronger I rule it, the more it is *my* earth. This authority to rule, which so peculiarly binds man to the created world and yet at the same time places him over against it, is bestowed upon him by nothing else than the word of God.

The fact that we no longer rule the world, but are its prisoners and slaves, is because we no longer know the world as God's creation and no longer receive our rulership from him, but seize it for ourselves. There is no "freedom from" without a "freedom for," no rulership without service to God; when one is lost, the other also necessarily falls by the way. Without God and without the brother, man loses the earth, because God, brother, and earth belong together. And, Bonhoeffer points out, for those who have once lost the earth there is no way back except the way to God and the brother. Indeed, from the very outset the way of man to the earth is only possible as the way of God to man. Only where God and the brother come to man can he find his way back to the earth. The *imago Dei* of the first man, then, is his being *free for* God and the other man and his being *free from* the created world in his lordship over it.

"And God blessed them." God's blessing on man is his promise, something which, like a curse, is laid upon man and is transmitted from generation to generation, often not understood, uncomprehended. It is not magical or bewitching, but something totally *real*. This blessing — be fruitful, multiply, rule — affirms man's whole empirical existence in the world of the living, his creatureliness, his earthliness. But, asks the author, what happens when this blessing is turned into a curse? For the time being the answer must be held in reserve.

"So God blessed the seventh day and hallowed it, because on it God rested from all his work which he had done in creation." "Rest" in the Bible, asserts Bonhoeffer, is really more than simply reposing; it means resting upon completion, the peace of God in which the world lies, glorification. It is never the rest of a lethargic

God, but the rest of the Creator who has completed his work. Thus the rest of God is at the same time the rest of his creation. God also hallows the day of his rest for Adam and for us, and our hearts are restless until they find rest in the rest of God! For us this rest is wholly a promise that is given to the people of God. Indeed, the day of rest is the same day that in the New Testament is the day of the resurrection of the Lord: day of rest, day of victory, of Lordship, of completion, of glorification, day of worship for us, day of hope, of looking toward the day of final rest with God!

Bonhoeffer now turns from the first Creation story (Gen., chs. 1 to 2:4a) to the second (Gen., chs. 2:4b to 3). He asserts that the two stories simply present two sides of the same thing, and both are equally necessary for an understanding of the whole. The first report sees things entirely from God's viewpoint, from above; man is here the final work of God's self-glorification, and the world remains the strange, distant world, the world in the deep. The second report, on the other hand, concerns the near world and the near Lord on the earth, living together in Paradise with Adam. In the former: man for God, here: God for man; there: the Creator and Lord, here: the close, fatherly God. There: man as the last act of God, the whole world created before man; here, just the opposite: man in the beginning, the animals, fowls, and trees created for him. There: God's action, here: history of man with God; there: God in his divinity, here: God in human form, the God of childlike anthropomorphism. Both reports, says Bonhoeffer, are only human, humble words about the same God and the same man.

"The Yahweh God formed man of dust from the ground, and breathed into his nostrils the breath of life; and man became a living being." The first thing to notice here is that God has his own name: no longer the *elohim* of Gen., ch. 1, with its somewhat abstract meaning of divinity, but "Yahweh." This proper name is God himself. Even today, asserts Bonhoeffer, we do not have God other than in his name; Jesus Christ — that is the name of God, utterly anthropomorphic and at the same time utterly real. Further, we should note that here Yahweh forms man with his own hands, and this signifies the bodily nearness of the Creator to the creature, his care and thinking about man, his intention with man. On the other hand, it also signifies his full power, his absolute superiority, his fatherliness. The man whom God creates in his own image, i.e., in freedom, is the man who is taken out of the earth. Out of God's earth man has his body, and this means that his body is not his prison or an outer shell, but is he himself. That is, man does not " have " a body and does not " have " a soul, but he " is " body and soul. The seriousness of human existence is shown in its integral connection with Mother Earth, man's being as a body. Finally, the fact that God breathes into man's body his own life-giving Spirit differentiates him from all other living things. God creates other life through his word, but to man he gives of his own Spirit, of his own life. The man who lives as a body in the Spirit is not differentiated from other life in his earthly origin, but he is unique in the fact that his body is the existence-form of God's Spirit on earth. God glorifies himself in this body, says Bonhoeffer, and when this original body in its created being is destroyed, God once more enters into the body, i.e., in Jesus Christ; and when this body is also rent, God enters in the forms of the sacrament of the body and blood. The body and blood of the Lord's Supper are the realities of the new creation of the promise for the fallen Adam. Because Adam is created as a body, he is also redeemed as a body, in Jesus Christ and in the sacrament. The man thus created is the image of God, and he is so, not in spite of, but precisely in his corporeality, because as a body he is related to the earth and to the other body; he is for the other, dependent on the other.

Bonhoeffer now comes to the story of Adam and Eve in the Garden of Eden. Myth, childlike, fantastic imagining of the hidden past — so says the world. God's word, *our* prehistory, our own beginning, fate, guilt, end — so says the church of Christ. Why fight one at the cost of the other, asks Bonhoeffer? Why not realize that all of our speaking of God, of our beginning and end, of our guilt, is *never* the thing itself, but only pictures, and if we are to be intelligent, we must realize that God reaches us and teaches us through these old pictures of a magical world as well as through the pictures of our modern technical concepts. The only difference between us and those who lived in this " magical world " is that Christ has appeared, but we are exactly the same in that, whether in hope or fulfillment, we can only live from Christ.

In the middle of the Garden stand two trees that bear special names and are bound together with human existence in a strange way: the tree of life and the tree of knowledge of good and evil. And connected with the latter is God's commandment not to eat of its fruit at the risk of death. Here, says the author, we are concerned with life, knowledge, and death, and we must understand the relation of the three.

The *tree of life* has no prohibition attached to it; in fact, this tree gains its peculiar significance only after man has fallen. Before this fateful event life is no problem; it is simply given life, and, to be sure, life before God. The significant thing at this point is that the tree of life is " in the center." The life that comes from God is in the center, which means that God, who gives life, is in the center! In the middle of the world over which Adam is to rule is not Adam, but the tree of divine life, and, adds Bonhoeffer, this is what is peculiar to man: the fact that his life continually revolves around life's center, but is never able to possess the same. Adam is not tempted to disturb the tree of life, nor would he understand a prohibition connected with it. He simply *has* life, to be sure, in this special way: first, *he* really has it (it does not have him!); and secondly, he has it in the unity of unbroken obedience to the Creator. Adam lives from the center and toward the center, but he himself is not in the center. He has his life from God and before God, but he has it, not as an animal, but as a man. He has it in his obedience, in his innocence, in his ignorance; but that means, he has it in his freedom! Man's life is lived in obedience out of freedom, and even if Adam could never be tempted to violate the tree of life because he *has* life, still it could be endangered indirectly from the other side, namely, from the freedom in unbroken unity of obedience in which Adam lives, which means: from the tree of the knowledge of good and evil.

The *tree of knowledge* also stands in the center of the Garden, and to it God attaches a prohibition and a threat. Naturally Adam could not possibly comprehend the meaning of " good " and " evil " and " death," but in these words he understands that God stands opposite him and indicates his limits. God points to what makes Adam a man, namely, his freedom (" for " and " from "), and at the same time he shows him his limitation, that is, his creatureliness. The tree that indicates man's limit stands in the center, which means that this limit is in the center of man's existence, not on the periphery. It is a limit, not of his condition or skill or possibility, but of his *reality*, of his existence in general. Adam knows that *God* is both the boundary and the center of his existence, and this knowledge is imbedded in his freedom for God, in his unbroken obedience to God. He understands the prohibition and threat only as a gift, as God's grace — not as a temptation. In a very real sense Adam lives beyond good and evil.

The words " good " and " evil," *tob* and *ra*, explains Bonhoeffer, have a broader meaning than in our common usage. They denote an ultimate discord in the world of man which goes beyond moral categories, so that *tob* would even mean perhaps " pleasureful " or " joyful " (*lustvoll*) and *ra* " painful " or " sorrowful " (*leidvoll*). *Tob* and *ra* are the concepts that indicate the deepest cleavage of human life in each direction, and one can only be calculated in terms of the other; that is, each has only relative significance. One is never without the other, and each exalts the other. Where absolute evil possesses man so that the joyful is completely destroyed by the sorrowful, there man has the sickness of the spirit which we call melancholia; there he has ceased to be a man. The healthy man is borne and nourished in the sorrowful by the joyful, is upset in the joyful by the sorrowful, in good by evil and in evil by good; he is in discord.

Of course, as yet Adam knows nothing of this, for only the fallen man lives in dissension. The man who knows about good and evil knows in the same moment about his death, for the tree of knowledge is the tree of death. In knowing about good and evil, man dies and is dead in both his good and his evil. Death defined as perishableness, asserts Bonhoeffer, is not the death that comes from God. What does being dead mean? Not the abolition of being created but being unable to live any longer before God and yet having to live before him! It means to stand before God as the lost and condemned, but not as the nonexisting. To be dead means no longer to receive life as grace coming from the limit and center of one's existence, but to receive it as commandment. God commands man to live in the knowledge of his death, and this commandment cannot be avoided, even through suicide! The commandment of life demands something of man which he cannot fulfill; he is to live out of his own self, and yet he cannot. This man who lives in contradiction, Bonhoeffer reminds us, is no fantasy; the story of Adam is also *our story,* with the decisive difference that for us the story begins where for Adam it ends. Our history is history through Christ, whereas Adam's history is history through the serpent. But as those who live and have a history alone through Christ, we cannot know about the beginning except from the new center, from Christ, as those who in faith are now freed from the knowledge of good and evil and from death and who only in faith are able to appropriate the picture of Adam.

The first man is alone. But, continues Bonhoeffer, Christ was also alone, and we are likewise alone. Adam is alone in the expectation of another human being, of fellowship. Christ is alone, because he alone loves the other man, because he is the way by which the human race returned to its Creator. We are alone, because we have driven the other man from us, because we hated him. Adam was alone in hope, Christ was alone in the fullness of divinity, we are alone in evil, in hopelessness. Adam's loneliness was not overcome by the creation of the animals and birds, so God caused a deep sleep to come over him and made from his own rib a woman, a " helper fit for him." But why does the man who lives completely from God need a " helper "? What is the significance of Eve? Bonhoeffer answers: She is to help Adam bear the limitation that is laid upon him by God. She is a gift of God's grace, for God knows that this free, creaturely life which is limited by the prohibition can only be borne if it is loved, and Eve is at once the embodiment of Adam's limitation and the object of his love. Indeed, love of the woman is now to be the real life of man. The untouchable, inaccessible center of Paradise about which the life of Adam revolves now assumes form and becomes man's helper. In love they belong to each other, and even though they remain two creatures of God, they become one body.

In the creation of the other human being freedom and creatureliness are bound together in love. In the common bearing of the limitation their fellowship assumes the character of church! From this, however, it follows that where love for the other is destroyed, man can only hate the other, who embodies his limitation; man wants to possess or to destroy the other, and thus to become limitless. This, claims Bonhoeffer, is our world! The grace of the other human being, who is to help us bear our limitation, that is, who is to help us live before God and in fellowship with whom we alone can live before God, has turned into a curse. The other has become the one who makes our hate toward God even more passionate, the one for whose sake we can no longer live before God, the one who again and again becomes a judgment upon us! As a result, marriage and communion with others receive an entirely new meaning.

"And they become one flesh." In this context Bonhoeffer speaks about human sexuality, which is nothing else than the last possible realization of human beings' belonging to each other. This, of course, points to the twofold truth of their being individuals and, at the same time, one. The communion of husband and wife is the communion of love that stems from God and that glorifies and worships him as the Creator. For this reason, asserts Bonhoeffer, it is church in its original form, and because it is church, it is an eternally bound communion. For *us,* however, these statements do not signify a glorification of *our* marriage, but indicate that the union of husband and wife as we know it does not stand in this clear reality, and that precisely the church's handling of the wedding is perhaps the most questionable of all its practices. The fellowship of love, which is completely rent by sexuality and has turned into passion, which rests on the claim of one upon the other, is just not a glorification of the Creator, but rather the seizing of the power and glory of the Creator, the heightening of the consciousness of one's own ego, of one's productive power.

"And the man and his wife were both naked, and were not ashamed." Shame, says Bonhoeffer, comes only from the knowledge of the alienation of man, of the alienation of the world in general, and thus of one's own estrangement. Shame is the expression for the fact that we no longer accept the other as a gift of God, for our passionate desire of the other and the accompanying knowledge that the other is no longer satisfied to belong to me, but desires something from me. Shame is the veiling of myself from the other for the sake of my own and the other's evil, i.e., on account of the alienation that has stepped between us. Shame first arises in the world of discord. In Paradise, where one accepted the other as a helper given him by God, man is not ashamed.

Bonhoeffer begins his exposition of Gen., ch. 3, with the statement that the commandment not to eat the fruit of the tree of knowledge, the creation of Eve, and the temptation of the serpent should be understood as a connected series of events that band together in the attack on the tree of life. All stem from God the Creator, and yet, strange to say, they now form a common front with man against the Creator! The prohibition, which had been heard by Adam as grace, becomes a law that incites the wrath of both man and God; the woman, who was created as a help for man, becomes a temptation; the serpent, who is one creature of God among others, becomes an instrument of evil. What happens here? The Bible, says Bonhoeffer, does not give an answer, at least no clear and direct answer, but speaks in a peculiar indirectness. It would be a complete distortion of the Biblical report, he asserts, if we here call on the devil or appeal to a false use of man's freedom or claim an imperfect creation, for it is characteristic and essential for the Biblical narrative that everything takes place in the world created by God and that no *diaboli ex machina* is brought into play to elucidate and dramatize this incomprehensible event. The twilight in which the created and evil appear here may not be dispelled without destroying what is decisive, because precisely this twilight, this ambiguity in which the creation here stands, is the only possible form in which this happening can be reported for us men who " stand in the middle." Only in this way can the twofold concern be preserved: to lay the guilt completely on man, and, at the same time, to express the incomprehensibility, inexplicability, inexcusability of the guilt! The Bible does not want to give information about the origin of evil, but wants to testify to its character as guilt and as an unending burden of man. No evil power suddenly breaks into creation from the outside, no previous fall of Lucifer is reported; instead, evil conceals itself completely in the creation. Man's fall is made ready and takes place in the midst of creation, and just thereby the complete inexcusability is most clearly asserted.

What, now, takes place? The serpent, who is obviously not the devil, but a creature of God more subtle than the others, takes up God's own word: " Did God say, ' You shall not eat of any tree of the garden '? " It does not dispute this word, but merely raises the possi-

THEOLOGICAL APPLICATION 133

bility that perhaps man has not heard God rightly, that perhaps God's word did not mean what it says. The decisive thing, states Bonhoeffer, is that this question suggests to man that he could *go behind* the word of God and establish it now from *his* side, from his own understanding of the nature of God. The question, which is apparently placed from God's own side, would destroy the given word of God on behalf of the "true" God, i.e., God as man understands him. The serpent pretends to know of a greater, nobler God for whom such a prohibition is not necessary, but it also knows that it has power only when it pretends to be informed from God's side! That is, explains the author, only as the *pious* serpent is it evil! Evil appears in the world with the first religious question. Its evil exists, not in the fact that it is asked, but in the fact that in this question the false answer is already included, that in it the basic attitude of the creature toward the Creator is attacked. Man presumes to be judge over God's word instead of simply hearing and doing it. On the basis of an idea, a principle, or some previously won knowledge about God, man is now to judge his concrete word; in other words, in the serpent's question *possibility* is played off against reality, and possibility undermines *reality!* But, Bonhoeffer reminds us, in the relation of man to God there are no possibilities, but only reality.

For the first man, who lives completely in this reality, the address to his possibility, namely, not to obey the word of God, is synonymous with an address to the freedom in which he belongs entirely to God, and it is only possible because this possibility of disobedience to God is enveloped in the reality of his "being for God." Only because the question is asked in such a way that Adam can understand it as a new possibility of "being for God" can it lead him to a "being against God." The possibility of man's *own* self-found "wanting to be for God," asserts Bonhoeffer, is the original evil in the pious question of the serpent. And by the clever insinuation embodied in the question the serpent had Eve on its side from the outset! When so stated, "Did God say, 'You shall not eat of any tree of the garden'?" Eve is straightway forced to the admission — no, naturally God has not said that — and, says Bonhoeffer, already this incident in which she has to restrict something in relation to the word of God (even though falsely presented!) must place her in utter confusion —

indeed, for the first time she must have felt the fascination of being a judge over God's word. Nevertheless, Eve remains in ignorance and can only repeat the commandment, yet she is thereby engaged in this clever conversation — the first discussion *about* God, the first religious, theological discussion!

The serpent, who has feigned an intimate knowledge of the secrets of God, now drops his pious pose and attacks openly. *Why* has God said it? Out of jealousy! God's word is a lie! This is the ultimate rebellion, says Bonhoeffer: when the lie calls the truth a lie. " You will not die. For God knows that when you eat of it your eyes will be opened, and you will be like God, knowing good and evil." God has promised death to the offender, the serpent promises that the offender will be " like God," *sicut deus*. Actually, asserts Bonhoeffer, both are the same thing! It is true that man becomes like God in the fall, but the man *sicut deus* can no longer live. Here we reach the climax; we stand before the abyss and stare into the incomprehensible, infinite chasm. " You will not die " — " You shall die ": in these two sentences the world now breaks apart for Adam. Proposition stands against proposition, God's truth against the serpent's truth. God's truth bound to the commandment, the serpent's truth bound to the promise; God's truth indicating man's limits, the serpent's truth indicating his limitlessness.

How can Adam understand the serpent's promise to " be like God "? Not otherwise, declares Bonhoeffer, than as the possibility to be more pious, to be more obedient, than he is in his *imago-Dei* structure. And yet he sees that this chance to deepen his being as a creature must be purchased at the cost of a transgression of God's commandment, and this fact must make him cautious. He is really *between* God and God, or better: between God and an idol that pretends to be the true God. But how can the idol keep from pointing Adam back to the real God of creation? Why does not the promise to be *sicut deus* simply make him hold faster to the given reality of the Creator and his word? How can the answer of Eve be other than a praise of the incomparable, incomprehensible grace of the Creator, a praise breaking forth from the ultimate depth of her creatureliness and freedom for God and the neighbor?

" She took of its fruit and ate; and she also gave some to her husband, and he ate." Instead of any answer, instead of any further discussion with the serpent — the act! What has happened? Just this: the center is entered, the boundary is transgressed; man now stands in the center and is boundless, which means that he is alone! To be in the center and to be alone means to be *sicut deus*. Man is now like God; he lives from himself, he creates his own life, he is his creator. He is no longer creature, but has seized his own creatureliness. He *is* like God, emphasizes Bonhoeffer, and this " is " is to be taken with complete seriousness. When Adam loses his limit, he loses his creatureliness, and thus he can no longer be addressed in terms of it. Here we have come to a basic fact: creatureliness and fall are not related in such a way that the fall is an act of creatureliness which is not able to destroy but at best only to modify or to deteriorate the creatureliness. Rather, the fall *really* makes of the creature (*imago-Dei*-man) the *sicut-deus*-creator-man, and henceforth there is no possibility to know him in his creatureliness. The unlimited man who is "like God" has no desire to be a creature. In fact, says Bonhoeffer, only God himself can now address man in terms of his creatureliness, and he does this in Jesus Christ, in the cross, in the church. He speaks of man's creatureliness only as the truth that he himself speaks and that we, for his sake, believe against all our knowledge of reality!

How have things developed till now? If we answer this question Biblically, says Bonhoeffer, we must, first, indicate again the series of events leading up to the act; secondly, point to the infinite chasm that lies between the end of this series and the act itself; and, thirdly, ask the question as such correctly, in that from the speculative we gain and answer the theological question.

(1) Fundamentally, it is never wrong to present the series of events that precedes the one evil act, but everything depends on never making the series responsible for the act, but letting the series lead up to the point where the chasm opens, where it is now completely incomprehensible how the act could take place. The prohibition given to Adam stands at the beginning of the series, and this indicates to him his creatureliness and freedom, which could only be understood as his freedom for God. This prohibition must have made the grace of the Creator clearer to Adam, but at the same time it pointed to the distance between the Creator and the creature, thus

intensifying Adam's awareness of his own being. Next, his knowledge of his own being is heightened by the unexpected creation of woman from his rib. Adam's boundary now assumes bodily form, moves near to him, and for that very reason becomes all the more sharply drawn. Adam's limitation has now stepped into the midst of the world of creation, so that now any transgression of the boundary set by God will simultaneously be a violation of another human being. But how can we talk of transgression where the boundary is known only as grace, where Adam lives in the unbroken unity of obedience?

What happens is this, states the author: man is made aware that his obedience and the object of obedience are two different things, which means that he becomes especially conscious of his freedom in unbroken obedience *next to* and apart from his creatureliness. Man now clearly knows about himself before God. But why does this knowledge not make Adam break forth in thanksgiving and praise of the Creator? Why does this not afford new strength for new obedience?

Eve falls first. She falls as the weaker, as the one partly taken from man, but she falls without excuse: she is completely herself. Yet the purpose of the story is the fall of Adam. First through Adam's fall does Eve fall completely, because the two are one. Adam falls through Eve; Eve falls through Adam. They fall together as one, but each alone bears the total guilt. How could it be that Adam did not see even in Eve's act a final pointing to his Creator? The Bible merely says, " And he ate "!

(2) Bonhoeffer asserts that three things must be stated: First, the act of disobedience is incomprehensible and inexcusable. The reason for this happening is not to be discovered in the nature of man or in that of the creation or in that of the serpent. No theory of *posse peccare* or *non posse peccare* can comprehend the actuality of the act. Every attempt to make it understandable is always only the accusation that the creature hurls against the Creator. Second, seen from man's standpoint, this act is final and irreparable. Otherwise, Adam could free himself from guilt. But then guilt would not be guilt, and Christ would have died in vain. Third, this act of man, whom God created as male and female, is an act of humanity from

THEOLOGICAL APPLICATION 137

which no man can separate himself. Each is guilty in the act of the other.

But, says Bonhoeffer, because the fall is as incomprehensible as it is final and unforgivable, the word disobedience does not exhaust the facts of the case. It is *rebellion,* the creature's becoming creator, destruction of creatureliness, falling away; and this downfall is a continuous falling, an ever-widening and deepening estrangement. We are concerned here, not merely with an ethical false step, but with the destruction of the creation by the creature. That is, the extent of the fall reaches the entire created world, and we must now speak of a fallen-falling world.

(3) The question about the " why? " of evil, says the author, is no theological question, for it presupposes a possibility of going behind our existence as sinners. If we could answer the " why? " then *we* would not be sinners! We could make something else responsible. Therefore, the question of "why?" can always only be answered with the " that," which lays the guilt completely on man. The theological question is not directed to the origin of evil, but to the real overcoming of evil on the cross; it asks about the forgiveness of guilt, about the reconciliation of the fallen world.

What results from the fall: " Then the eyes of both were opened, and they knew that they were naked." Are we to understand this whole story as being concerned simply with the question of the origin of the love of man and woman? Are we to understand the eating of the fruit of the tree of knowledge as the great, proud, liberating act of man by which he has attained the right to love and to create life? Was the knowledge of good and evil essentially the knowledge of a boy become man? The element of truth in all these assertions, says Bonhoeffer, is that here we are dealing with the problem of *sex.* The fall brings Adam the knowledge of the duality of *tob* and *ra,* the pleasureful-good and the sorrowful-evil, and this disjunction must first express itself in the relation of Adam to Eve. Eve, the other human being, was the embodiment of Adam's limitation, which he recognized in love, in the undivided unity of his devotion. Now, however, he has overstepped the boundary. He first knows that he is limited; he no longer accepts the limitation as God's creational grace, but hates it as God's creational envy. And in the same act in which Adam transgresses God's boundary, he also transgresses the God-given embodiment of that boundary. He now sees Eve, no longer as an expression of God's grace, but of God's hate, God's wrath, God's jealousy; no longer in love, but in estrangement. Man and woman are now alienated, and this means two things.

First, in alienation man appeals to his share in the body of the woman, or, speaking more generally, one human feels entitled to another, claims the right to possess another. The passion of one for the other first finds expression in sexuality, which is passionate hate of every limitation, self-will, an impassioned, weak will for unity in an estranged world. Sexuality, asserts the author, desires the annihilation of the other human as a creature, and in this annihilation of the other one's own life is to be preserved, to be propagated. That is, in the act of annihilating man is creative; in sexuality the human race is preserved in its annihilation! Unbridled or uncreative sexuality, therefore, is annihilation in the highest degree, an insane acceleration of the falling. Passion and hate, *tob* and *ra* — that is the fruit of the tree of knowledge.

Second, following his estrangement man covers himself. The boundless, hating, passionate man does not display his nakedness. Nakedness is the essence of unity, is revelation, is innocence. Veiling is the essence of the world divided into good and evil, and for that reason even revelation must be veiled in the world of good and evil. And paradoxically enough, the very fact that man feels shame and covers himself means that, without wanting to, he recognizes his boundary. Man's shame is an unwilling indicator to revelation, to the boundary, to the other, to God. Thus the preservation of shame in the fallen world is the sole possibility of a reference to the original nakedness and the sanctification of this nakedness; not that shame in itself is something good — that is a moralistic, puritanic, completely un-Biblical view — but that shame must give a reluctant witness to man's fallen condition.

Therefore, states Bonhoeffer, when church dogmatics saw the essence of original sin in sexuality, it was not so wrong as a Protestant moralistic naturalism has often said. The knowledge of good and evil is originally not an abstract recognition of ethical principles, but precisely sexuality, that is, perversion of the relation between human beings. And because the essence of sexuality exists in being creative in annihilation, so the ongoing propagation of the original sinful nature of man is preserved from generation to generation. The protest that appeals to the naturalness of sexuality is simply not aware of the extremely ambiguous character of all the so-called " natural " in our world. The consecration of sexuality is given in its restraint through shame, i.e., through the veiling, and by the reference of the restrained fellowship of marriage to the church. The deepest reason for this is that man has lost his creatureliness; it is destroyed in his being " like God." The entire creaturely world is now veiled; it has become speechless and inexplicable, opaque and enigmatic.

" The man and his wife hid themselves from the presence of the Lord God among the trees of the garden." The estranged pair now try to flee, as if they could hide from God! This flight from God we call the conscience. Before the fall man had no conscience, but in his alienation from the Creator he becomes divided within himself. This is the twofold function of the conscience: to pursue man in his flight from God in order thereby to acknowledge God against his will, and yet, at the same time, to let man feel secure in his hiding place. And hidden from God, man now plays the judge and lives from his own knowledge of good and evil, from his own inner estrangement. Conscience is by no means the voice of God in sinful man, stresses Bonhoeffer, but a *defense* against this voice, and yet as a defense it unwillingly points to that voice.

" The Lord God called to the man, and said to him, ' Where are you? ' " With these words, says Bonhoeffer, the Creator calls the fleeing Adam forth from his conscience. Man may not remain alone in his sin. God speaks to him, halts him in his flight. God kills the conscience. The fleeing Adam must know that he cannot escape his Creator, yet he does not recognize God's call as grace, attempts to excuse himself, remains fallen.

God now speaks to Adam in terms of curse and promise. Paradise is destroyed, and Adam's life is now preserved in a world between curse and promise. The curse and promise connected with the life of fallen man is stated in these four great thoughts: enmity with the serpent, pain of childbearing, toil of work, death. The curse is that man *must* live in this fallen world as the man " like God "; the promise is that he *may* live in it, that he is not without the word of God in it, even though it be the word of the wrathful God.

Curse and promise are first attached to the eternal enmity between man and the serpent, that is, between man and the power of pious godlessness. In the fallen world man does not have God's word directly and simply, but perceives it in the distortion of the pious question; nevertheless, in this fate the promise of the victory, which must be always won anew through struggle, is given, in that man bruises the head of the serpent! In the enmity against the serpent *man's relation to God* is placed under the law of *tob* and *ra*. In the fate of the wife *tob* and *ra* enter into the *fellowship of man and wife*. The new that stems from the fall is shame and passion, but the fruit of Eve's passionate communion with Adam is the pain in which she bears children. Pain and the pleasure of passion are indissolubly bound together. In the word directed to Adam concerning the toil of work, the destruction and alienation of the original *relation of man and nature* is expressed. Adam is cursed in having to earn his food by the sweat of his brow, but he is promised that he thereby may live.

The world in which Adam now lives, says Bonhoeffer, is the world of the curse, but just because it is *God's* curse that it bears, it is not a world completely abandoned by God, but one that he preserves. And to what end does God preserve the world? The answer is clear, asserts the author: " Till you return to the ground, for out of it you were taken; you are dust, and to dust you shall return." The fallen Adam lives for his *death;* his life is preserved for the goal of death. Why? Because in eating the fruit of the tree of knowledge Adam, the man " like God," has also taken into himself death. Adam is dead before he dies. The serpent was right: " You will be like God; you will not die," namely, the death of no longer being. But the Creator was also right: " In the day that you eat of it you shall die," namely, the death of being " like God." The serpent, who brings man to fall with his lie, must speak the truth of God! The man " like God " is dead, because he has cut himself off from the tree of life. He lives from his own self and yet cannot live — which is what it means to be dead! Nevertheless, this death, this having to return to dust, is a promise of the gracious God. It must be understood by

Adam as the death of his present state of being dead, of his being "like God." Death of death — that is the promise character of this curse. Adam understands it as a sinking back into the nothingness out of which God created the world. Nothingness is for him the final promise, nothingness as the death of death. For that reason, says Bonhoeffer, Adam sees his life preserved toward nothingness. How is Adam, who has fallen from faith, to know that the real death of death is never *das Nichts,* but alone the living God? That the promise of the death of death is never nothingness, but alone life, Christ himself? How is he to know that in this promise of death God spoke already of the end of death, of the resurrection of the dead?

"The man called his wife's name Eve, because she was the mother of all living." Eve is the mother of the old humanity; all pleasure and all sorrow had its beginning with her. For Adam she is the symbol for the new life which is torn from the Creator and is propagated in passion. Eve, the fallen, knowing, clever mother of man — that is one beginning. Mary, the innocent, unknowing mother of God — that is the second beginning.

"And the Lord God made for Adam and for his wife garments of skin and clothed them"! The Creator, explains Bonhoeffer, is now the Preserver, the created world is now the fallen, preserved world. God accepts and affirms man as fallen, and he does not simply place Adam and Eve before each other in their nakedness, but covers them himself. That is, God's action is still concerned with man, but now his work is *ordering,* restraining action. It is not action which breaks through the new earthly and human laws, but enters into them and, in doing so, orders and restrains them. In other words, God now acts in reference to man's evil, to his being fallen. By making garments for Adam and Eve, God shows them that this is necessary for the sake of their evil. He thereby *restrains* their passion, but he does not destroy it. This is the preserving action of God with the world: that he says "Yes!" to the sinful world and through order shows it its limits. However, none of these orders as such are eternal, for they are only there for the sake of the preservation of life. For Adam, as we have already seen, the preservation of life is directed toward death; for us it is directed alone toward — Christ! Not orders of creation, but orders of preservation for the sake of Christ! God's new act with man is to preserve him in his fallen world toward death, toward the resurrection, the new creation, Christ. Man remains between good and evil, in discord; even with his *tob*-good he remains on the other side of God's good. In his entire divided *Dasein* he remains remote from God, in the fallen-falling world, and for that reason he is in twilight. All of his thinking about creation and fall — even the thinking of the Biblical author — is bound to this twilight. He cannot return to the original unity and must speak of Paradise and the fall as the Bible speaks to them.

Man has become like God, knowing good and evil, and to prevent his eating from the tree of life, God drives him from the garden and places the cherubim with the flaming sword to guard the way to the tree of life. Man is now in this paradoxical situation, explains Bonhoeffer: he wants to live, he is not able to live, and yet he must live; and this means that the *sicut deus* man is dead. Man thirsts after life, but because he is now his own creator, because he lives from himself, he thirsts after himself. In its essence, man's search for life is a search for death. Just in his dying, Adam hopes to save his life from the enforced situation of having to live without being able to live. It is flight from life and at the same time grasping after life, flight from God and seeking after God, wanting to be like God and grasping after the tree of life. But now this grasp is decisively prevented. The limitation has not shifted; it is where it always was: in the inaccessible center of the tree of life. But Adam now stands in another place! His limitation is no longer in the center of his life, but oppresses him from without, stands in his way. The tree of life is guarded by the powers of death and remains inaccessible, but the life of Adam before the gate is a continuous attack on the closed kingdom.

"And Adam knew Eve his wife, and she conceived and bore Cain." Adam and Eve preserve their new fellowship in a new way. They become proud creators of new life, but this new life is produced in passionate human fellowship, in the fellowship of death. Cain is the first man who is born on the *cursed* earth; with him history begins, the history of death. Adam, who is preserved from death and is consumed by his thirst for life, produces Cain, the *murderer*. The man who may not eat of the tree of life reaches all the more greedily after the fruit of death, the annihilation of life. Only the Creator can destroy life, and now Cain presumes this final right of the Creator and becomes a murderer. Cain is greater than Adam, asserts Bonhoeffer, because his hate of God and his yearning after life is greater. The whole history of death stands under the sign of Cain.

Christ on the cross, the murdered Son of God: that is the end of Cain's history and therewith the end of all history. That is the last confused storming of the door to Paradise, and under the cutting sword, under the cross, the human race dies. But Christ lives. The wood of the cross becomes the tree of life. In the midst of the world, on the cross of Christ, the spring of life wells up, and all who thirst after life are called to this water. Whoever eats from this tree of life will nevermore hunger and thirst! Strange Paradise, this hill of Golgotha, this cross, this blood, this broken body; strange tree of life, this trunk on which God himself must suffer and die — but precisely the kingdom of life which is given again by God in grace, the resurrection, opened door of imperishable hope, of waiting, and of patience. Tree of life, cross of Christ, center of the fallen and preserved world of God — that, concludes Bonhoeffer, is the end of the story of Paradise for us.

b. " King David "

King David (*König David*) is a series of three Bible lessons that Bonhoeffer conducted with the brotherhood of Pomeranian vicars. These were published in 1936 in the biweekly journal *Junge Kirche*. The author's intention was to furnish a guide to the proper reading of the books of Samuel and, at the same time, to contribute to the problem that is generally designated " Christ in the Old Testament."

From the beginning to end, asserts Bonhoeffer, the problem of David is determined by the fact of his anointment to be king. The first words concerning him tell of God's commanding Samuel to anoint David, whom God himself has chosen to be king, and only as the elected and anointed king does this shepherd boy take on Biblical stature and become important and interesting. With the anointing, David receives the Spirit of God, the Spirit of the Messianic Kingdom, the same Spirit that descends on Jesus at his baptism and seals him as the Messianic King. At the same time the Spirit departs from

Saul, who has been rejected, and Saul becomes mad. The entire episode of Saul's subsequent persecution of David can only be understood as the action of one who is possessed by the " evil spirit."

The anointing leads David straightway into the struggle with the powers of the world. He knows that he must battle for his people, who are in dishonor and danger, so he steps into the middle between his people and the Philistines, being led by the Lord himself. But now temptation sets in; Saul wants to equip him with heavy armor. But David refuses, for he may not be strong in the eyes of the world. Weaponless and defenseless he engages Goliath as God's anointed. He is mocked and cursed and despised by the enemy, but he holds fast to the God of Israel, who has called him to be the king of his people. He knows that God triumphs not by the sword and spear, but by the faith of his anointed. As the one anointed to the Messianic Kingdom, as a prototype (*Vorbild*) and shadow of Jesus Christ, David triumphs over Goliath. It is Christ's victory in him, because Christ was in David.

The anointed David cannot evade the hate and persecution on behalf of his anointment. The time preceding his accession to the throne is a time of continuous enmity toward him from all sides. The demon in Saul hates and shuns him, for he recognizes him as the anointed, just as the demons recognized Christ. The struggle against David is one of life and death, and Saul's hate drives him to idolatry and magic and finally to suicide. David becomes a fugitive in his own land and in the land of the Philistines and has no place to lay his head. He has few companions. Jonathan, the son of Saul, makes an eternal fraternal covenant with him, and in his love for David he recognizes that the election and anointing is not inherited by flesh and blood, but rests upon the free grace of God. David's other companions are those who are distressed and burdened, hopeless and dejected. He shares their life; he is their chief, leader of a band of outcasts and sinners, and as such he is God's anointed!

David's great temptation during the years of flight and persecution, says Bonhoeffer, is to seize hold of his kingdom by force, to shed blood, to set up the kingdom prematurely, before it pleases God. But the erection of the Messianic Kingdom has its own time, which is established by God, and David can only obey. He suffers for the sake of the kingdom. He remains free from violence and bloodshed, although he is sorely tempted when Saul is twice given into his hands, but because he rewards evil with good, he forces Saul to a recognition of his sin. Not through power but through love David wins the heart of the rejected Saul. He who cursed David must finally bless him.

In order that it should become clear that God's gracious providence alone preserves David from bloodguiltiness, David is once again led to the brink of sin. He wants to kill Nabal, who has mocked and scorned him, but God sends Abigail, and David's hand remains unspotted. Everything, asserts Bonhoeffer, depends on this: God's anointed may not help himself with his own hand; he must wait and suffer until God helps him. This David has done. When he has shed blood in battle, it has been *God's* war, at God's explicit commandment. And when Saul is struck down by the Lord, and Jonathan with him, David *suffers* for the last time for their sake. Instead of shouting for joy, he suffers and weeps over their death. So as the obedient anointed one who has been tried by many temptations, as the persecuted and suffering one who rewards evil with good, David is raised by God to the throne of the Messianic Kingdom.

The divine anointment by Samuel is followed by an anointment by the men of Judah, then by the elders in Israel. This second anointing, explains Bonhoeffer, is the visible attestation of the first, which took place in secret. David has withstood temptation and persecution, and God now says " Yes " to him through his people, who name him king. David is king for the sake of the people of Israel, for the sake of the church. This means, says Bonhoeffer, his kingship is service. He comes not to be served, but to serve!

David's first act is the capture of Jerusalem, the fortress Zion. He succeeds in what had till then been impossible, and he establishes in Jerusalem a permanent dwelling place for the Ark of the Covenant in which God abides. The wandering of the Children is over, and God's Kingdom stands fast in the throne of David on Mount Zion. When the Ark is brought into Jerusalem, David and the people learn that God needs no help from man in carrying out his work. The Ark totters, and when Uzzah reaches out his hand to steady it, he is immediately smitten by God in his anger. God needs no help from man, not even if it is piously conceived. God's holiness forbids any rash human grasp after his work.

As the Ark of God is carried into the city, David humbles himself, and then, dancing in the clothes of a priest, he leads his people in the worship of God. As a priest-king he steps next to his people, among the servants and maids; he is one of them, God's elect, but their brother. This action, continues Bonhoeffer, wins for David the derision of Michal, the daughter of Saul, who had expected the king to act with more dignity, but David affirms his intention to be a servant of his people. David's triumphal entry into Jerusalem with the Ark is carried out in lowliness and meekness. " Blessed be he who comes in the name of the Lord! " shouted the people to Jerusalem when Jesus entered. " The name of the Lord " — precisely this, says Bonhoeffer, is the meaning of the *Ark,* which *David* brings into Jerusalem! His throne is now firmly established, and he can rest from his enemies.

This time of rest and peace is understood by David as a fulfillment of the promise given to Moses (Deut. 12:10-11), which he interprets as a commandment to build for God a temple in which He may dwell. Kingship and priesthood belong together in the city of God. However, David shows his humble obedience by refusing to begin the work on his own authority. Instead, he follows the instructions of the prophet Nathan, whom God has given him. Nathan receives God's word in the night, and it contains both a " no " and an immeasurably great " yes " to David's question. David is not to build the temple for two reasons: first, God wants to continue dwelling in the tent, which is a sign that the promise given to Moses is not yet fulfilled. David is not the king who has rest from all his enemies and will dwell securely. The temple of God stands in the kingdom of peace. Who is this king? Solomon, says Bonhoeffer, later considered the promise to be related to him and built the Temple — but it was destroyed. The question, then, must be repeated: Who is this king of peace?

The second reason is this: God asks, " Would you build me a house to dwell in? . . . The Lord declares to you that the Lord will make you a house." (II Sam. 7:5, 11.) What is the house of God? What is the temple, the church? It is not a house that any man can build, declares Bonhoeffer, not even the anointed priest-king David, but it is God's own house and therefore his own work, built from above. David's mistake was to think that he could build for the Lord a church. This was a religious but a godless thought! God alone builds his church.

" The Lord will make you a house " — that, says Bonhoeffer, is the " yes " to David's question! The gracious God answers David's ungodly question with a new promise. He promises him not only his kingship, but a house, a kingdom, a church, which God himself builds. Who will see this house? David will die, and when he is asleep with his fathers, his offspring, who comes from his body, will be raised up and will build the house of God. David's son will be God's Son. David's lordship will be God's Lordship and eternal Kingdom. The Temple that Solomon later builds is perishable and thus is only a foreshadowing of the imperishable temple which is to come. The house that God himself will build, says Bonhoeffer, is the body of Christ, his Son, and this body is Christ and in him his congregation. This body of the Son of God is the humanity that is created from the seed of David according to God's promise through and in Jesus Christ. The promise, which David receives in faith, is the promise that in him the body of Christ, the church of Christ, is already hidden! The promise has to do with Jesus Christ, and David answers with humbleness and thanksgiving and prayer.

Now the story of David's sin begins. His sin, declares Bonhoeffer, is the sin of the great, the sin that threatens all those who are especially blessed and gifted by God, namely, the sin of *false security* (*securitas* instead of *certitudo*). David feels secure in the city of God and begins to lose his fear of the Lord. He sees Bathsheba, the wife of Uriah the Hittite, commits adultery, and when his sin cannot be hidden because of her subsequent pregnancy, he finally resorts to the murder of her husband and takes her to be his own wife. David, God's own anointed, has become a sinner, and yet he does not recognize his sin, but hardens his heart. God's promise has become too great and too heavy for David. He remained not in humility, but sinned against God's grace. David, concludes Bonhoeffer, was too weak for such grace, namely, to bear in himself the Christ of the world.

Nevertheless, David's sin cannot nullify God's promise, for the promise is given for eternity. God acts through his prophet Nathan. The hardening of David's heart is so great that he can only recognize his sin when Nathan says to him: "Thou art the man." This is the essence of hardness of heart, says the author: that we see our own situation before God as different from that of others, that we believe that we are blessed with some special privilege. Through Nathan, however, the king is able to see his real situation before God. David has scorned the word of God, and for that reason the judgment that God has already threatened for his seed is now already executed on David. He wants to chastise him with the scourges of man, but he does not want to destroy him. David has shed innocent blood; therefore the sword comes over his house forever. David has broken the marriage of another; therefore his women are to be dishonored by others. Wherein one sins, therewith will he also be punished.

The punishment falling on David's house begins during the last years of his reign, persists during the reign of Solomon and beyond. David's kingdom should be a kingdom of peace, but it is continually threatened by the sword. The struggle between the power that bears the sword and the church of God is announced and now remains "eternally." David's descendant, Christ and his church, is struck by the power of the sword, and this sword chastises and even kills bodily, but it does not kill the promise. Instead — and this is the miracle of divine chastisement — the sword that is directed against the house of David brings life and promise again to the church! The crucified Christ rises; the church under the cross, under the discipline of the sword, receives new life! Thus in David's punishment is included the whole grace of God; God adheres to his promise precisely through the punishment that he visits on the house of David. God remains true to the house of David in its fall!

From David's own house comes the one who shames him, who dishonors his wives. The dishonor of the church of God, says Bonhoeffer, comes from within itself, not from without. Absalom — he is the shadow of all those sons of the church who have shamed the church throughout its history. But woe to them, for they bring themselves to judgment and fall. Absalom remained hanging by his hair from a tree and so met his death!

David has now heard the word of God for the first time since his sin. He first knows his sin when God's word is spoken to him by another man. God, explains Bonhoeffer, waits a long time; he lets the fallen man follow the way of his sin to the end, he lets him harden his heart. The word of God has its own time, but then it breaks in and judges. " David said to Nathan, ' I have sinned against the Lord.' And Nathan said to David, ' The Lord also has put away your sin; you shall not die.' " David confesses his sin under the word of God, and because it is real confession and genuine penitence, Nathan informs him that God has already forgiven his sin. It is the same word of God that judges and acquits, the same word that drives one to repentance and humiliation, and pardons. God comes in the cross as the one who punishes and forgives his church. But if God is again there, then David cannot die in his sin, but he lives before God as a justified sinner. God comes in Christ to the sinner.

However, because God is a God who visits the sins of the father on the children, the son of the adultery must die. He is not to be the right seed of David. Nevertheless, in his concern for his child, David again learns to pray and to fast; in faith David accepts God's judgment, knows that it is a righteous judgment, and worships his God. Once again he finds peace with God, and, as a justified sinner, he again takes Bathsheba to be his wife. David cannot simply separate himself from his past guilt, and Bathsheba is for him a constant reminder of his fall, of his humiliation, of God's judgment and grace. And Bathsheba bears David a second son, whom David names Solomon, which means " the son of peace." Solomon is the son of a marriage that began with adultery and bloodshed, but he is also the son on whom the peace of God rests. The seed of David who is to bear his promise comes into this world in the flesh of sin (" in the likeness of sinful flesh," Rom. 8:3). Asks Bonhoeffer: Who is this offspring of David?

The last years of David's rule bring him daily to a consciousness of the reality of God's threat of punishment. The forgiveness of sin, asserts Bonhoeffer, does not take away from us the punishment of sin. However, the punishment is now no longer experienced as the wrath of God, but as his gracious chastisement. One should humbly submit to this punishment and not resist it, for sin demands its punishment either in this world or the world to come. David now submits and again becomes humble. David's sins are repeated in his sons: Ammon disgraces the house by raping his half-sister, and Absalom murders Ammon. Later Absalom tries to murder his father as well, and he dishonors the wives of his father and thereby shames the house of David. Through it all, however, David does not resist, but submits to God's punishment. He finally has to leave Jerusalem and crosses the Brook Kidron, the same brook that the Son of David crossed on the night before his crucifixion, as he prepared to bear the punishment of the world outside the gate (Heb. 13:12).

David refuses the priest's suggestion that he should take the Ark of God with him, he bears the curses of Shimei as he departs from Jerusalem, and he withstands the temptation of Abishai, who urges revenge. David wants to bear the whole punishment of God, and by doing so God again acknowledges David. His enemies are destroyed, and he returns home to his people.

Our question, says Bonhoeffer, is this: How is David, who became a sinner, a prototype and shadow of Christ? This is his explanation: David is a man, of sinful flesh; he is not Christ; he is not of heaven, but of earth. David is not (and never was!) a " prototype and shadow " of Christ in his moral qualities, in his holiness, but he is and remains a " prototype and shadow " of Christ through the election and anointing and the grace of God, who remains faithful to him. As the one whom God humbles and humiliates and punishes, and who as a sinner bears God's judgment and takes upon himself God's punishment and so receives the full grace of God, that is, precisely as the *justified sinner,* David, the anointed King, is the " prototype and shadow " of Christ, of the crucified Christ!

David's house, concludes Bonhoeffer, is the bearer of the promise. David himself is indeed righteous, but precisely as one who is justified as a sinner; David fears God, but he does so as a sinner who has experienced his grace. David's house is again the witness of the temple of God, namely, of Jesus Christ and his body. Jesus Christ will be righteous without sin, will fear God without transgression. David prophesies of him whom he knows in his loins, according to the promise. The eternal covenant is the covenant in Christ.

c. "The Cost of Discipleship"[31]

The Cost of Discipleship (*Nachfolge*), which appeared in 1937, was the largest and most influential book published by Bonhoeffer during his lifetime. It may rightly be considered the epitome of his theological thinking during the 1930's, and its profundity quickly won for him fame and a firm reputation as one of Germany's leading theologians. Within its pages one can discover a reiteration, in some form or other, of almost everything the author had hitherto written, but beyond this Bonhoeffer sounded a new note and issued a stinging challenge, namely, *the call to Christian discipleship*. What it means to follow Jesus: this is the burning question for Bonhoeffer! Not man-made dogmas and institutional demands that oppress and alienate, but the simple and obedient discipleship that liberates. Not the hard yoke of ecclesiasticism, but the easy yoke of Jesus. Not doctrinairism, but the Christian life. The church, says Bonhoeffer, must cease placing nonessential obstacles in the way of the common man, the man who yearns to hear Jesus, but is repelled by a type of preaching which seems hopelessly irrelevant to life and makes demands that only a pious few can afford. The church must once again preach what is central in the Christian faith, and this Bonhoeffer sums up in one word: discipleship! The purpose of this book is to elucidate the meaning of discipleship for the Christian.

The work is divided into two parts: first, a consideration of the relation between grace and discipleship, centering about an exposition of the Sermon on the Mount; second, an attempt to show the connection between discipleship and the church. Although Bonhoeffer's interpretation of the Sermon on the Mount (Matt., chs. 5 to 7) stands at the heart of the book, each of the other sections fairly bristles with incisive exegeses of pertinent Biblical passages. It is no accident that Bonhoeffer stays close to the text, for he is convinced that what the modern man wants and needs is not the human

---

[31] This is the title of the abridged English translation of *Nachfolge* (literally, "following after," "discipleship") by R. H. Fuller, which was published by the S.C.M. Press, Ltd., London, in 1948, and by The Macmillan Company in 1949. The following five scattered chapters were omitted: "The Simple Obedience"; "The Messengers" (Exposition of Matthew, ch. 10); "The Church of Jesus Christ and Discipleship — Preliminary Questions"; "The Visible Community"; "The Saints." Where possible, citations will be taken from this translation.

ballast, but the pure word of Jesus himself.

" Cheap grace is the deadly enemy of our church. We are fighting today for costly grace " (37). With these opening words Bonhoeffer sets the stage for everything that is to follow. By cheap grace he means " grace sold on the market like cheap-Jack's wares," " grace as a doctrine, a principle, a system," " the justification of sin without the justification of the sinner " (37). Cheap grace is " the preaching of forgiveness without requiring repentance, baptism without church discipline, communion without confession, absolution without contrition. Cheap grace is grace without discipleship, grace without the cross, grace without Jesus Christ, living and incarnate " (38). On the other hand, costly grace is " the treasure hidden in the field," for the sake of which " a man will gladly go and sell all that he has," " the pearl of great price to buy which the merchant will sell all his goods," " the kingly rule of Christ, for whose sake a man will pluck out the eye which causes him to stumble," " the call of Jesus at which the disciple leaves his nets and follows Him " (38 f.). " Costly grace is the gospel which must be *sought* again and again, the gift which must be *asked* for, the door at which a man must *knock*. Such grace is *costly* because it calls us to follow, and it is *grace* because it calls us to follow Jesus Christ. It is costly because it costs a man his life, and it is grace because it gives a man the only true life. It is costly because it condemns sin, and grace because it justifies the sinner " (39).

The early Christians, contends the author, lived lives in which grace and discipleship were inseparable, but as the church became secularized and the world " Christianized," grace remained costly within the Roman Church only in monasticism. This movement, however, led to the fatal conception of a double standard of obedience within the church, and God subsequently raised up Martin Luther to show that " the following of Christ was not the achievement or merit of a select few, but an obligation laid on all Christions without distinction " (41). Luther left the cloister and returned to the world and thereby dealt the world its greatest blow since the early days of Christianity, because he brought into sharpest relief the contrast between the Christian life and the life of the world. He was driven from the cloister, explains Bonhoeffer, not by the justification of sin, but by the justification of the sinner, and this was the secret of the Reformation. However, Luther's proclamation of "by grace alone" (and even his statement: "Sin boldly, but believe and rejoice in Christ more boldly still!") came as a result of the costly following of Jesus and was looked upon as an *answer to a sum,* whereas his followers changed this "answer" into a datum of calculation, a principle for having grace at low cost. "We Lutherans," charges Bonhoeffer, "have gathered like eagles round the carcass of cheap grace" (47), and the collapse of organized religion today (the German Church Struggle!) is the inevitable result of this policy. The most urgent problem of today's church is expressed in the question that the author intends to answer in this book, namely, How can we live the Christian life in the modern world?

The call of Jesus to discipleship, says Bonhoeffer, demands a response of immediate obedience. Not a confession of faith, not a religious decision, but *obedience* to the word of Jesus, who as the Christ has authority to call and to demand obedience! Discipleship offers no program, no set of principles, no ideal, no law; discipleship means Jesus Christ and him alone, and its sole content is: "Follow me." "When we are called to follow Christ," he asserts, "we are summoned to an exclusive attachment to his person" (51). The call of Jesus is grace and commandment in one and thus transcends the difference between law and gospel. It means adherence to the *living* Christ, the Son of God who became Man, the sole Mediator, the God-Man. An abstract Christology, a doctrinal system or a general knowledge on the subject of grace or on the forgiveness of sins may be enthusiastically accepted and even put into practice, but an idea can never be followed in personal obedience. "Christianity without the living Christ is inevitably Christianity without discipleship, and Christianity without discipleship is always Christianity without Christ" (52).

One must take certain steps if he is to follow Jesus, and the first of these is to break away from the past. "The first step places the disciple in the situation where faith is possible" (54), and it has no other justification than that it brings the disciple into fellowship with Jesus. Bonhoeffer fully realizes the danger of distinguishing between a situation where faith is possible and one where it is not, and he emphasizes that there is nothing in the situation itself that tells us to which category it belongs. A situation where faith is possible can never be demonstrated from the human side, never possesses any intrinsic worth or merit of its own, is itself rendered possible only through faith. The situation is entirely dependent on the call of Jesus, and it may be described by two propositions that are equally true: *only he who believes is obedient,* and *only he who is obedient believes.* Of course, admits Bonhoeffer, from the point of view of justification the two must be separated; nevertheless, there must be no chronological distinction that dissolves their essential unity, for " faith is only real when there is obedience, never without it, and faith only becomes faith in the act of obedience " (56).

The first step is an external work that any man is capable of taking, but it is never more than " a purely external act and dead work of the law, which can never of itself bring a man to Christ " (57). The first step is necessary, but it can never be looked upon as a precondition for faith and grace. But how can this be avoided? Only by fixing our eyes, says Bonhoeffer, " not on the work we do, but on the word with which Jesus calls us to do it. . . . In the end, the first step of obedience proves to be an act of faith in the word of Christ " (58).

The commandment of Jesus, insists Bonhoeffer, calls for *simple, literal* obedience. To be sure, there may be cases where a paradoxical understanding of a commandment is Christianly justified. For instance, the commandment of Jesus to the rich young man to sell all his possessions, give the proceeds to the poor, and follow him, may be so construed that in the end everything depended upon the young man's *faith,* not upon whether he was rich or poor, and thus one may conclude that it is possible for a wealthy man to believe in Christ and to hold his possessions as if he did not have them. Nevertheless, a paradoxical understanding must never destroy the primary, simple understanding, and it is only possible for one who has already taken seriously the simple understanding at some point in his life, who thus stands in the fellowship of Jesus, in discipleship, in anticipation of the end. Therefore, in a paradoxical understanding the literal must always be included! The call of Jesus is completely concrete, and wherever the simple obedience has been eliminated, there costly grace has become the cheap grace of self-justification, there a false law has been set up, there an unevangelical principle of Scriptural interpretation has been introduced.

" If any man would come after me, let him deny himself and take up his cross and follow me." Discipleship, asserts Bonhoeffer, means the *cross*. Jesus as the Christ must suffer and be rejected and die on the cross, and so " the disciple is a disciple only in so far as he shares his Lord's suffering and rejection and crucifixion " (71). Christ bids one to count the cost and freely decide; he asks one to deny himself, which means to know Christ and cease to know oneself. " Only when we have become completely oblivious of self," says Bonhoeffer, " are we ready to bear the cross for his sake " (72).

The endurance of the cross is not an accidental tragedy, but a necessary suffering that is the fruit of an exclusive allegiance to Jesus Christ. It is suffering and rejection for the sake of Christ alone, and no Christian need go out looking for a cross or run after suffering per se. God has destined and appointed a cross for everyone who becomes a disciple. " It begins," explains the author, " with the call to abandon the attachments of this world. It is that dying of the old man which is the result of his encounter with Christ. . . . When Christ calls a man, he bids him come and die " (73). Not only is the Christian committed through his baptism to a daily warfare against the world, the flesh, and the devil, but he also must undergo temptation and bear the sins of others. Indeed, stresses Bonhoeffer, *only* the sufferings of Christ are *redemptive,* but in his grace Christ lets his disciples share the fruits of his Passion by bearing the burdens of others and by participation in the work of forgiving men their sins. In fact, the only way to bear the burden or sin of another, and thereby fulfill the law of Christ, is by forgiving it in the power of the cross of Christ. " Forgiveness is the Christlike suffering which it is the Christian's duty to bear " (74). By drinking the cup of suffering to the dregs on the cross, Jesus overcame the suffering of mankind in its separation from God and made fellowship with God again possible, and the church that follows Christ beneath the cross will find itself suffering before God on behalf of the world.

" Through the call of Jesus," says the author, " men become individuals " (78). Each man is called individually, each must make his own decision and each must follow alone. When Christ brings men into direct contact with himself through his call, he delivers them from all direct contact with the world, from all the natural ties of life. "We cannot follow Christ," asserts Bonhoeffer, "unless we are prepared to accept that breach as a *fait accompli*" (78). Why is this so? Because by virtue of his incarnation Christ has come between man and his natural life, and henceforth everything that happens must happen through him alone. "*He is the Mediator,* not only between God and man, but between man and reality" (79). Even in the most intimate relationships of life, in our kinship with father and mother, brothers and sisters, in our love for our wives, and in our community obligations, direct relationships are impossible. There is an unbridgeable gulf, an "otherness" and strangeness between us, and we can get in touch with each other only through Christ the Mediator!

Nevertheless, the same Mediator whose call makes us individuals is also the founder of a new fellowship. Through him we are united to one another in the church, and the one who has severed close ties for the sake of Christ finds himself compensated a hundredfold in a visible brotherhood, yet with the proviso — " with persecutions." This, concludes Bonhoeffer, is the grace and the promise held out to the followers of Christ: "They will be members of the community of the cross, the people of the Mediator, the people under the cross" (85).

Bonhoeffer now begins his exposition of the Sermon on the Mount, which he divides into three sections dealing with different aspects of the life of discipleship. Matthew, ch. 5, is concerned with the "extraordinariness" of the Christian life; Matt., ch. 6, with its hidden character; Matt., ch. 7, with the separation of the disciple community.

At the beginning of the Sermon on the Mount, Jesus calls his disciples blessed and addresses the Beatitudes to them and to the people. He calls blessed *the poor in spirit* (those who accept privation for *his* sake); *those who mourn* (those who refuse to be in tune with the world, who mourn on account of its guilt, its fate, its fortune, and who *bear* the sorrow and suffering that come their way as they follow him); *the meek* (those who renounce every right of their own and live for the sake of Christ); *those who hunger and thirst for righteousness* (those who renounce their own righteousness, who get no praise for their achievements or sacrifices and who must always look forward to the renewal of the earth and the perfect righteousness of God); *the merciful* (those who renounce their honor and dignity for Christ's sake and show mercy by seeking all those who are enmeshed in the toils of sin and guilt and taking upon themselves their distress and humiliation and sin); *the pure in heart* (those who have surrendered their hearts completely to Jesus that he may reign in them alone); *the peacemakers* (those who have found their peace in Christ and who now renounce all violence and tumult and endure suffering for his cause); *those who are persecuted for righteousness' sake* (those who suffer for *any just cause*). Is there any place on earth where such a community as the Beatitudes describes still remains? It has become clear, answers Bonhoeffer, that there is only one place, namely, the place where the poorest, the meekest, the most sorely tried of all men is to be found: the cross at Golgotha! " The community which is the subject of the Beatitudes is the community of the Crucified. With him it has lost all, and with him it has found all. It is the cross which makes the Beatitudes possible " (97).

Jesus calls his disciples the *salt* of the earth, because he entrusts his work to them. It is important to note, says Bonhoeffer, that Jesus said, " You *are* the salt," not " You *must be* the salt " or " You *have* the salt." The call of Christ makes those who respond to it the salt of the world, and the Reformers' identification of the salt with the apostolic proclamation robbed the saying of all its sting. Again, Jesus calls the disciple community the *light* of the world. But, contends the author, what becomes visible is not the disciples, but their good works; and " these works are none other than those which the Lord Jesus himself has created in them by calling them to be the light of the world under the shadow of his cross. The good works are poverty, estrangement, meekness, peaceableness, and finally persecution and rejection " (102). These good works will glorify God, for " it is by *seeing* the cross and the community beneath it that men come to believe in God " (103).

Jesus binds his disciples to the Old Testament law. Christians have no " better law," but there is a " better righteousness " that is expected of them. " The call of Christ, in fact Christ himself, is the *sine qua non* of this better righteousness " (105). Now it is evident why Jesus thus far has said nothing about himself in the Sermon on the Mount. " Between the disciples and the better righteousness demanded of them stands the person of Christ, who came to fulfill the law of the Old Covenant. This is the fundamental presupposition of the whole Sermon on the Mount " (105). Jesus himself is the righteousness of the disciples, and their righteousness consists precisely in their following him! It is something that must be *done*. " It is the sincere and spontaneous practice of righteousness through faith in the righteousness of Christ. It is the new law, the law of Christ " (109).

In what follows, says Bonhoeffer, Jesus tells the disciples how to practice this better righteousness, and in doing so he makes it clear that he is in full agreement with the law of the Mosaic covenant, but declares war on all false (Pharisaic!) interpretations of it. " But I say unto you " — Jesus means that he, the Son of God, is the Author and Giver of the law, and only those who recognize this fact can fulfill the law. The first law that Jesus commends concerns the brother. The disciples are to let the brother live and to care for his welfare. Anger and insults have no place in the community of Christ, but service and self-denial do — for this is the way of the cross. Man's relation to woman is sanctified by Christ, for adherence to him allows no free rein to desire unless it be accompanied by love. Lust is impure because it is unbelief. Jesus does not forbid the disciples to look at anything, but bids them look at him. " If they do that, he knows that their gaze will always be pure, even when they look upon a woman " (115). By affirming the indissolubility of marriage and prohibiting the innocent party from remarrying when the marriage is broken by adultery, Jesus consecrates marriage to the service of love. The purity and chastity that mark the Christian marriage are only possible for those who follow Jesus and share his life.

Because of his concern for absolute truthfulness, Jesus commands his disciples not to swear oaths, since such an action would only throw doubt on all their other statements. Bonhoeffer seriously questions the general rule of the Reformation Churches that Jesus did not mean to prohibit oaths exacted by the state in a court of law, a rule based on the assumption that in this case an oath is desirable in the interest of the truth and presupposing the distinction between the spiritual and the worldly realms. Each case must be decided on its own merits. In any case, says the author, only those who follow Jesus and know their sin revealed upon the cross can be genuinely truthful. Further, the disciples are not to requite evil with evil, because they live only for Christ's sake and renounce every personal right. " The only way to overcome evil is to let it run its course, so that it does not find the resistance it is looking for " (122). This removes the church from the sphere of politics and law; it is not to be a national community like the Old Israel, but a community of believers without political or national ties. Bonhoeffer sharply rejects the Reformers' distinction between *personal* sufferings and those incurred by Christians in the performance of duty as *bearers of an office* ordained by God, with the accompanying assertion that the precept of nonviolence applies to the former but not to the latter. " This distinction between person and office is wholly alien to the teaching of Jesus " (123). On the other hand, nonresistance is not to be made into a principle for general application or a piece of worldly wisdom. The Passion of Christ on the cross, where divine love conquers the powers of evil, is the sole justification for the precept of nonviolence and the only supportable basis for Christian obedience. " On the cross Jesus practices what he preaches, and at the same time, by enjoining this precept upon the disciples, he helps them to realize their share in the cross " (125).

The word " love " sums up the whole message of the Sermon on the Mount, and " love is defined in uncompromising terms as the love of our enemies " (126)! Furthermore, the New Testament conception of enemies refers only to those who are hostile to us, for Jesus refuses to reckon with the possibility of his followers' cherishing hostility toward others. How does love conquer? " By asking not how the enemy treats her but only how Jesus treated her. The love of our enemies takes us along the way of the cross and into fellowship with the Crucified " (129).

In the final analysis, how do the disciples differ from the heathen?

What does it really mean to be a Christian? *One word,* asserts Bonhoeffer, spells the difference: *perisson* (Matt. 5:47)! This word, which means the "peculiar," the "extraordinary," the "unusual," that which is not "a matter of course," sums up all that has been said thus far. "This is the quality whereby the better righteousness exceeds the righteousness of the scribes and Pharisees. It is 'the more,' the 'beyond all that.' The natural is *to auto* (one and the same) for heathen and Christian, the distinctive quality of the Christian life begins with the *perisson*. . . . What is the precise nature of the *perisson?* It is the life described in the Beatitudes, the life of the followers of Jesus, the light which illuminates, the city set on the hill, the way of self-renunciation, of absolute purity, truthfulness, and meekness. It is unreserved love for our enemies, for the unloving and the unloved, love for our religious, political, and personal adversaries. In every case it is love which is fulfilled in the cross of Christ. What is the *perisson?* It is the love of Jesus Christ himself, who went patiently and obediently to the cross — it is in fact the cross itself. The cross is the differential of the Christian religion, the power which enables the Christian to transcend the world and to win the victory. The *passio* in the love of the Crucified is the supreme expression of the 'extraordinary' quality of the Christian life" (131 f.). And in practice this "extraordinary" is something that the disciples of Jesus do, something that is visible to all, but is at the same time simple, unreflecting obedience to the will of Christ.

Although Matt., ch. 5, has demanded the "extraordinary" that is visible to others, Matt., ch. 6, begins with a warning against practicing one's piety in order to be seen by men! "Our activity," explains Bonhoeffer, "must be visible, but never be done for the sake of making it visible" (136). Jesus calls us to reflection, but this reflection is intended to prevent us from reflecting on our extraordinary position! Bonhoeffer resolves the paradoxical relation of chs. 5 and 6 by answering three questions. First: From whom are we to hide the visibility of our discipleship? Answer: Not from men, but from *ourselves!* A follower must look only to his leader, so that the "extraordinary" is simply the natural, ordinary, and thus hidden fruit of obedience. Second: How can the visible and invisible aspects of discipleship be combined? Answer: Only in the cross of Christ beneath which the disciples stand. The cross is the hidden and necessary, and at the same time the visible and extraordinary. Third: How is the contradiction between the fifth and sixth chapters to be resolved? Answer: By exclusive adherence to Christ. This implies looking only to the Lord and not to the extraordinary quality of the Christian life, and doing only the will of God, which is without alternatives and thus quite natural. Who can live a life that combines the demands of both chapters? Only those in whom through Christ the old man has died and a new life has been found in the fellowship of the disciples! Love as an act of simple obedience is the death of the old man, and the true nature of man is recovered in the righteousness of Christ and in his fellow men. The love of Christ crucified is the love that lives on in his disciples, so that henceforth the Christian finds himself only in Christ and in his brethren.

The devout life of discipleship is a hidden life of prayer and fasting, an unending struggle of the spirit against the flesh. There is an ascetic discipline to the life of faith, but, warns the author, our asceticism (voluntary suffering, *passio activa* rather than *passiva!*) must not lead us to imagine that we can imitate the sufferings of Christ! Instead, the motive of asceticism is much more limited, namely, to equip us for better service and deeper humiliation. The hidden life of devotion and obedience is the life of *carefree simplicity*. The Christian allows nothing — neither the law nor personal piety nor the world — to come between him and Christ, but with singleness of eye and heart he looks solely to Christ, walks with him and accepts everything as it comes from God. The Kingdom of God and his righteousness, i.e., communion with Jesus and obedience to his commandment, *come first,* and all else follows.

Chapters 5 and 6 have portrayed a clear distinction between the old life and the new, but what of the distinction between Christians and their non-Christian neighbors? Do Christians possess certain criteria by which they may judge others? Bonhoeffer points out that ch. 7 begins with an admonition that immediately stifles any illusion of superiority. The disciples are not to judge! A disciple possesses his righteousness exclusively *within* his association with Jesus Christ, so it can never become an objective criterion to be applied at will. " His righteousness," says Bonhoeffer, " is hidden from himself and possessed in fellowship with Jesus. . . . Again, there is no standard of judgment with which to judge a nondisciple, for between them there is only Jesus Christ. Christians always see other men as brethren to whom Christ comes; they meet them only by going to them with Jesus. . . . Discipleship does not afford us a point of vantage from which to attack others; we come to them with an unconditional offer of fellowship, with the sincerity of the love of Jesus" (158). And not only may disciples not judge others, but they also may not *force* the word of salvation upon them. The gospel is no ideology that requires fanatics to run after people and to proselyte them. No, the gospel in its weakness takes the risk of meeting the scorn of men and of being rejected; it reckons with impossibilities! When the disciples encounter opposition, they have only one recourse, namely, *prayer to God,* who alone judges and forgives, closes and opens.

Bonhoeffer now speaks of what he calls "the great divide." The call of Jesus alone separates his disciples from the world. The way of discipleship is a narrow way that can only be trod by following Jesus step by step! As a citizen of two worlds the Christian treads the narrow path "on the razoredge between this world and the Kingdom of Heaven" (163). The call of Jesus not only separates church and world, however, but also nominal Christians and real ones, appearance and reality. Thus the division runs right through the middle of the confessing church, a division between those who simply confess "Lord, Lord," and those who do the will of God. Yet even here the division is not ended! Within the church there will appear people who do all sorts of wonderful deeds and seem to be true disciples, but who do all this *without love.* Here, asserts Bonhoeffer, is a demonic faith, the most incredible satanic possibility in the church. The ultimate division will not come until the Last Day, when the crucial question will be whether or not Jesus has known us. Everything depends on the word of Jesus Christ: "I have known you" — which is his eternal word and call. "The end of the Sermon on the Mount echoes the beginning. The word of the Last Judgment is foreshadowed in the call to follow. But from beginning to end it is always *his* word and *his* call, his alone. If we follow Christ, cling to his word, and let everything else go, we shall find support in this word at the day of judgment. His word is his grace " (167).

The hearer of the Sermon on the Mount, concludes Bonhoeffer, might conceivably understand it and interpret it in a thousand different ways, but " Jesus knows only one possibility: simple surrender and obedience, not interpreting it or applying it, but doing and obeying it. . . . Jesus has spoken: his is the word, ours the obedience " (168).

Bonhoeffer now turns his attention to Christ's commissioning of the Twelve to be his messengers (Matt. 9:35 to 10:42). Where the scribes and Pharisees see only barren wasteland, Jesus sees ripe fields to be harvested for the Kingdom of God, so he calls the Twelve and sends them to the lost sheep of the house of Israel, for Israel must first hear the message of Christ and reject it in order that the Gentiles may come in. The disciples are armed with the word, " The kingdom of heaven is at hand," and as the word of Almighty God it is act, event, miracle. It is Jesus Christ himself who accompanies the disciples and does his work. To indicate their freedom Jesus commands them to serve in the uniform of poverty (not as beggars!), and in the same freedom they are to accept lodging and food (again not as beggars!), for a laborer deserves his food. Their work should be carried out in those houses " which are worthy " to lodge the messengers of Jesus, and in these a small group should be formed to stand as a deputy for the entire community. The preaching of the messengers is to be short and clear, and for those who do not want to hear, the time of grace is past! They have brought judgment upon themselves! But is this not unmerciful haste? No, says Bonhoeffer; nothing is more unmerciful than to delude a person into thinking that he still has time for conversion. And nothing is more merciful than the good news that the Kingdom of God is very near! Where the word of God is rejected, the messengers should simply depart, and the shaking of the dust from their feet is a sign of the curse that will befall the place, a curse in which they will have no part.

Jesus tells his disciples to expect opposition and cautions them to be " wise as serpents and innocent as doves." How often this passage has been misused to justify worldly cunning and disobedience! But, declares Bonhoeffer, it is not *our* judgment of the situation that can show us what is wise, but solely the truth of the word of God. The *only* wise thing that we can ever do is to remain by the truth of God, for only here is God's promise of help and faithfulness. The messengers can expect to suffer for the sake of the word, but even this will present an opportunity for the " good confession " and thus serve to spread the word.

Bonhoeffer next turns to some questions that modern man asks concerning discipleship. For the first disciples Jesus was bodily present with his word, but this Jesus has died and risen. Since he can no longer walk past us and call " Follow me " as when he called the tax collector Levi, how can we hear his call to discipleship today? That which was so unambiguous for his contemporaries seems for us an extremely questionable matter. And what makes us think that the call of Jesus to the tax collector is also meant for us? Who are we to want to do the unusual and the extraordinary? Who can say that we are not acting under our own power and enthusiasm?

All these questions, declares the author, are impure questions by which we again and again place ourselves outside the living presence of Christ. These questions fail to recognize that Jesus Christ is not dead, but is living today and still speaks to us through the witness of Scripture. He is present with us today, bodily and with his word, and if we want to hear his call to discipleship, then we must hear it where he is. The call of Jesus Christ today is issued *in the church through his word and sacrament!* The very same Jesus who encountered the disciples is found in the church; indeed, now he is the victorious and glorified Christ! Because discipleship never essentially concerns a decision for this or that act, but always a decision for or against Jesus Christ, the situation was no clearer for the disciples of old than it is for us today. Both then and now it is the *hidden* Christ who calls, and this Christ is only recognized and obeyed *in faith*. We hear the word and believe in him!

But did not the first disciples have the distinct advantage of knowing Christ when they received his commandment, whereas we are left with a commandment alone? Does not Christ speak to us in a different way than to those? If that were true, asserts Bonhoeffer, then we would surely be in a hopeless situation! No, Christ speaks to us exactly as he spoke to them. The first disciples did not first know Christ and then receive his commandment; rather, they knew him only through his word and commandment. They believed his word and commandment and recognized in them the Christ.

Finally, if we say that the commandment to the first disciples was clear and unambiguous, but that we have to decide for ourselves which of his words is valid for us, then we have again misunderstood not only the disciples' situation, but also our own. The purpose of Jesus' command, says Bonhoeffer, is always to call forth faith from undivided hearts; it demands love of God and love of neighbor. Only in this was and is the commandment clear. On the other hand, we are not deprived of knowing the *concrete* commandment, because in every word of proclamation in which we hear Christ it is spoken clearly — to be sure, in such a way that we know that its fulfillment takes place solely in faith in Jesus Christ. Thus the gift of Jesus to his disciples, namely, his gracious call, is preserved for us in every respect. In fact, for us it has come even nearer through the departure of Jesus, the knowledge of his glorification, and the sending of the Holy Spirit.

Bonhoeffer now undertakes the task of correlating the Synoptic category of discipleship with the " churchly " language of Paul. Whereas in the Synoptic Gospels the relationship between the disciples and their Lord is expressed almost exclusively in terms of *following him,* in the Pauline epistles this conception gives way to a *new set of terms,* which deal less with the earthly life of Jesus and more with the presence of the risen and glorified Christ and his work in us. Nevertheless, emphasizes Bonhoeffer, these terms " confirm those of the Synoptists, and vice versa. Neither set of terms is intrinsically preferable to the other " (173). We have to do with the *one* Christ in the whole of Scripture, and differences of terminology and testimony do not break the unity of the Biblical witness.

" Where the Synoptic Gospels speak of Christ calling men and their following him, St. Paul speaks of *baptism* " (174). Baptism is an offer made by Christ to man, an essentially passive act (*being baptized!*) in which man becomes Christ's own possession. Baptism is a visible act of obedience in response to Christ's gracious call, and it signifies a breach with the world, a dying of the old man, which means justification from sin. The gift of baptism is the Holy Spirit, who gives us assurance and discernment. From now on man's relationship to all the God-given realities of life is possible only through Christ the Mediator. Baptism means the death of the old man as a gift of grace and new life in the fellowship of Christ, that is, in the fellowship of the cross. "The cross to which we are called," explains Bonhoeffer, "is a daily dying in the power of the death which Christ died once and for all. In this way baptism means sharing in the cross of Christ" (176). Nevertheless, "the baptized live, not by a literal repetition of this death, but by a constant renewal of their faith in the death of Christ as his act of grace in us. The source of their faith lies in the once-and-for-allness of Christ's death, which they have experienced in their baptism" (178).

The first disciples lived in the bodily presence of Jesus and enjoyed bodily communion with him; Paul tells us that through baptism we are made members of the body of Christ and thereby enjoy the same bodily fellowship and presence! In fact, ours is a richer and surer bodily communion because it is with the glorified Lord. "Our faith," says Bonhoeffer, "must be aware of the greatness of this gift. The body of Christ is the ground and assurance of that faith. It is the one and perfect gift whereby we become partakers of salvation. It is indeed newness of life" (180).

Bonhoeffer now gives this concise understanding of the incarnation in order to indicate the importance of the body of Christ:

After the fall of Adam, God never ceased to send his word to sinful men. He sought after them in order to take them to himself. The whole purpose for which the word came was to restore lost mankind to fellowship with God. The word of God came both as a promise and as a law. It became weak and of no account for our sake. But men rejected the word, refusing to give ear and return to God. They offered sacrifices and performed works which they fondly imagined God would accept in place of themselves, but with these they purchased their independence from him. Then the supreme miracle occurs. The Son of God becomes man. The word is made flesh. He who had existed from all eternity in the glory of the Father, he who in the beginning was the agent of creation (which means that the created world can be known only through him and in him) he who was very God . . . accepts humanity by taking upon himself our human nature, "sinful flesh" as the Bible calls it, and human form. . . . God takes humanity to himself, not merely as heretofore through the spoken word, but in the body of Jesus. Of his mercy God sends his Son in the flesh, that therein he may bear the whole human race and bring it to himself. The Son of God takes to himself the whole human race bodily, that race which in its hatred of God and in the pride of its flesh had rejected the incorporeal, invisible word of God. Now this humanity, in all its weakness, is, by the mercy of God, taken up in the body of Jesus in true bodily form.

As they contemplated the miracle of the incarnation, the early fathers became passionately convinced that while it was true to say that God took human nature upon him, it was wrong to say that he chose a perfect individual man and united himself to him. God was made man, and while that means that he took upon him our entire human nature with all its infirmity, sinfulness, and corruption, it does not mean that he took upon him the man Jesus. Unless we draw this distinction we shall misunderstand the whole message of the gospel. The body of Jesus Christ, in which we are taken up with the whole human race, has now become the ground of our salvation. (180 f.)

Thus the incarnate Son of God existed simultaneously as himself and as humanity. In Adam, who had also been an individual man and at the same time a representative of the whole human race, mankind had fallen, but in Christ, the Second Adam, humanity is created anew. Christ is the Second Man, the New Man! Now we can understand why the bodily fellowship and communion of the disciples with Christ is so important. Discipleship means to cleave to Jesus Christ *bodily,* and this is a natural consequence of the incarnation. "Had he been merely a prophet or teacher," explains Bonhoeffer, "he would not have needed followers, but only pupils and hearers. But since he is the incarnate Son of God who came in human flesh, he needs a community of followers, who will participate not merely in his teaching, but also in his body" (182). But how do we today participate in the body of Christ, who has borne human nature on the cross and carried it onward to his resurrection? We participate, answers the author, through the two sacraments of his body: Baptism and the Lord's Supper. "The word of preaching," he asserts, "is insufficient to make us members of Christ's body; the sacraments also have to play their part. Baptism incorporates us into the unity of the body of Christ, and the Lord's Supper fosters and sustains our fellowship and communion (*koinōnia*) in that body. ... The communion of the body of Christ, which we receive as the disciples received it in the early days, is the sign and pledge that we are 'with Christ' and 'in Christ,' and that he is 'in us.' Rightly understood, the doctrine of the body is the clue to the meaning of these expressions" (183).

The incarnation means that *all men* are "with Christ," for he bore our whole human nature, and his life, death, and resurrection are events in which all men really participate. But, continues Bonhoeffer, Christians are "with Christ" in a special way; for the rest of humanity it means death, but for Christians it is a means of grace. "The Christian who is baptized into (*eis*) Christ is baptized into the fellowship of his sufferings. Thus not only does the individual become a member of the body of Christ, but the fellowship of the baptized becomes a body which is identical with Christ's own body. The Christians are 'in Christ' (*en*) and 'Christ in them'" (184). All of this can be summed up, asserts Bonhoeffer, in the single phrase: Christ is "for us"! He suffers and dies in our stead, and he incorporates us in his body, which is in fact the church. To be in Christ is to be in the church, and the church is the real presence of Christ. "We should think of the church not as an institution, but as a *person*, though of course a person in a unique sense" (185).

The church, asserts Bonhoeffer, is *One Man*, the New Man. And the New Man is both Christ and the church; indeed, Christ is the church. In Baptism the individual believer "puts on" Christ and at the same time is incorporated into the church, into the One Man. When we have recognized this unity between Christ and his church, warns Bonhoeffer, we must hold fast to the complementary truth of Christ's Lordship over the body. Paul calls Christ the Head of the body, which means that Christ stands over against the church. Furthermore, Christ's ascension and his Second Coming rule out any idea of a mystical fusion between Christ and his church. "The church is One Man; it is the body of Christ. But it is also many, a fellowship of members" (187). The members of the body cannot transcend their own individuality, but their separate identity and function are preserved only as members of the one body, as a fellowship united in service. This is the fellowship of the cross, participation in the suffering and glory of Christ, freely suffering "for him." It is a suffering that first takes the form of the baptismal death, and after that a daily dying in the power of that baptism. "Although Christ has fulfilled all the vicarious suffering necessary for our redemption, his suffering on earth is not finished yet" (188). In his grace, Christ has left a "residue" of suffering for the benefit of his church, and those who share in this suffering (in a representative capacity "for" the church) live the very life of Christ, who wills to be formed in his members!

The body of Christ, emphasizes the author, occupies space on earth; that is, *it is visible*. Unlike a truth or a doctrine or a religion, all of which need no space, but are merely to be heard, learned, and understood, the incarnate Son of God needs not only ears and hearts, but *real men* who follow him. The body of the Lord is the visible body in the form of the *congregation*. And how does this body become visible? It does so, says Bonhoeffer, in these three realms of activity: proclamation, church order, and life in the world. First, the church becomes visible when the congregation assembles to hear the preaching of the word of God and to participate in Baptism and the Lord's Supper. Secondly, the body of Christ as a congregation implies and demands visible church organization and order. To be sure, the triune God establishes the offices in the congregation in order to serve it, not to rule, and the organization is flexible to the extent that it may assume the form that best serves the situation. Those who occupy the offices of the church are also responsible for the purity of the administration of the word and the sacraments, and where false doctrine becomes evident, there full separation is mandatory. Finally, the body of Christ becomes visible in the daily life of the members, in fellowship and brotherly love, in worldly callings and under worldly authorities. The disciples are completely in the world, but not of the world, and in their encounter with the world the visible congregation will always become more like the form of the suffering Lord!

Those who follow Christ are called "saints." The saints, explains the author, are the people of God who have been elected and placed in a covenant relationship by the holy God himself, and for this reason they become holy. " You shall be holy; for I the Lord your God am holy." (Lev. 19:2.) As God in his holiness is set apart from the profane and from sin, so also is the congregation of his sanctuary. But his sanctuary is the temple, and the temple is the body of Christ! Thus in the body of Christ the will of God for a holy congregation is fulfilled. The church is God's sanctuary in the world, and for the congregation of the saints this means three things: first, its sanctification will be confirmed in its clear separation from the world; second, its sanctification will be confirmed in a behavior that is worthy of God's sanctuary; and third, its sanctification will be hidden in waiting for the day of Jesus Christ. The good works of the saints of the church are hidden from their eyes, for they look only toward their Lord!

" For those whom he foreknew he also predestined to be conformed to the image of his Son, in order that he might be the firstborn among many brethren." (Rom. 8:29.) This, declares Bonhoeffer, is the promise which passes all understanding: that the disciples of Christ are destined to bear his image, to be his brethren, to become " like Christ "! With his image before them their own lives will be so transformed that they become sons of God, bearing like him the image of God. Adam, who was created by God in his own image, was destined to be " like God," but he was persuaded by the serpent that he still had to do something to *become* like God, and in choosing to achieve that likeness by deciding and acting for himself, Adam fell. He became " like God " in his own way, which is to say, he ruled in solitude as a creator-god in a Godforsaken world! " With the loss of the Godlike nature God had given him, man had forfeited the destiny of his being, which was to be like God. In short, man had ceased to be a man. He must live without the ability to live. Herein lies the paradox of human nature and the source of all our woe " (193).

The divine image is lost forever to the sons of Adam, yet God does not abandon his creature, but plans to re-create his image in him. But how can this be accomplished? Since man can no longer be like the image of God, God must become like the image of man in order to effect a complete transformation, a metamorphosis. " The Son of God, who dwelt in the form of God the Father, lays aside that form, and comes to man in the form of a slave (Phil. 2:5 ff.). The change of form, which could not take place in man, now takes place in God. The divine image which had existed from eternity with God assumes the image of fallen, sinful man. God sends his Son in the likeness of sinful flesh (Rom. 8:2 f.)" (194). A Man comes to men, and in him the divine image is re-created on earth. "But," Bonhoeffer reminds us, "it is not the same image as Adam bore in the primal glory of Paradise. Rather, it is the image of one who enters a world of sin and death, who takes upon himself all the sorrows of humanity, who meekly bears God's wrath and judgment against sinners, and obeys his will with unswerving devotion in suffering and death, the Man born to poverty, the friend of publicans and sinners, the Man of sorrows, rejected of man and forsaken of God. Here is God made man, here is man in the new image of God" (194).

The image lost in the fall can be recovered only by being conformed to the image of the suffering Christ, letting the form of Christ be manifest in us. Only those who share his shame will share his glory! The Christian life (or better: Christ living in us) is a life of crucifixion which begins with the impression of the form of Christ's death in baptism and continues through a daily dying in the war between the flesh and the spirit, and in the mortal agony inflicted daily by the devil. When Christians suffer and die for his sake, Christ takes on visible form in his church. Christ lives on in the lives of his followers, and where he lives, there the Father also lives, and both the Father and the Son through the Spirit. "The Holy Trinity himself has made his dwelling in the Christian heart, filling his whole being, and transforming him into the divine image. Christ, incarnate, crucified and glorified, is formed in every Christian soul, for all are members of his body, the church. . . . In the body of Christ we are become 'like Christ'" (197).

Because (and *only* because!) Christ became like us, we can become like him! "By being transformed into his image," concludes Bonhoeffer, "we are enabled to model our lives on his. By simply following him we can perform deeds and live a life that is one with the life of Christ. We are now able to render spontaneous obedience to the word of God. We no longer regard our own lives or the new image that we bear, for then we should at once have forfeited it. No, we must look steadfastly on the reflection of the image of Jesus Christ. The disciple looks solely at his Master. But when a man follows Jesus Christ and bears the image of the incarnate, crucified, and risen Lord, when he has become the image of God, we may at last say that he has been called to be the ' imitator of God.' The follower of Jesus is the imitator of God. ' Be ye therefore imitators of God, as beloved children ' (Eph. 5:1) " (197 f.).

d. " Temptation " [32]

Temptation (*Versuchung*) is a short Bible study that Dietrich Bonhoeffer conducted during the reunion of the members of his first Finkenwalde class in 1937. The manuscript survived his death and was edited and published by his friend Eberhard Bethge in 1953. It is an attempt to interpret theologically what the Bible means when it speaks of " temptation."

In the Lord's Prayer we are taught to pray, " Lead us not into temptation." " Natural man and moral man," says Bonhoeffer, " cannot understand this prayer " (9). Natural man welcomes temptation as an opportunity to pit his strength against the adversary and to win life at the risk of death; moral man calls forth evil in order that he may test the power of good within him. But none of this has anything to do with the temptation of which Christ speaks. When the Bible talks about temptation, it is not at all concerned with the testing of one's strength, but refers to that horrible, immobilizing time when one's strength is turned against him, when all one's powers (yes, even the strength of one's faith!) fall into the hands of the enemy and are now led into the field against him. " This is the decisive fact in the temptation of the Christian, that he is *abandoned,* abandoned by all his powers — indeed, attacked by them — abandoned by all men, abandoned by God himself " (10). Man is alone in temptation and is delivered defenseless into the hands of Satan. The Christian knows that this is a dark hour which can be irrevocable, so he does not seek for his strength to be proved,

---

[32] An English translation of *Versuchung* by Kathleen Downham was published in 1955 by the S.C.M. Press, Ltd., London, and The Macmillan Company. Used by permission of The Macmillan Company.

but prays, "Lead us not into temptation."

Natural man considers all life a struggle and moral man views each hour as a time of temptation, but " the Christian knows hours of temptation, which differ from hours of gracious care and preservation from temptation as the devil is different from God " (11). That is, explains the author, the Christian does not see his life in terms of abstract principles (such as: Every moment of life is a time of decision!), but only in its relation to the living God. He lives from the times of God and not from his own conception of life, and for that reason he knows that temptation is a concrete event that can come upon him suddenly during the course of his life. Therefore, during the time when he is preserved from temptation he prays that God may not let the time of temptation come upon him. But if temptation seems bound to come, should we not rather pray for the strength to overcome temptation? " Such a thought," states Bonhoeffer, " claims to know more about temptation than Christ himself, and wants to be better than he who knew the hardest temptation " (12). *We* do not sit in God's counsel, and if temptation must come, by virtue of some *divine* " must," then we can only hold to Christ's summons to pray against the divine " must " — not to yield in Stoic resignation to temptation, but to flee from that dark " must " in which God lets the devil have his way and to call to that revealed divine freedom in which God tramples the devil underfoot.

Bonhoeffer asserts that, unlike a book of edification, which tells many stories of men's temptations and their overcoming, the Bible tells essentially only *two* temptation stories: the temptation of the first man and the temptation of Christ; that is, the temptation that led to man's fall and the temptation that led to Satan's fall. " All other temptations in human history have to do with these two stories of temptation. Either we are tempted in Adam or we are tempted in Christ. Either the Adam in us is tempted — in which case we fall. Or the Christ in us is tempted — in which case Satan is bound to fall " (14).

From Adam's temptation in Paradise, says Bonhoeffer, we can learn these three things. First, the tempter is to be found only where there is innocence. Second, it is the sudden, unmediated, and inscrutable appearance of the tempter in the voice of the serpent that brings out his character as seducer; that is, the denial of the origin belongs to the essence of the seducer. Third, in order to win access to innocence, the denial of the origin must be maintained to the end. The serpent must introduce himself in the name of God, and place before innocence, which clings unquestioningly to the word of God, the seductive question: " Did God say? " Adam is faced with the dreadful possibility of being robbed of his only strength, the word of God! Here there is no chance for ethical struggle; Adam is delivered up defenseless to the tempter and is left quite alone. Adam sinks into the abyss of the godless question, " Did God say? " and with him the entire human race, for thereafter every man is born with this question of Satan in his heart, a doubting of the word of God. The seduction of Adam brings all flesh to death and condemnation.

Jesus Christ, the Son of God who came upon earth in the likeness of sinful flesh, undergoes an infinitely more difficult temptation than Adam, for whereas Adam carried nothing in himself that could have given the tempter a claim and power over him, Christ bore in himself the whole burden of the cursed and condemned flesh — yet without sin. Jesus takes upon himself the whole temptation experience of the flesh in order to bring salvation to all flesh! He is led by the Spirit into the wilderness, which means he is completely abandoned by God in the face of temptation, and in contrast to the temptation of Adam and all human temptations, the tempter does not make use of creatures, but comes himself to Jesus. Satan tempts Jesus in his flesh (Turn stones into bread!), in his faith (Demand a sign from God!), and in his allegiance to God (Accept the kingdoms of the world and worship me!). And, says Bonhoeffer, all three are the one temptation, namely, to separate Jesus from the word of God.

In his temptation Jesus is no heroic figure struggling against evil powers; rather, he is robbed of all strength and is abandoned by God and man. He has fallen into deepest darkness, and there is nothing left " but the saving, supporting, enduring word of God, which holds him firmly and which fights and conquers for him. The night of the last words of Jesus — ' My God, my God, why hast thou forsaken me? ' — has fallen; it must follow the hour of this temptation as the last fleshly-spiritual, complete temptation of the Savior " (20). Jesus' suffering of abandonment is God's word and judgment for him, and in his defenseless, powerless submission to the power of Satan reconciliation arises. Jesus holds fast to God's word and promise and thereby overcomes temptation. And as in the beginning God had abandoned him, now the tempter abandons him — and angels come and minister to him! " That is the end of the temptation," declares Bonhoeffer, " that he who has entered into all weakness, but who has been upheld by the word, receives from an angel of God refreshment of all his powers of body, soul, and spirit " (21).

Because Christ has overcome temptation and thus brought the temptation of Adam to an end, we can pray: " Lead us not into temptation " and know that it *is* granted in Jesus Christ himself. From now on, insists Bonhoeffer, *we* are not tempted, but *Jesus Christ* is tempted in us. Because of his failure to bring about the fall of the Son of God, Satan now pursues Christ through the members of his body, the church, but by their participation in his suffering of temptation Christians are assured of participation in his victory. The practical task of the Christian, then, is " to understand all the temptations which come upon him as temptations of Jesus Christ in him, and thus he will be aided " (24).

The Bible speaks of three authors of temptation: the devil, the lust of man, God himself. When Scripture calls the devil the author of temptation, it means that temptation is perpetrated by the enemy of God; that in temptation God's enemy shows his power to act contrary to God's will and thus to be stronger than any creature; that temptation is seduction, which means that the devil is a liar who wants to make man believe that he can live without God's word; and that temptation comes from the devil, because here the devil becomes man's accuser, compelling God to judge the sin that has been exposed. That is, " there are two parts to every temptation: man must be alienated from the word of God, and God must be forced to reject man, because the accuser has exposed his sins " (25). Accordingly, Job's is the prototype of all temptations!

Concerning the lust of man as the author of temptation, the Bible (James 1:13 ff.) says these things. First, the source of temptation lies in one's own self, so that each man's fall is inexcusable, and the guilt of temptation cannot be laid at the door of the devil or God or another man. Further, temptation is punishment; it originates in man's own evil desires, which entice him to let go of the word of God. Finally, desire in itself does not make one sinful; man is sinful only when he submits to the temptation of his desire, which means that he himself is the source of sin.

The most difficult question of all concerns what the Bible says about God as the author of temptation. God tempts no one, says James; yet the Bible cites many cases where temptation is looked upon as the judgment of God. For Bonhoeffer this means two things: first, Satan is in God's hands and must — against his will — serve him, i.e., Satan could not tempt man unless God first abandoned him; second, God gives Satan opportunity because of man's sin. Satan must execute the death of the sinner in order that the new man can rise from the dead, and thus he must unwillingly serve God's plan of redemption. In temptation Satan does his work by leading men to the knowledge of their sin, by letting the flesh suffer to such an extent that the sinner is driven into the very hands of God, and by giving death to the sinner and thus making him ready for life. " But how can the Bible say that God tempts man? " asks Bonhoeffer. " It speaks of the wrath of God, of which Satan is the executor. . . . The wrath of God lay upon Jesus Christ from the hour of the temptation. It struck Jesus because of the sin of the flesh which he wore. And because the wrath of God found obedience . . . the wrath was propitiated, the wrath of God had driven Jesus to the gracious God, the grace of God had overcome the wrath of God, the power of Satan was conquered. But where the whole temptation of the flesh, all the wrath of God, is obediently endured in Jesus Christ, there the temptation is conquered in Jesus Christ, there the Christian finds behind the God of wrath who tempts him the God of grace who tempts no one " (30).

The interpreter next considers the concrete temptations of believers as temptations of Christ in his members and thus analogous to the temptation of Christ. The concrete temptations that are analogous to Jesus' first temptation, the temptation of the flesh, are desire and suffering. When desire seizes mastery over the flesh, there is only one stronger reality to set against it: the image and the presence of the Crucified! In times of temptation the Bible teaches us to flee! If we trust in our own strength, we are lost, so we must flee from our lustful desires to our only refuge, to the Crucified. We must patiently endure the humiliation of the temptations of the flesh, seeing in the midst of Satan's deadly work the righteous and merciful punishment of God, and finding refuge in the death and victory of Jesus Christ. From this it is obvious that, for the Christian, temptation by desire always means suffering. "Temptation to desire," explains Bonhoeffer, "always includes the renunciation of desire, that is to say, suffering. Temptation to suffering always includes the longing for freedom from suffering, that is to say, for desire. Thus temptation of the flesh through desire and through suffering is at bottom one and the same " (35).

Bonhoeffer differentiates two kinds of suffering that tempt the Christian: the general suffering of the world, which afflicts all men, and the suffering for the sake of Christ, in which only Christians participate. The Christian can understand the first as a consequence of the fallen and sinful condition of all flesh in which he too shares, and by understanding it as the temptation of Christ within him, it becomes " a protest against the devil, a recognition of his own sin, the righteous judgment of God, the death of his old man, and communion with Jesus Christ " (38). Suffering for Christ's sake, on the other hand, is a much more difficult temptation for the Christian because of its voluntary character. However, the Christian should understand that here he is led into the communion of the sufferings of Christ (I Peter 4:13) and so should recognize in this suffering, " first, the devil, and his temptation to fall from Christ; second, the joy to be allowed to suffer for Christ; third, the judgment of God at the house of God. He knows that he suffers according to the will of God (I Peter 4:19) and, in the fellowship of the cross, he grasps the grace of God " (40).

In the second temptation Satan tempted Jesus to ask for a visible acknowledgement of his divine Sonship, not to let himself be satisfied with God's word and promise, and to want more than faith, but Jesus repelled this temptation with the words, " Thou shalt not tempt the Lord thy God." Temptation that tries to undermine our faith in salvation, declares the author, brings us into the danger of tempting God. Thus the temptations of the spirit which the devil inflicts on Christians have this double aim: " the believer is to fall into the sin of spiritual pride (*securitas*) or perish in the sin of despair (*desperatio*). But in both sins there is the one sin of tempting God " (41). In the sin of spiritual pride the devil tells us that God is a God of grace and tempts us to disregard God's law and wrath; the man who succumbs ends by making the God of grace into an idol that he serves and thus tempts God by testing the seriousness of his wrath and by demanding a sign beyond his word. In the temptation to despair, on the other hand, it is not God's law and wrath, but his grace and promise, that are attacked and put to test. The devil suddenly places our sin and guilt before us and tempts us to rebel against the word of God by demanding an experience, some proof of God's grace; the man who succumbs ends either in the sin of blasphemy or in self-destruction or in the attempt to make himself into a saint by his own strength.

" As to how Satan repeats the third temptation of Jesus on believers," concludes Bonhoeffer, " there is not much to be said " (44). Here Satan appears openly and tempts man to a willful and final defection from God, and the one who succumbs to this temptation commits what the Bible calls " wanton sin," for which there is no forgiveness. " Just as temptations of the spirit are not experienced by all Christians, since they would go beyond their powers," explains the author, " so this last temptation certainly comes only to a very few men. . . . He who has experienced this temptation and has conquered, has indeed won the victory over all temptations " (45).

Bonhoeffer ends this work with a short section on " The Legitimate Struggle," in which he reminds us that the Christian's sole defense against temptation is Jesus Christ, his blood, his example, his prayer. In temptation the believer is led into the deepest solitude, into abandonment by men and by God, but in this solitude he finds Jesus Christ, man and God. " Believers suffer the hour of temptation without defense. Jesus Christ is their shield. And only when it is quite clearly understood that temptation must befall the God-forsaken, then the word can at last be uttered which the Bible speaks about the Christian's struggle. From heaven the Lord gives to the defenseless the heavenly armor before which, though men's eyes do not see it, Satan flees. . . . It is the garment of Christ, the robe of his victory, that he puts upon his struggling community. . . . The Spirit teaches us that the time of temptations is not yet ended, but that the hardest temptation is still to come to his people. . . . So we pray, as Jesus Christ has taught us, to the Father in heaven: 'Lead us not into temptation,' and we know that our prayer is heard, for all temptation is conquered in Jesus Christ for all time, unto the end. . . . The promise of Jesus Christ proclaims: ' Ye are they which have continued with me in my temptations, and I appoint unto you a kingdom ' " (46 f.).

e. "Life Together "[88]

Life Together (*Gemeinsames Leben*) is a small work that Bonhoeffer published in 1939 as the sixty-first contribution to the well-known series of theological monographs, *Theologische Existenz heute*. This book, which grew out of his two-year experience of living communally with his vicar-students in the Brother-house at Finkenwalde, added to Bonhoeffer's growing stature as a significant Christian thinker, and the fact that it has since gone through numerous editions in Germany testifies to its importance and widespread influence. In the foreword the author emphasizes that this work is merely one individual contribution to the comprehensive question of fellowship, which faces the whole Christian church and which demands the mutual assistance of all responsible Christians. He hopes that it will at least help to clarify the whole question and to show how " life together " can be put into practice.

This book, which is simply written, powerfully convincing, and unusually quotable, probably deserves less to be categorized as " theological interpretation of Scripture " than any of Bonhoeffer's writings during this period. Of course, it is interspersed with Biblical passages that illustrate and support the text and it presupposes the author's understanding of the Biblical message, but it is not intended to be exegesis. Rather, it is an attempt to give practical guidance to those who want to take their lives as Christians seriously, and it is based for the most part on concrete practical experience. The work

---

[88] English translation of *Gemeinsames Leben* by John W. Doberstein (Harper & Brothers, 1954; S.C.M. Press, Ltd., London, 1955. Quotations are used by permission of Harper & Brothers.

is divided into these five chapters: "Community"; "The Day with Others"; "The Day Alone"; "Ministry"; "Confession and Communion."

Life in visible community with Christian brethren, begins Bonhoeffer, is not something that can be taken for granted. Like Jesus, who lived in the midst of enemies, Christians live in the midst of the world, dispersed among unbelievers and united only in Christ. When they are permitted to live in visible fellowship with other Christians and to gather visibly to share God's word and sacrament, it must be recognized as the pure grace of God, who allows them the extraordinary, the "rose and lilies" of the Christian life.

"Christianity," states Bonhoeffer, "means community through Jesus Christ and in Jesus Christ" (21). This means three things. First, a Christian needs others because of Jesus Christ; that is, the Christian is wholly dependent for his salvation upon the truth of God's word in Jesus Christ which is spoken to him through the mouth of a brother. Second, a Christian comes to others only through Jesus Christ; that is, Jesus Christ is the Mediator who has opened up egocentric man's only way to God and to his brother. Third, in Jesus Christ we have been chosen from eternity, accepted in time, and united for eternity. According to the eternal counsel of the triune God, the Son of God out of pure grace bodily took on human nature, and as a result of this being chosen and accepted with the whole church in Jesus Christ, we are now in him and belong to him in eternity *with* one another. That the fellowship between Christian brothers means fellowship through and in Jesus Christ is the presupposition for all the Biblical directions and precepts for the communal life of Christians. Christian brotherhood is not an ideal, but a divine reality! It has nothing to do with man's visionary dreaming of what a fellowship *should* be, but is concerned with the reality that God has bound us together in one body in Jesus Christ for eternity, and we can only be thankful recipients of this divine gift.

Likewise, because Christian brotherhood is founded solely on Jesus Christ, it is a spiritual (pneumatic) and not a psychic (human) reality. That is, it is created solely by the Holy Spirit, who brings Jesus Christ into our hearts as Lord and Savior, and it does not derive from the natural urges, powers, and capacities of the human spirit.

It is not a fellowship of devout and pious souls, but a fellowship of those who are *called* by Christ. Its basis is truth, not desire; its essence is light, not darkness. It is ruled by the word of God, not by the word of man. Its love is *agapē*, not *erōs*. " Human love," says Bonhoeffer, " makes itself an end in itself. It creates of itself an end, an idol which it worships, to which it must subject everything. It nurses and cultivates an ideal; it loves itself and nothing else in the world. Spiritual love, however, comes from Jesus Christ; it serves him alone; it knows that it has no immediate access to other persons " (35). " Human love lives by uncontrolled and uncontrollable dark *desires;* spiritual love lives in the clear light of service ordered by the *truth*. Human love produces human subjection, dependence, constraint; spiritual love creates *freedom* of the brethren under the word. Human love breeds hothouse flowers; spiritual love creates the *fruits* that grow healthily in accord with God's good will in the rain and storm and sunshine of God's outdoors. The existence of any Christian life together depends on whether it succeeds at the right time in bringing out the ability to distinguish between a human ideal and God's reality, between spiritual and human community " (37). It is faith in this reality that binds us together, not the experience of Christian brotherhood per se.

Bonhoeffer now takes the reader through an entire day of activities in a Christian community. " Common life under the word begins with common worship at the beginning of the day " (42), and this should include the reading of Scripture, singing, and praying. He recommends the use of the psalms as a beginning prayer, and if one feels that he cannot repeat some of the psalms as his own prayer, states Bonhoeffer, then he has not yet learned the secret of the Psalter. This secret is that it is not merely we, but the *Man* Jesus Christ, who prays here. That is, the Psalter is God's word and at the same time prayer to God, for Jesus Christ prays through the Psalter in his congregation. The psalms are Christ's vicarious prayers for his church and thus belong in a peculiar way to the whole Christian church. The Psalter teaches us what prayer means, what we should pray, and to pray as a fellowship.

The praying of a psalm should be followed by a hymn of praise and then the Scriptural reading. Instead of reading a few brief, selected verses to form the guiding thought of the day, Bonhoeffer recommends that the family hear a chapter of the Old Testament and at least half a chapter of the New Testament each morning and evening. " Holy Scripture," he explains, " does not consist of individual passages; it is a unit and is intended to be used as such " (50 f.). Because the Bible as a whole is the word of God, it should be read consecutively so that we are torn out of our own existence and set down in the midst of the holy history of God on earth, the history of the Christ. " And only in so far as we are *there* is God with us today also " (54)! We must learn to know the Scriptures again for the sake of our own salvation, in order to attain certainty and confidence that our personal and church activity rests on a firm Biblical foundation, and so that we can help a Christian brother who is in difficulty and doubt by speaking to him God's own word.

After the reading of Scripture the fellowship should sing another hymn, and Bonhoeffer emphasizes that in doing so they join the whole church in singing together the word of God. What is important about a hymn is the *word,* and because the music is merely the servant of the word, Bonhoeffer believes that unison singing is most desirable. The devotion period should end with prayer, and the author recommends that one person take the responsibility of praying in his own words for the entire fellowship over an extended period of time.

Now that the fellowship has been nourished and strengthened by the bread of eternal life, it gathers to receive from God the earthly bread for this temporal life. " Giving thanks and asking God's blessing, the Christian family receives its daily bread from the hand of the Lord " (66). Jesus blesses the table fellowship with his presence; to know him in the presence of the gift of earthly bread is to know him as the Giver of all gifts and to believe that Christ wills to be present when his congregation prays for his presence. Christian table fellowship should be a *festive* occasion that constantly reminds us in the midst of our everyday work of God's resting after his work. Further, it should remind us of our obligation to share our bread with one another.

" After the first morning hour," continues Bonhoeffer, " the Christian's day until evening belongs to work " (69). Here the Christian

THEOLOGICAL APPLICATION

moves from the world of personal encounter into that of impersonal things, i.e., into an " it-world " that God has designed to liberate man from himself. There is a definite distinction between work and prayer, and yet "to find, back of the 'it' of the day's work, the 'Thou,' which is God, is what Paul calls 'praying without ceasing ' (I Thess. 5:17). Thus the prayer of the Christian reaches beyond its set time and extends into the heart of his work . . . promotes it, affirms it, and lends it meaning and joy " (70 f.).

" The noonday hour, where it is possible, becomes for the Christian family fellowship a brief rest from the day's march. . . . The fellowship thanks God and prays for protection until the eventide " (72). When the work of the day is finished, the group is again united at the evening table and the last devotion, in which the psalm-prayer, a hymn, the reading of Scripture, and common prayer close the day. This is the appropriate place for common intercessions, the petition of forgiveness for every wrong done to God and to our brothers, and the prayer for preservation during the night from the devil, from terror, and from an evil, sudden death.

Now that Bonhoeffer has spoken of the "day with others," he turns to its counterpart: " the day alone." He begins by issuing this warning: " Let him who cannot be alone beware of community. Let him who is not in community beware of being alone " (78). For the Christian there should be a time of fellowship and a time of solitude, and both of these begin with the call of Jesus. The mark of the former is speech (not idle chatter!), whereas the latter is marked by silence (not dumbness!). To misinterpret silence as a ceremonial gesture or a mystical desire to get beyond God's word is to miss the essential relationship of silence to the word. " Silence is the simple stillness of the individual under the word of God . . . waiting for God's word and coming from God's word with a blessing " (79). This sort of silence will exert an influence upon the entire day and will not only lead to the right hearing, but also to the right speaking of the word of God at the right time.

The Christian needs to be alone during a definite period of each day for meditation on Scripture, for prayer, and for intercession. " In our meditation," says Bonhoeffer, " we ponder the chosen text on the strength of the promise that it has something utterly personal to say to us for this day and for our Christian life, that it is not only God's word for the church, but also God's word for us individually " (82). It is not necessary that we finish any given passage, for often one verse or even one word engrosses our whole attention. Furthermore, it is not necessary that we express our thoughts and prayers in words, discover new ideas, or have any extraordinary " experiences " during our meditation. The main thing is that we faithfully and patiently adhere to our daily meditation period, even during times of spiritual drought and apathy, and humbly center all our attention on the word of God, trusting that God will hold to his promise.

Meditation on Scripture leads quite naturally to prayer, which means " nothing else but the readiness and willingness to receive and appropriate the word, and, what is more, to accept it in one's personal situation, particular tasks, decisions, sins, and temptations. What can never enter the corporate prayer of the fellowship may here be silently made known to God " (84 f.). All our prayers that conform to the word are heard and answered in Jesus Christ, for God's word has found its fulfillment in him. In our prayer, stresses Bonhoeffer, we should include our intercessions, because a Christian fellowship lives or falls by the intercession of its members for one another. " Intercession means no more than to bring our brother into the presence of God, to see him under the cross of Jesus as a poor human being and sinner in need of grace . . . to grant our brother the same right that we have received, namely, to stand before Christ and share in his mercy " (86).

The test of true meditation and true Christian fellowship comes during the many hours of the day when the Christian is alone in an unchristian environment. At this time it is determined whether the fellowship has made him strong and mature or weak and dependent, whether his meditation has afforded only a momentary spiritual ecstasy or has lodged the word of God so securely in his heart that it holds and fortifies him and impels him to active love, obedience, and good works. " Only the day can decide," concludes Bonhoeffer. " Blessed is he who is alone in the strength of the fellowship and blessed is he who keeps the fellowship in the strength of aloneness. But the strength of aloneness and the strength of the fellowship is solely the strength of the word of God, which is addressed to the individual in the fellowship " (89).

The main thesis of Bonhoeffer's chapter on the ministry is brought forth in these two statements: " Self-justification and judging others go together, as justification by grace and serving others go together " (91); " Not self-justification, which means the use of domination and force, but justification by grace, and therefore service, should govern the Christian community " (94). In order that service should govern, the members should learn to hold their tongues and to be meek. " It must be the decisive rule of every Christian fellowship," asserts the author, " that each individual is prohibited from saying much that occurs to him " (92). This, of course, does not concern the giving of friendly advice and guidance, but the sort of talking and judging and condemning that is a covert excuse for self-justification. Where a discipline for the tongue is practiced, each individual will discover that he can refrain from constantly scrutinizing and judging others and can allow them to exist as the completely free persons that God made them to be! By the practice of meekness Bonhoeffer means to consider the neighbor's will and honor more important than one's own and, in the final anaylsis, to consider oneself as the greatest of sinners. " Only he who lives by the forgiveness of his sin in Jesus Christ will rightly think little of himself " (95).

True brotherly service within the Christian community does not exist exclusively in ministering to one another the word of God, although this is certainly the greatest service and the service for which all the others are performed. Besides it there is a *ministry of listening*, which can often be a greater service than speaking. In fact, " brotherly pastoral care is essentially distinguished from preaching by the fact that, added to the task of speaking the word, there is the obligation of listening " (98). A second service is that of *active helpfulness*, which means to give simple assistance in trifling, external matters. Bonhoeffer reminds us that " only where hands are not too good for deeds of love and mercy in everyday helpfulness can the mouth joyfully and convincingly proclaim the message of God's love and mercy " (100).

A third ministry consists in *bearing others*. Here the author quotes as his basic authority the words of Paul: " Bear one another's burdens, and so fulfil the law of Christ " (Gal. 6:2). The law of Christ, which was fulfilled in the cross, is a law of bearing, and Christians must share in this law by suffering and enduring the burden of the brother. This burden involves the *freedom* of the other person, which includes all that we mean by a person's nature, individuality, endowment, weaknesses, and oddities, and also the *abuse of that freedom,* namely, the sin of the other person. This latter, says Bonhoeffer, is the more difficult to bear, because in sin, fellowship with God and man is broken, yet " as Christ bore and received us as sinners, so we in his fellowship may bear and receive sinners into the fellowship of Jesus Christ through the forgiving of sins " (102). Forgiveness is a daily service that occurs, without words, in the intercessions for one another.

The author now discusses the ultimate and highest Christian service: the *ministry of the word*. Here he is not concerned with the ordained ministry, which is bound to a particular office, time, and place, but with the free communication of the word from one person to another. " We are thinking," asserts Bonhoeffer, " of that unique situation in which one person bears witness in human words to another person, bespeaking the whole consolation of God, the admonition, the kindness, and the severity of God " (103 f.). This is a dangerous undertaking, for only the person who has really listened and served and borne with others can say the right, convincing, and liberating word, and yet this is the very person who is apt to say nothing because of a profound distrust of everything that is merely verbal or because of a fear of forcing himself upon his brother! Nevertheless, it is inevitable that a time of crisis will arise when one person should and must declare God's word and will to another, and the only basis on which this can be done is that " each knows the other as a sinner, who, with all his human dignity, is lonely and lost if he is not given help. This is not to make him contemptible nor to disparage him in any way. On the contrary, it is to accord him the one real dignity that man has, namely, that, though he is a sinner, he can share in God's grace and glory and be God's child " (106). God's word demands reproof of a brother who falls into open sin, but this is a ministry of mercy that brings the healing judgment of God himself.

Finally, there is a *ministry of authority* within the Christian community, but this authority in no way depends upon the personality or admirable qualities of a man himself, but lies solely in the exercise of his ministry of hearing, helping, bearing, and proclaiming. That authority is dependent upon brotherly service is clear not only from the word of Jesus, " Whoever would be great among you must be your servant " (Mark 10:43), but also from the New Testament description of a bishop (I Tim. 3:1 ff.). " The church will place its confidence only in the simple servant of the word of Jesus Christ because it knows that then it will be guided, not according to human wisdom and human conceit, but by the word of the Good Shepherd " (109).

In his final chapter Bonhoeffer speaks of confession and communion. Taking the words of James: " Confess your faults one to another " (James 5:16) as his point of departure, he maintains that many Christians participate in the worship and prayer and service of the community without ever breaking through to fellowship, and the reason for their loneliness is that they have fellowship with others as believers and as devout people, but not as the undevout, as sinners! The pious fellowship permits no one to be a sinner and is horrified when a real sinner is suddenly discovered in its midst, so everyone remains alone with their sin, living in lies and hypocrisy, when in fact they *are* sinners. " It is the grace of the gospel, which is so hard for the pious to understand, that it confronts us with the truth and says: You are a sinner, a great, desperate sinner; now come, as the sinner that you are, to God who loves you. He wants you as you are. . . . He wants to be gracious to you. You do not have to go on lying to yourself and your brothers, as if you were without sin; you can dare to be a sinner. Thank God for that; he loves the sinner but he hates sin. . . . The misery of the sinner and the mercy of God — that was the truth of the gospel in Jesus Christ. It was in this truth that his church was to live. Therefore, he gave his followers the authority to hear the confession of sin and to forgive sin in his name " (110 f.).

Jesus Christ, who became our Brother in order to help us, has made the church a blessing to us by commissioning our Christian brother to stand in his stead, to become a Christ for us. " Our brother," asserts Bonhoeffer, " stands before us as the sign of the truth and the grace of God. He has been given to us to help us. He hears the confession of our sins in Christ's stead and he forgives our sins in Christ's name. He keeps the secret of our confession as God keeps it. When I go to my brother to confess, I am going to God " (111 f.).

In confession, continues Bonhoeffer, there is a break-through to community, to the cross, to new life, and to certainty. Isolating sin is brought to light and fellowship established; the sin of pride is destroyed by the public dying of the old man and the sharing in the humiliation of Christ's cross. The break with the past leads to conversion and discipleship, the delusion of self-forgiveness is overcome by the concrete assurance of forgiveness spoken by a brother in the name of God. But is confession a divine law? No, says Bonhoeffer, it is rather an offer of divine help for the sinner. Some may find the joy of fellowship, the cross, the new life, and certainty in confession to God alone, but for those who do not, God offers the blessing of mutual confession. And to whom shall we make confession? To any Christian brother but more specifically, to the Christian brother *who lives beneath the cross,* for he alone understands the wickedness of the human heart and the mercy of God's forgiveness. There is no need of confession to the whole community; confession to one other Christian is quite sufficient, because where there is one member of the church, there is the whole church.

Bonhoeffer cites two dangers that must be avoided in the practice of confession in the Christian community. First, it is not a good thing for one person to be confessor for all the others; furthermore, only he who practices confession should listen to the confession of others. Second, for the salvation of his soul the confessant must guard against making a pious work of his confession, because the only basis for confession is the promise of absolution. " Confession as a routine duty is spiritual death; confession in reliance upon the promise is life. The forgiveness of sins is the sole ground and goal of confession " (120).

Although confession is an act complete in itself that should be practiced as often as needed, Bonhoeffer believes it is especially significant for the Christian community as a preparation for the common reception of the Lord's Supper. No one should go to the altar with a heart unreconciled to his brother or with anxiety about particular sins that are known only to God. Confession brings the reconciliation with God and the brethren and the assurance of forgiveness that makes the day of the Lord's Supper a joyful occasion that brings the ultimate fulfillment of Christian fellowship. Concludes Bonhoeffer: " The life of Christians together under the word has reached its perfection in the sacrament " (122).

f. " The Prayer Book of the Bible "

Except for some contributions to books of sermons, *The Prayer Book of the Bible: An Introduction to the Psalms* (*Das Gebetbuch der Bibel: Eine Einführung in die Psalmen*) was Bonhoeffer's last publication during his lifetime. In this small pamphlet which appeared in 1940 he attempts to make clear the role of the psalms within the prayer life of the church, and from it one begins to understand why the Psalter was his favorite book of the Bible.

The author begins by saying that the words of the disciples to Jesus: " Lord, teach us to pray," mean that man cannot pray naturally, but must be taught how to pray. We so often confuse our wishing, hoping, sighing, complaining, and rejoicing with praying and thereby confuse earth and heaven, man and God! Prayer, declares Bonhoeffer, does not mean simply to pour out one's heart, but, with filled or even empty hearts, to find the way to God and to speak with him. No man can do this alone. In order to pray we need Jesus Christ, and only when we enter into his prayer with our whole hearts can we pray rightly and have the happy assurance that God will hear us.

A child learns to speak, says Bonhoeffer, because his father speaks to him; he learns the speech of the father. In like manner we learn to speak to God because God has spoken and speaks to us. We begin to pray to God by repeating his own words, the speech that he has spoken to us in Jesus Christ, and we find this in Holy Scripture. Therefore, if we want to pray with certainty and joy, then the word of Scripture must be the firm ground of our prayer. Now within Scripture there is one book that is differentiated from all others by the fact that it contains nothing but prayers, and this is the book of The Psalms. Since the Bible is the word of God and prayers are the words of men, it is really quite surprising that it contains a book of prayers. This seeming incongruity can be understood only when we remember that we can learn to pray properly from Jesus Christ alone and that in the psalms it is the incarnate Son of God, who lives with us men, praying to God the Father, who lives in eternity. In the mouth of Jesus Christ the word of man becomes the word of God, and when we pray his prayer with him, the word of God becomes the word of man!

When we read and pray the psalms, therefore, we must not ask first of all what they have to do with us, but rather what they have to do with Jesus Christ. Our use of the psalms should not depend on whether they express the present feeling of our heart, but on what God wants us to pray. That the Bible contains a prayer book teaches us that the word of God contains not only the word that God speaks to us, but also the word that he wants to hear from us. This is God's grace, which we can receive by praying in the name of his Son. The psalms are given to us in order that we may learn to pray in the name of Jesus Christ!

In response to his disciples' request Jesus gave them the Lord's Prayer, in which he summarizes all the prayers of Holy Scripture, but he does not thereby make the other prayers superfluous. Rather, they represent the inexhaustible richness of the Lord's Prayer, just as the Lord's Prayer is their crown and unity. It is quite sensible, then, that the Psalter should be bound together with the New Testament, for it is the prayer of the church of Jesus Christ and belongs to the Lord's Prayer.

The Psalter, continues Bonhoeffer, is connected in a special way with the name of David. Of the 150 psalms, seventy-three are attributed to King David, and many others to his choirmaster and to his son Solomon. According to Scripture, David, as the anointed king of the elect people of God, is a prototype (*Vorbild*) of Jesus Christ, so that whatever befalls him happens for the sake of Jesus Christ, who is in him and shall go forth out of him. Not only is David a witness of Christ in his office, his life, and his words, but the New Testament audaciously asserts that in the psalms of David the promised Christ already speaks (Heb. 2:12; 10:5), or, as it can also be interpreted, the Holy Spirit (ch. 3:7). In the words of David the future Messiah spoke, so that when David prays, Christ prays with him, or better: Christ himself prayed the prayers in David! Thus the New Testament refers the psalms to Christ. Of course, all the psalms are not from David, and the New Testament never puts the whole Psalter in the mouth of Christ. Nevertheless, the fact that the psalms are so decisively connected with the name of David, and the further fact that Christ himself says that the psalms proclaim his death and resurrection and the preaching of the gospel, permits the reference of the whole Psalter to Christ.

But how is it possible that a man and Jesus Christ pray the psalms at the same time? For no other reason, asserts Bonhoeffer, than that it is the incarnate Son of God, who has borne all human weakness in his own flesh, who here pours out the heart of all humanity before God, who stands in our place and prays for us. He has known agony and pain, guilt and death, more deeply than we, so that the prayer that here comes before God is that of the human nature that was assumed by him. It is really our prayer, but because he knows us better than we know ourselves, because he was a truer man than we, it is also really his prayer and can only become our prayer because it was his.

Who, then, prays the psalms? David (Solomon, Asaph, etc.) prays, Christ prays, we pray. We — that means the whole church, in which alone the entire richness of the psalms can be prayed, but it also means each individual, in so far as he has a share in Christ and his congregation and prays their prayer. David, Christ, the church, I myself: whenever we reflect on this, says the author, we perceive the wondrous way that God takes in order to teach us to pray.

After explaining some of the background of the psalms, e.g., that they are both hymns and prayers, that they were originally used in worship services and were set to music, and that their structure is such that they can be sung antiphonally, Bonhoeffer urges that we use the psalms daily. If this is no longer the custom in our churches, then we must make them a part of our morning and evening devotions, reading and praying them together. Only through this daily regularity can one grow to the point where this divine prayer book becomes his own. Furthermore, we should not pick and choose, but should pray *all* the psalms. Otherwise, we dishonor God by presuming to know better than he what we should pray.

Finally, Bonhoeffer classifies the psalms according to their subject matter and finds that the following themes are represented: creation, law, history of salvation, Messiah, church, life, suffering, guilt, the adversaries, the end-time. It would not be difficult, he asserts, to arrange all of these as parts of the Lord's Prayer and to show how the Psalter can be taken up completely into the prayer of Jesus. However, he chooses to follow The Psalms' own division and proceeds to select certain exemplary psalms from each category and to indicate in a few words how they interpret their subjects and how they are fully understood only in connection with Jesus Christ. No complete report can be given here, but in what follows a few of Bonhoeffer's theologically significant observations will be noted.

Creation: God is known as the Creator only because he has already revealed himself to his people in his redeeming word. The creation with all of its gifts exists on behalf of Jesus Christ. *Law:* Under " law " is to be understood God's entire act of redemption and the instructions for a new life of obedience. That God can hide his commandment from us is the deepest anxiety of the new life. It is pure grace to know God's commandments; they are given to be fulfilled, and for those who have found salvation in Jesus Christ they are not burdensome. *Sacred history:* All of God's action with his people in the history of Israel should be looked upon as action done for us. The whole history of God with his congregation is fulfilled in Jesus Christ. *Messiah:* God's history of salvation comes to its completion in the sending of the Messiah. Jesus fulfills the prophecies of the psalms and so makes them his own.

Church: What Mount Zion and the Temple are for the Israelites is for us the world-wide church of God, where God constantly dwells with his congregation in his word and sacrament. The gracious God who in Christ is present to his congregation is the fulfillment of all the thanksgiving, joy, and yearning of the psalms. Because God has promised to be present in his congregation's service of worship, the church gathers together for worship. But because Jesus Christ has offered the perfect service of worship by bringing all previously ordered sacrifice to completion in his voluntary, sinless sacrifice, there remains for us only the offering of praise and thanksgiving in prayer, song, and a life lived according to God's commandments.

Life: Just as Jesus taught us to pray for our daily bread, it is proper that we pray in the psalms for life, health, and visible evidences of the friendliness of God, so long as we recognize these as proofs of God's gracious fellowship and know that God's goodness is better than life. Life is given and preserved by the Creator solely for the sake of Jesus Christ, and so he wants us to be prepared at any time to forfeit all of life's possessions in death in order to win eternal life with Christ.

Suffering: The psalms squarely recognize the dreadful and manifold sufferings of man on earth. No one can pray the psalms of lamentation and complaint from his own experience alone, for this is the distress of the entire church of all times, which has been experienced completely only by Jesus Christ. The complaints are rightly directed against God, for nothing happens without his knowledge and will, but the only answer to the "why?" of suffering is — Jesus Christ! He has borne all of man's suffering, and from now on there is no more suffering in which Christ is not with us, suffering with us, praying with us, helping us. *Guilt:* The Christian experiences no difficulty in praying for forgiveness, but why should Christ, who is sinless, pray for the forgiveness of sins? For the sole reason that he bore the sins of the whole world and was made sin for us! But how is the Christian to understand all the psalms in which the devout protest their innocence? This can be true from two points of view: first, through God's grace and the merit of Jesus Christ, the Christian has become completely righteous and innocent in the eyes of God; second, when one suffers at the hands of God's adversaries for the sake of God's own affair, he can rightly claim his innocence. The notion that we can never suffer innocently so long as within us there still hides some kind of defect is a thoroughly unbiblical and demoralizing thought. In identifying ourselves with the cause of God and suffering with him, God forgives our sins and looks upon us as innocent.

The adversaries: Can we understand the imprecatory psalms as God's word for us and as a prayer of Jesus Christ? Can we as Christians pray these psalms of vengeance? Here several things are to be noted. The adversaries in question are the enemies of the affairs of God; these psalms are not concerned with any personal fight. Prayer concerning the vengeance of God has to do with the execution of his righteousness in judgment over sin, and this judgment must come to pass if God remains true to his word. It is a judgment under which we all stand and which we should not want to hinder. It must be fulfilled and, indeed, has been fufilled in a miraculous way. The vengeance of God did not strike sinners, but the one who alone is sinless, who has stepped into the sinner's place, the Son of God. Jesus Christ bore God's vengeance, stilled God's wrath against sin, and prayed in the hour of the execution of God's judgment: " Father, forgive them; for they know not what they do." This was the end of all those false ideas about the love of God which do not take sin seriously. God hates and judges his enemies in the one who is alone righteous, and this one prays for the forgiveness of the enemies of God! The love of God is to be found only in the cross of Jesus Christ! Thus the imprecatory psalms lead to the cross of Jesus and to the enemy-forgiving love of God. Of course, in praying these psalms it makes a decisive difference whether we stand in the time of promise or in the time of fulfillment; we Christians can pray a psalm of vengeance with the certainty of its wonderful and gracious fulfillment. It is Christ's cross that makes the difference, and only through it can we today believe in God's love and forgive enemies.

The end-time: The hope of Christians is directed toward the Second Coming of Jesus and the resurrection of the dead. In the Psalter this hope is not expressed in these words, and yet there is prayer for life in fellowship with the God of revelation, the ultimate victory of God in the world and the setting up of the Messianic Kingdom. In essence this is not different from the New Testament, except that the Christian finds the yearned-for life in the resurrection of Jesus Christ.

At the end of this short introduction into the *Prayer Book of the Bible,* Bonhoeffer expresses the hope that with fidelity and love we will begin anew to pray the psalms in the name of our Lord Jesus Christ and reminds us that in order to pray aright we must ask God to bestow upon us the Spirit of prayer.

Chapter III

Theological Fragmentation

Bonhoeffer said to the world: Your theme, forsakenness, is God's own theme! (Eberhard Bethge.)

A. BIOGRAPHICAL INTRODUCTION (1940–1945)

On his return from the United States to Germany in 1939, Dietrich Bonhoeffer stopped off for a short visit in England, arriving in London about the middle of July. By the end of the month he was back in Germany, where he resumed his work as leader of the makeshift *Sammelvikariat* at the Pomeranian village of Köslin, and in August he penned his unusally perceptive impressions of American Christtendom in an essay with the suggestive title " Protestantism Without Reformation " (" Protestantismus ohne Reformation ").[1]

On September 1, 1939, Hitler's armies invaded Poland, and this infamous attack brought forth an Anglo-French declaration of war two days later. In the face of such tumultuous events the German Church Struggle faded into the background. Bonhoeffer began his lecturing for the winter semester, wrote a meditation on " The Mystery of the Incarnation " (" Das Geheimnis der Menschwerdung Gottes ") just before Christmas, and finally had to disband the pseudo seminary in March, 1940. By this time most of the ministerial candidates had been drafted into military service anyhow, but the decisive reason for discontinuance was an order from the Gestapo forbidding even this sort of ecclesiastical activity.

Ever since 1938, Bonhoeffer had been forbidden to reside in Berlin, although his father had been able to secure permission for him to

[1] GS I, pp. 323–354.

visit from time to time. Now he was compelled to give up his teaching, and soon he was also forbidden to speak in public anywhere in the Reich. Furthermore, " he was also forbidden by the Reich Chamber of Literature to publish any kind of written work because, it was said, he had neither ' signed on ' nor asked exemption from ' signing on ' as a Nazi propagandist." [2] Fortunately, prior to this prohibition Bonhoeffer's introduction to the psalms, *The Prayer Book of the Bible* (*Das Gebetbuch der Bibel*), had already been published; but other writings from 1940, such as " Concerning Thankfulness " ("Von der Dankbarkeit") and " The Exaltation of Jesus Christ " ("Die Erhoehung Jesu Christi"), were destined to be printed only after his death.

Faced with so many prohibitions, one would surmise that Bonhoeffer's further usefulness would be at an end, but in reality this marked the beginning of a three-year period of fruitful activity, during which he undertook various tasks on behalf of the Brethren Council (*Brüderrat*) of the Confessing Church, entered into active participation in the underground resistance movement against Hitler, and wrote as much as possible on his *Ethics*.

Eberhard Bethge reports that already in 1937, upon completion of *The Cost of Discipleship*, " Bonhoeffer was planning a new approach to the problems of Christian ethics," which he considered to be " the beginning of his actual lifework. In June, 1939, he was invited by Professor John Baillie, on behalf of the Croall Lectureship Trust, to lecture in Edinburgh, and he hoped to make his lectures the basis for his book. The war put an end to his preparations, and he did not take up this work again until 1940." [3] The brilliant but unfinished work which was posthumously edited by Bethge as Bonhoeffer's *Ethics* is a compilation of manuscripts that were written and hidden between 1940 and 1943 in such varied places as Berlin, the Benedictine Abbey of Ettal in Upper Bavaria, the summer estate of Frau von Kleist in Klein-Krössin in Pomerania, and Kieckow.[4]

The nature and extent of Bonhoeffer's ecclesio-political activities during the period 1940–1943 are still largely shrouded in mystery, al-

---

[2] Editor's Preface to Bonhoeffer's *Ethics*, p. xi.
[3] E, p. xi.
[4] *Idem.* See also *Gebetbuch*, p. 23.

though the details of two of his spectacular journeys outside Germany (Switzerland in 1941, Sweden in 1942) are now known.[5] One can only be amazed by the paradoxical fact that on the one hand Bonhoeffer's life was hedged about by prohibitions from the Gestapo, while on the other hand he was at the same time able to obtain passports and courier identification papers that were ordinarily accessible only to those privileged Germans who were trusted by the Nazi regime. To understand how this was possible one must be aware of Bonhoeffer's connections with the men in high positions who plotted to wrest control of the government from Adolf Hitler. His brother-in-law was Hans von Dohnanyi, a former high official of the German Supreme Court, who was one of the closest confidants of Colonel (later Major General) Hans Oster, the co-ordinator of the resistance movement during the early years. Oster was a high-ranking officer in the German Military Intelligence Service, headed by Admiral Wilhelm Canaris, a confirmed opponent of Hitler and National Socialism who encouraged Oster to use the facilities of the Intelligence organization to further the cause of the movement. It was through Dohnanyi that Dietrich and his brother Klaus and another brother-in-law, Rüdiger Schleicher, became involved in the plans to overthrow the Nazi dictatorship.

As early as 1938, Bonhoeffer became aware of the resistance to Hitler that was instigated by two important figures: Colonel General Werner von Fritsch, Army Commander in Chief, who was forced to resign his position because of a fabricated immorality charge diabolically conceived by Gestapo Chief Heinrich Himmler; and Colonel General Ludwig Beck, Chief of the General Staff, who resigned as a protest to Hitler's policy of conquest after the "annexation" of Austria. Although he had long advocated a near-pacifist position — what has been called "an unheard-of position in the Germany of that time" — Bonhoeffer gradually came "to see pacifism as an illegitimate escape, especially if he was tempted to withdraw from his

[5] The historical research is continuing. See Jørgen Glenthøj's "Bonhoeffer und die Oekumene" in MW II; also Bishop George Bell's address on "The Church and the Resistance Movement" in GS I, pp. 399–413, and his chapter on "The Background of the Hitler Plot" in *The Church and Humanity (1939–1946)*; W. A. Visser 't Hooft's "Begegnung mit Dietrich Bonhoeffer" in *Das Zeugnis eines Boten,* and the various articles by E. Bethge.

increasing contacts with the responsible political and military leaders of the resistance. He no longer saw any way of escape into some region of piety." [6] Bonhoeffer became convinced that he, acting as an individual under the compulsion of Christ, must oppose Hitler and his diabolical regime with direct political action. He explained his decision in this way: " It is not only my task to look after the victims of madmen who drive a motorcar in a crowded street, but to do all in my power to stop their driving at all." [7]

After the outbreak of war Bonhoeffer's participation in the resistance became resolute. In July and August, 1940, when despair had seized all those engaged in subversive activities, a meeting was held at which " it was proposed that further action should be postponed, so as to avoid giving Hitler the character of a martyr if he should be killed. Bonhoeffer's rejoinder was decisive: ' If we claim to be Christians, there is no room for expediency. Hitler is the Antichrist. Therefore we must go on with our work and eliminate him whether he be successful or not.' " [8]

Some of Bonhoeffer's most significant journeys on behalf of ecclesiopolitical interests were his visits to Switzerland in 1941 and his flight to Sweden in 1942. In September, 1941, Bonhoeffer traveled to Geneva to confer with Visser 't Hooft, General Secretary of the World Council of Churches, in an attempt to enter into conversation with British church leaders concerning Allied peace aims and the church's responsibility for future international order. Together they wrote and forwarded to friends in England a document concerning " The Church and the New Order in Europe," [9] which presented a Continental reaction to William Paton's then-new book, *The Church and the New Order*. Bonhoeffer's main objective was to encourage the Allies to offer the kind of realistic peace terms that would strengthen the resistance movement in Germany.[10]

An interesting episode connected with an earlier journey took

[6] PFG, p. 8.
[7] CD, pp. 22 f.
[8] G. K. A. Bell, *The Church and Humanity 1939–1946*, p. 175.
[9] GS I, pp. 362–371.
[10] The Allies' subsequent demand for "unconditional surrender" was a bitter blow to resisting forces within Germany and is considered by many to have been a tragic blunder second only to the dropping of the atomic bomb on Hiroshima.

place as Bonhoeffer tried to cross the German-Swiss border at Basel. Confronted by Swiss border guards, suspicious of anyone bearing a pass issued by Nazi officialdom, Bonhoeffer telephoned Karl Barth and asked that he vouch for him. With some uneasiness Barth, who had not seen or heard from the young theologian in several years, provided the needed assurances. Bonhoeffer then proceeded at once to Geneva, but promised Barth that he would stop for a proper visit on his way back to Germany. While he was gone, however, Barth was questioned by Swiss friends about the wisdom of vouchsafing such a suspicious character, and he resolved to ask Bonhoeffer point-blank about the nature of his visit upon his return. This he did, and Bonhoeffer told him quite openly of his participation in the resistance movement.

On May 31, 1942, Bonhoeffer, at great personal risk, flew to Sweden to confer with the Bishop of Chichester, who was visiting Sweden at the request of the British Ministry of Information. The two friends, long associated in the ecumenical movement, met in the little town of Sigtuna near Stockholm, and Bonhoeffer forthrightly revealed the extensive plans for overthrowing Hitler and the Nazi regime, named the chief conspirators, and asked that this information be relayed to the proper authorities in the British Government, requesting a prompt reply as to whether the Allied governments would negotiate a reasonable peace settlement if the revolution were successful. The Bishop of Chichester relates these reactions of Bonhoeffer to the whole affair:

> I could see that as he told me these facts he was full of sorrow that things had come to such a pass in Germany, and that action like this was necessary.... He was obviously distressed in his mind as to the lengths to which he had been driven by force of circumstances in the plot for the elimination of Hitler.... "There must be punishment by God. We should not be worthy of such a solution. We do not want to escape repentance. Our action must be understood as an act of repentance."[11]

The Gestapo arrested Bonhoeffer at the home of his parents in Berlin on April 5, 1943, a few hours after the arrest of Hans von

---

[11] Bell, *op. cit.*, pp. 171 f.

Dohnanyi. During the following eighteen months he was confined in the military section of Tegel Prison in Berlin, and it was from here that he wrote the majority of the letters and papers which were collected and edited for publication in 1951 by Eberhard Bethge.[12] Letters to his parents were sent through regular postal channels and thus came under the scrutiny of prison censors, but through the assistance of friendly prison wardens and medical orderlies Bonhoeffer was able to carry on uncensored correspondence with a number of people on the outside, chief among them being Bethge. He also wrote many letters to his fiancée, Maria von Wedemeyer, but these were never published.[13] His letters from prison reveal much about the routine of prison life in a city suffering frequent Allied bombing attacks, but they pre-eminently expose the intimate thoughts of a sensitive and profoundly Christian man.

Not only did Bonhoeffer engage in this extensive correspondence while at Tegel, but he also undertook an intensive program of reading and writing. He assiduously read through the Bible, concentrating his study on the Old Testament, and from the prison library or family and friends he was able to secure many books in the fields of theology, philosophy, science, music, literature, and history. He was especially intent on familiarizing himself with the rich intellectual and spiritual heritage bequeathed by the nineteenth century. At the same time he began experimentally to express his thoughts in new literary forms, the result being a number of striking poems, an unfinished drama, and an incomplete novel. Beyond this he wrote essays on " The Sense of Time " (" Zeitgefühl "), " What Is Meant by ' Telling the Truth '? " (" Was heisst: die Wahrheit sagen? "), " On the Possibility of the Word of the Church to the World " (" Ueber die Möglichkeit des Wortes der Kirche an die Welt "), and an exposition of the first three commandments.

[12] The German edition, published by the Chr. Kaiser Verlag, is entitled *Widerstand und Ergebung (Resistance and Surrender)*; an English translation by R. H. Fuller has been published in England as *Letters and Papers from Prison* (S.C.M. Press, Ltd., London, 1953) and in America as *Prisoner for God* (The Macmillan Company, 1954; used by permission of the publisher).
[13] The poem *Vergangenheit (The Past)*, which appears in the supplement to the sixth German edition of *Widerstand und Ergebung*, was Bonhoeffer's poetic attempt to say good-by to his beloved.

The unsuccessful attempt on Hitler's life on July 20, 1944, and the subsequent discovery in September of the Zossen papers, which provided incriminating evidence against many participators in the resistance movement, led to Bonhoeffer's removal on October 8, 1944, to closer confinement in the ill-famed Gestapo prison in the Prinz Albrecht Strasse, Berlin. Here Bonhoeffer had little opportunity for contact with the outside, but we learn something of the man and his prison life from these words of Fabian von Schlabrendorff, the fellow inmate who lived to tell his tale:

Bonhoeffer told me of his interrogations, how he had been threatened with torture the first time, and how the proceedings had been sheer blackmail. Outwardly he showed no emotion. He was always in good spirits, and invariably kind and considerate to everyone — so much so that, to my surprise, even his guards soon fell under his spell. In our relationship it was always he who remained hopeful, while I sometimes suffered from depression. He never tired of repeating that only that fight is lost in which you admit defeat. How often did he smuggle a scrap of paper into my hands on which he had written words of comfort and faith from the Bible! He was also optimistic regarding his own situation. He repeatedly said that the Gestapo had not been able to trace his really important activities. His acquaintance with Goerdeler [14] he had been able to explain away as incidental; and the real purpose behind his meetings with the Bishop of Chichester during the war had never been detected by the Gestapo. If his investigation continued to proceed so slowly, it might well drag on for years. . . . During this time I shared joy and sorrow with Bonhoeffer. We also shared our few possessions and whatever our families were allowed to bring us. With sparkling eyes he used to tell me of the letters from his fiancée and from his parents, feeling their love and care surrounding him even in the Gestapo prison.[15]

One day in February, 1945, Bonhoeffer disappeared from the Prinz Albrecht Strasse. His parents could gain no information concerning his whereabouts from the Gestapo, and it was not until summer, after the collapse of Germany, that they learned the bitter truth. From Berlin he had been taken to the concentration camp at Buchen-

[14] The reference is to Dr. Karl Goerdeler, former mayor of Leipzig, who was the outstanding civilian in the struggle against Hitler. General Beck has been called the "head" and Dr. Goerdeler the "heart" of the resistance movement.

[15] *They Almost Killed Hitler*, pp. 138, 142.

wald, where he became associated with prisoners from all over Europe. These included such prominent Germans as his cellmate, General von Rabenau, Dr. Josef Müller, General von Falkenhausen, Commander Franz Liedig, former Secretary of State Pünder, and Captain Gehre; Englishmen such as Squadron Leader Hugh Falconer and Intelligence Officer Payne Best; and the Russian flyer Wassilli Kokorin, nephew of Molotov. During this time Bonhoeffer became a pastor to the heterogeneous group. Payne Best writes:

Bonhoeffer . . . was all humility and sweetness; he always seemed to me to diffuse an atmosphere of happiness, of joy in every smallest event in life, and of deep gratitude for the mere fact that he was alive. . . . He was one of the very few men that I have ever met to whom his God was real and ever close to him.[16]

On the evening of April 3, 1945, the Tuesday after Easter, these international prisoners were loaded into an army truck and began a journey to the Gestapo concentration camp at Flossenbürg, but because of its overcrowded conditions their destination was changed to the Bavarian village of Schönberg, where they arrived on Friday and were billeted in the schoolhouse. On Sunday, April 8, Bonhoeffer was asked to conduct a short worship service for the group, and he gave a brief meditation based on the Bible verses for the day: "With his wounds we are healed" (Isa. 53:5) and "Blessed be the God and Father of our Lord Jesus Christ! By his great mercy we have been born anew to a living hope through the resurrection of Jesus Christ from the dead" (I Peter 1:3). Payne Best tells what happened in the following words:

Pastor Bonhoeffer held a little service and spoke to us in a manner which reached the hearts of all, finding just the right words to express the spirit of our imprisonment and the thoughts and resolutions which it had brought. He had hardly finished his last prayer when the door opened and two evil-looking men in civilian clothes came in and said: "Prisoner Bonhoeffer, get ready to come with us." Those words "Come with us" — for all prisoners they had come to mean one thing only — the scaffold. — We bade him good-by — he drew me aside — "This is the end," he said. "For me the beginning of life," and then he gave me a message to

---

[16] *The Venlo Incident*, p. 180. Used by permission of Hutchison & Co.

give, if I could, to the Bishop of Chichester, a friend to all evangelical pastors in Germany.[17]

From Schönberg, Bonhoeffer was taken to Flossenbürg, where, along with Canaris, Oster, and others implicated in the plot of July 20, he was tried at a most dubious court martial that same night and sentenced to death. The camp doctor observed Bonhoeffer kneel and pray in his preparatory cell. At dawn on Monday, April 9, 1945, Dietrick Bonhoeffer was executed by hanging, and on the same day Hans von Dohnanyi was murdered in Sachsenhausen.[18] Only a few days later Flossenbürg was liberated by the rapidly advancing American Army.

Thus ended the life of a great Christian whose story, as Reinhold Niebuhr rightly says, " belongs to the modern Acts of the Apostles." [19]

B. THEOLOGICAL EXPOSITION

The development of Bonhoeffer's thought during the last five years of his life must be extracted mainly from his fragmentary *Ethics* and his letters and papers from prison. Everything was written under extremely difficult conditions, and nothing is in the form the author would have desired. All that is available to us is either fragmentary or intimate in character, and yet the theology that emerged under the stress of extraordinary external pressures is perhaps for that very reason more profound and provocative.

There can be little doubt that the theology of Bonhoeffer expressed in his *Ethics* is a fairly direct development of his thought of the earlier periods. Bonhoeffer's former concentration on the *exclusive* claim of Jesus Christ, which was necessary during the German Church Struggle, led ineluctably to the recognition and exposition of Jesus Christ's *total* claim upon all spheres of life in the world. The more firmly one believes in Christ as Lord, the more extensive becomes the dominion of his Lordship. On the other hand, there is a genuine question as to whether or not Bonhoeffer's thoughts in the letters and papers from

[17] *Op cit.,* p. 200. For the message to the Bishop of Chichester, see GS I, p. 412.
[18] On April 23, 1945, his brother Klaus and Rüdiger Schleicher were executed in Berlin.
[19] For an account of Bonhoeffer's last seven days read Eberhard Bethge's report in the sixth German edition of *Widerstand und Ergebung,* pp. 287–293. This new material has been added to the second edition of the English translation.

prison represent a break with his former theological position. Certainly such notions as the " world's having come of age," the " non-religious interpretation of Biblical concepts," and the " this-worldly " character of the Christian faith are startlingly new, at least in the sense that they could hardly have been anticipated.

1. " Ethics "[20]

Bonhoeffer's *Ethics* has been divided into two general parts by the editor, the first being material that was clearly to be incorporated in the framework of the book, the second being a collection of unrelated essays pertaining to various ethical themes. While there is a definite continuity of theological understanding undergirding the whole, the work suffers from its fragmentary character and its somewhat arbitrary organization.

The author begins with a section on " Ethics as Formation," in which he introduces the basic theme of the entire book. In discussing the relation between the theoretical ethicist and reality he states that the man who is able to deal effectively with evil today is not the man of reason or moral fanaticism or conscience or duty or free responsibility or private virtue, but alone the man who can combine simplicity with wisdom. To be simple is to belong to God and to look only to him, and to be wise is to see reality as it is — to see into the depths of things. But since true reality is only in God, to combine simplicity with wisdom is " to look in freedom at God and at reality, which rests solely upon him " (8). Yet as long as the world and God are torn asunder, how can man keep his eyes on both at the same time? Bonhoeffer answers that there is *one* place where God and cosmic reality are reconciled, where God and man have become one, and this place does not lie beyond reality in the realm of ideas, but in the midst of history as a divine miracle. " It lies," he asserts " in Jesus Christ, the Reconciler of the world. . . . Whoever sees Jesus Christ does indeed see God and the world in one. He can henceforward no longer see God without the world or the world without God " (8).

To live lives of simple wisdom, then, Bonhoeffer exhorts us to be-

[20] Unless otherwise noted, quotations will be cited from the English translation by Neville Horton Smith, which was published in 1955 by S.C.M. Press, Ltd., of London and The Macmillan Company.

hold the God-Man Jesus Christ. *Ecce homo!* Behold the man in whom the *real* world was reconciled (not overthrown!) by the lived love of God. Behold the God *who has become man* and thus has mercifully decided to bear and to suffer to the end the fate of all mankind. Behold the man *sentenced by God,* the figure of the Crucified, in whom every man, successful or unsuccessful in the world, is judged and found wanting. Behold the man whom God has taken to himself, has sentenced and executed and *awakened to a new life*. The miracle of the resurrection means that God's loving " yes " to man is stronger than judgment and death, that God wills to create a new man, a new life, a new creature. " It is true," confesses Bonhoeffer, " that mankind is still living the old life, but it is already beyond the old. It still lives in a world of death, but it is already beyond death. It still lives in a world of sin, but it is already beyond sin. The night is not yet over, but already the dawn is breaking " (17). The new world takes form whenever it is drawn into the form of Jesus Christ.

For Bonhoeffer, then, Christian ethics is a matter of " formation " (*Gestaltung*) into the likeness of Jesus Christ, of " conformation " (*Gleichgestaltung*) with " the unique form of him who was made man, was crucified, and rose again " (18). Formation is not something that can be accomplished by man himself, but rather it " is achieved only when the form of Jesus Christ itself works upon us in such a manner that it molds our form in its own likeness (Gal. 4:19). Christ remains the only giver of forms " (18). To be conformed to the *Incarnate* is to be the man one really is, or better, to be a *real* man who is an object not for deification, but an object of the love of God. To be formed in the likeness of the *Crucified* means to die daily before God for the sake of sin, to bear all suffering with the knowledge that it " serves to enable him to die with his own will and to accept God's judgment upon him " (19). To be conformed with the *risen One* means to be a new man before God, even though the glory of the new life remains " hidden with Christ in God " (Col. 3:3).

The author points out that the form which takes form in man is neither the form of God, which would be alien to man, nor merely an imitation or repetition of the form of Christ, but it is Christ's form itself. Christ bore the form of mankind as a whole and longs to take form in all men, but this longing is still unsatisfied except in the small number of men who are his church. The church is the body of Christ, and the body is the form. "The church," explains Bonhoeffer, "is not a religious community of worshipers of Christ but is Christ himself, who has taken form among men. The church can be called the body of Christ because in Christ's body man is really taken up by him, and so too, therefore, are all mankind. The church, then, bears the form which is in truth the proper form of all humanity. . . . The church is nothing but a section of humanity in which Christ has really taken form . . . , is the man in Christ, incarnate, sentenced, and awakened to new life" (20 f.).

"The point of departure for Christian ethics," therefore, "is the body of Christ, the form of Christ in the form of the church, and the formation of the church in conformity with the form of Christ" (21). Inasmuch as Christ became not an idea or doctrine or teaching or principle but a real man like ourselves, the form of Christ is the same at all times and in all places, but inasmuch as Christ is willing for his form to take form in the real man, it assumes different guises. That is, Christ does not dispense with, but gives effect to, human reality. For this reason the Christian ethic is never abstract, but always entirely concrete. Christ takes form among us here and now, and this means in the sphere of our decisions and encounters, the sphere of concrete problems, tasks, and responsibilities. Lest we conclude that he endorses an unrestrained individualism, however, Bonhoeffer hastens to add that "by our history we are set objectively in a definite nexus of experiences, responsibilities, and decisions from which we cannot free ourselves again except by an abstraction" (24). This nexus is "the world of the peoples of Europe and America in so far as it is already united through the form of Christ" (24).

Bonhoeffer next begins a discussion of what he terms "Inheritance and Decay." Unlike the East, where existence is timeless and history assumes the character of mythology, the Christian West is impressed with an awareness of temporality and a historical heritage which is consciously or unconsciously effected by the entry of God into history at a definite place and a definite point of time. God's "yes" to history in his incarnation in Jesus Christ and his "no" in the crucifixion of Jesus Christ introduce into each moment of history an infinite and unresolvable tension. "Here," says Bonhoeffer, "history becomes a serious matter without being canonized" (26). With the life and death of Jesus Christ, history becomes for the first time truly temporal and as such " history with God's consent."

Since Western history finds its continuity in Jesus Christ, it is *directly* connected with the entire history of Israel in that Jesus was the promised Messiah of the Israelite-Jewish people, and *indirectly* related to Greco-Roman antiquity in that it was the time and world chosen for the incarnation (its nearness to Christ) but also the time of the crucifixion (its opposition to Christ). " It is the Roman heritage," asserts Bonhoeffer, " which comes to represent the combination and assimilation of antiquity with the Christian element, and it is the Greek heritage which comes to represent opposition and hostility to Christ " (27). The former is more characteristic of Roman Catholicism and the Western European countries, the latter of the Reformation and Germany. Bonhoeffer explains the difference and also the possibility of unifying the two in this way:

Wherever the incarnation of Christ, his becoming man, is more intensely in the foreground of Christian consciousness, there one will seek for the reconciliation of antiquity with Christianity. And wherever the cross of Christ dominates the Christian message, there the breach between Christ and antiquity will be greatly emphasized. But Christ is both the Incarnate and the Crucified, and he demands to be recognized as both of these alike. For this reason the due acceptance of the historical heritage of antiquity is a task which the Christian West has yet to complete, and with the completion of this task as their common purpose the West European peoples and the Germans will draw more closely together. (28)

It is Bonhoeffer's conviction that during the Middle Ages the unity of the West through the form of Christ was striven for by pope and emperor alike. Together they fought for, ruled, and consolidated the *corpus Christianum* in the name of Jesus Christ, and this heritage still remains today in the form of the Roman Church, i.e., the papacy. But the *corpus Christianum* was broken by the Reformation into its two constituent parts, the *corpus Christi* and the world, and this because Luther was compelled by the word of the Bible to conclude that the true unity of the church was not to be found in any political power, but only in Jesus Christ as he lives in his word and sacrament.

The guilt toward Christ incurred by the schism of faith, which was ratified in the Peace of Westphalia, and by the subsequent political disunity, which was evidenced in the Thirty Years' War, is a guilt shared by the whole of Western Christendom. On the other hand, the fact that both sides called upon the name of Jesus Christ means that the common guilt was not destined to destroy the unity of the West.

Nevertheless, the author points out, the process of secularization quickly set in and continues until today. Luther's doctrine of the two kingdoms, the kingdom of the church, which is ruled by the preached word of God, and the kingdom of the world, which is ruled by the sword, was misinterpreted to imply " the emancipation of man in his conscience, his reason, and his culture, and as the justification of the secular as such " (33). On the Catholic side the process rapidly became anticlerical and even anti-Christian, and the result was the terror of the French Revolution, with its emphasis on the emancipated reason, an emancipated class, and an emancipated people. The emancipation of reason, which brought about a healthy respect for intellectual honesty, led to the discovery of " that mysterious correspondence between the laws of thought and the laws of nature," and so fostered " the unparalleled rise of technology " (34). Besides technology the Revolution also bequeathed to the Western world the stirring of the masses and nationalism, so that the total result was the creation of a new unity of mind in the West which was rooted in the emancipation of man as reason, as the mass, and as the nation. But, asserts Bonhoeffer, while these work together in harmony during the struggle for freedom, they become deadly enemies as soon as freedom is achieved. " The masses and nationalism are hostile to reason. Technology and the masses are hostile to nationalism. Nationalism and technology are hostile to the masses " (38). Therefore, the seeds of decay are found within the new unity itself, and the net result can only be nihilism.

The new unity, the crisis of which we are experiencing today, is really Western godlessness, a religion of hostility toward God that cannot but acknowledge God and the concomitant deification of man. This godlessness is essentially hostile to the church, and yet the fact that the churches lose few members points to its ambiguous character. Bonhoeffer gives this unusual insight into the problem:

It would be quite wrong simply to identify Western godlessness with enmity toward the church. There is the godlessness in religious and Christian clothing, which we have called a hopeless godlessness, but there is also a godlessness which is full of promise, a godlessness which speaks against religion and against the church. It is the protest against pious godlessness in so far as this has corrupted the churches and thus, in a certain sense, if only negatively, it defends the heritage of a genuine faith in God and of a genuine church. There is relevance here in Luther's saying that perhaps God would rather hear the curses of the ungodly than the alleluia of the pious. (39 f.)

It is the author's conviction that the American Revolution, which was almost contemporary with, and certainly not unconnected from, the French Revolution, was profoundly different in character. A peculiar historical convergence of the Calvinist idea of original sin and the wickedness of the human heart and the Dissenters' idea that the Kingdom of God on earth cannot be built by the authority of the state but solely by the congregation of the faithful led to a democracy " not founded upon the emancipated man but, quite on the contrary, upon the Kingdom of God and the limitation of all earthly powers by the sovereignty of God " (40). Nevertheless, even the Anglo-Saxon countries, which consider democracy to be the only Christian form of the state, have not escaped the process of secularization. " The cause," asserts Bonhoeffer, " does not lie in the misinterpretation of the distinction between the two offices or kingdoms, but rather in the reverse of this, in the failure of the enthusiasts to distinguish at all between the office or kingdom of the state and the office or kingdom of the church " (41). In the end, the church inadvertantly capitulates to the world, and the godlessness simply remains more covert.

Bonhoeffer believes that the Western world's loss of the unity it possessed through the form of Jesus Christ constitutes a crisis without equal, a decisive struggle of the last days. We are rapidly approaching an apostate, rebellious void (*Nichts*) that threatens to engulf every facet of life, at once shaking off the burden of yesterday and refusing any responsibility for tomorrow. " With the loss of past and future," states Bonhoeffer, " life fluctuates between the most bestial enjoyment of the moment and an adventurous game of chance.

An abrupt end is put to any kind of inner self-development and to any gradual attainment of personal or vocational maturity. There is no personal destiny, and consequently there is no personal dignity. Serious tensions and inwardly necessary periods of waiting are not sustained. . . . If we ask what remains, there can be only one answer: fear of the void " (42 f.).

For Bonhoeffer the really significant sign of our time is man's willingness to sacrifice anything and everything when confronted by the void, and he sees only two things that are still powerful enough to save us from plunging into it: first, the miracle of the new awakening of faith, which is proclaimed by the church; and second, the restraining force of the state, which is able to establish and maintain order. Church and state, unlike in their nature, are allies in the struggle against the forces of destruction.

Today, affirms Bonhoeffer, the church faces a unique situation and is called to an unparalleled task. The Western world has repudiated its inheritance by turning its back on Christ, and the church now must prove that Christ is the living Lord of a hostile world. As a bearer of a historical inheritance the church has an obligation to the historical future, even while it waits for the eschatological " Last Day." Its preaching of the risen Lord " strikes a mortal blow at the spirit of destruction," and its suffering " presents an infinitely greater danger to the spirit of destruction than does any political power which may still remain " (45). However, the church is not simply concerned for the preservation of the past, for its message judges even the forces of order and justice which ally themselves with it. Instead, the church " leaves it to God's governance of the world to decide whether he will permit the success of the forces of order and whether it, the church, while still preserving the essential distinction between itself and those forces, even though it unreservedly allies itself with them, will be allowed to pass on to the future that historical inheritance that bears within it the blessing and the guilt of past generations " (45).

Bonhoeffer follows his analysis of the inheritance and decay of the Western world with a discussion of " Guilt, Justification, and Renewal." He reiterates his assertion that the real man is the man who is taken up in Christ, and concludes that " man's apostasy from

Christ is at the same time his apostasy from his own essential nature " (46). The only way for man to realize his true form is to confess the guilt of his defection from Christ, and this marks the beginning of his conformation with Christ. The true acknowledgment of guilt arises, not from the experiences of disruption and decay, but solely from an encounter with Christ, who in his grace " stretches out his hand to save the one who is falling away " (46). The place where this occurs is the church, which is precisely "that community of human beings which has been led by the grace of Christ to the recognition of guilt toward Christ " (46 f.).

The recognition by the true repentant that *he* is entirely guilty for both his own apostasy from Christ and that of the Western world brings forth an acceptance of the burden of guilt, with no attempt to transfer any blame to another. And yet, continues Bonhoeffer, the very fact that the origin of this confession of guilt is the form of Christ denotes that it is not unconditional and entire, for " Christ subdues us in no other way more utterly than by his having taken our guilt upon himself unconditionally and entirely, declaring himself guilty of our guilt and freeing us from its burden " (47). Thus from confession there arises the possibility of forgiveness. Only by confession are the church and the individual sentenced in their guilt and justified by him who takes upon himself all human guilt and forgives it. Thereby they become partakers of the form of Christ, sharing in his cross and in the glory of his new righteousness and new life.

It is Bonhoeffer's conviction that the justification and renewal of the Western world lie solely in the divine justification and renewal of the church. Whereas the church is justified and renewed *directly* through faith in Christ (submission to his form), the Western world's " justification and renewal " takes place *indirectly* through the faith of the church. " The church," he says, " experiences in faith the forgiveness of all her sins and a new beginning through grace. For the nations there is only a healing of the wound, a cicatrization of guilt, in order to return to order, to justice, to peace, and to the granting of free passage to the church's proclamation of Jesus Christ " (52). This restoration of justice, order, and peace in the West, concludes Bonhoeffer, can come about only gradually. Past guilt must be forgiven; it must no longer be imagined that what has been done can be undone by means of punitive measures and reprisals, and the church must be given room to carry out its work among the nations. Just as the guilt of the apostasy from Christ is shared by all the Western nations, the justification and renewal must likewise be shared by the whole of the West.

Bonhoeffer's second section is entitled "Christ, Reality, and Good." He begins with a discussion of the concept of reality and asserts that neither the self nor the world constitutes ultimate reality, but only the reality of God, the Creator, Reconciler, and Redeemer. Thus the Christian who is concerned with an ethical problem does not ask: "How can I be good?" or "How can I do good?" but "What is the will of God?" The point of departure for all Christian ethics is faith in the ultimate reality and goodness of the God who reveals himself in Jesus Christ, and the problem of Christian ethics is how the revelational reality of God in Christ becomes real among men. Bonhoeffer explains what he means in these words:

> The place which in all other ethics is occupied by the antithesis of "should be" and "is," idea and accomplishment, motive and performance, is occupied in Christian ethics by the relation of reality and realization, past and present, history and event (faith), or, to replace the equivocal concept with the unambiguous name, the relation of Jesus Christ and the Holy Spirit. The question of good becomes the question of participation in the divine reality which is revealed in Christ. (57)

The good, then, is the real, and the real is not abstract, but possesses reality only in the reality of God. Therefore, only when we share in this reality do we share in the good. For this reason neither an ethic of motive, which inquires about the goodness of the person, nor an ethic of consequences, which asks about the goodness of the action, can commend itself to the Christian. Furthermore, our common distinctions between a man and his work and between "moral man" and "immoral society" are purely abstract. "The question of good," states the author, "embraces man with his motives and purposes, with his fellow men and with the entire creation around him; it embraces reality as a whole, as it is held in being by God. . . . With respect to its origin this indivisible whole is called 'creation.' With respect to its goal it is called the 'Kingdom of God.' Both of these are equally remote from us and equally close to us, for God's creation and God's Kingdom are present with us solely in God's self-revelation in Jesus Christ " (59 f.).

The Christian understanding of reality is not at all that which underlies the positivistic approach to ethics. The positivist believes that reality itself teaches what is good, but by " reality " he means that which is empirically verifiable, a conception that implies denial of the origin of this reality in God and " surrender to the contingent, the casual, the adventitious, and the momentarily expedient " (60). The Christian, on the other hand, sees both the reality of the world and the reality of God in Jesus Christ. " The reality of God," claims Bonhoeffer, " discloses itself only by setting me entirely in the reality of the world, and when I encounter the reality of the world it is always already sustained, accepted, and reconciled in the reality of God. This is the inner meaning of the revelation of God in the man Jesus Christ " (61). Christian ethics inquires about the way this reality is being realized in the present, the way in which life may be conducted in this reality, and therefore, the way one participates in the reality of God and of the world in Jesus Christ today.

This brings the author to a discussion of what he calls " Thinking in Terms of Two Spheres." The understanding of reality that he has delineated cuts across the main stream of Christian ethical thought. With the exception of Reformation and New Testament times, this thought has been informed by " the conception of a juxtaposition and conflict of two spheres: the one divine, holy, supernatural, and Christian, and the other worldly, profane, natural, and unchristian " (62). According to this scheme, reality is divided into two parts, and ethics is concerned with the proper relation between the two. Medieval scholasticism subordinated the realm of nature to the realm of grace; the pseudo-Lutheranism that followed the Reformation set in opposition the autonomous orders of this world and the law of Christ; and the Enthusiasts exhorted the congregation of the elect to struggle with a hostile world for establishment of God's Kingdom on earth. Bonhoeffer is convinced that the presupposition underlying all these schemes is false, for it assumes that there are realities which lie outside the reality which is in Christ, and he draws the following consequences of this type of thinking:

So long as Christ and the world are conceived as two opposing and mutually repellent spheres, man will be left in the following dilemma: He abandons reality as a whole, and places himself in one or other of the two spheres. He seeks Christ without the world, or he seeks the world without Christ. In either case he is deceiving himself. Or else he tries to stand in both spaces at once and thereby becomes the man of eternal conflict, the kind of man who emerged in the period after the Reformation and who has repeatedly set himself up as representing the only form of Christian existence which is in accord with reality. (63)

In contrast, both New Testament and Reformation thought affirm only *one* reality, " the reality of God which has become manifest in Christ in the reality of the world " (63 f.). Secular and Christian, natural and supernatural, profane and sacred, rational and revelational — these are neither ultimate static antitheses nor identities. Instead, the world, the natural, the profane, and reason have been taken up into the divine and cosmic reality in Christ and must always be seen in the movement of being accepted and becoming accepted by God in Christ. The unity of the reality of God and of the world in Christ is such that what is Christian is to be found only in what is of the world, the " supernatural " only in the natural, the holy only in the profane, the revelational only in the rational. Yet in no case are they identical; their unity is a polemical one, in which neither element allows the other to assume a kind of static independence in regard to the other. On the contrary, this mutual polemical attitude witnesses to their shared reality and to their unity in the reality that is in Christ. Bonhoeffer believes that Luther's doctrine of the two kingdoms was originally intended in this sense, i.e., as a polemical unity, and it is only in this sense that it can be accepted.

In the final analysis, however, are there no ultimate static contraries, no spaces that are permanently separated? Is not the church a space that is separate from the space of the world, and is not the kingdom of the devil a space that will never enter into the Kingdom of Christ? Bonhoeffer is the first to admit that the church occupies a definite space in the world, " a space delimited by its public worship, its organizations, and its parish life," but he insists that this space is not something that exists on its own account. The church is the place where Jesus Christ's reign over the *whole world* is evidenced and proclaimed, and it is therefore continually reaching out beyond itself and extending its boundaries. " The church," says the author, " is the place where testimony and serious thought are given to God's reconciliation of the world with himself in Christ, to his having so loved the world that he gave his Son for its sake " (68). The church desires only enough space to serve the world by bearing this witness, so that if we speak of a space or a sphere of the church, we must be aware that the confines of this space are at every moment being overrun and broken down by the testimony of the church to the Lordship of Christ. " The only way in which the church can defend its own territory," explains Bonhoeffer, " is by fighting not for it but for the salvation of the world. Otherwise the church becomes a ' religious society ' which fights in its own interest and thereby ceases at once to be the church of God and of the world." (68 f.)

At first sight the Kingdom of Christ and the kingdom of the devil seem to represent an ultimate antimony which would justify thinking in terms of two spheres. But Bonhoeffer points out that, although Christ and his adversary are mutually exclusive contraries, the devil must serve Christ even against his will. The author explains further:

He [the devil] desires evil, but over and over again he is compelled to do good; so that the realm or space of the devil is always only beneath the feet of Jesus Christ. But if the kingdom of the devil is taken to mean that world which " lies in disorder," the world which has fallen under the devil's authority, then here, especially, there is a limit to the possibility of thinking in terms of spheres. For it is precisely this " disordered " world that in Christ is reconciled with God and that now possesses its final and true reality not in the devil but in Christ. The world is not divided between Christ and the devil, but, whether it recognizes it or not, it is solely and entirely the world of Christ. (70)

In its relation to the world " as such," i.e., the world as it understands itself, the church must take its cue from the relation of God to the world. Even as the world resists and rejects the reality of the love of God, the church must open the eyes of precisely this rebellious world to this reality and to its reconciliation with God. In this way the lost and sentenced world is incessantly drawn into the event of Christ.

Although he recognizes the difficulty of abandoning a picture that has long been used for the ordering of our ideas and concepts, Bonhoeffer is firmly convinced that the picture of the two spheres must be left behind. But what is to take its place? Bonhoeffer would have us direct our gaze to the body of Christ! " In the body of Jesus Christ," he explains, " God is united with humanity, the whole of humanity is accepted by God, and the world is reconciled with God. . . . Whoever sets eyes on the body of Jesus Christ in faith can never again speak of the world as though it were lost, as thought it were separated from Christ; he can never again with clerical arrogance set himself apart from the world " (71). But is the church not distinct from the world? Yes, but solely by virtue that it affirms in faith the reality of God's acceptance of mankind as a whole and allows this reality to take effect within itself. If the difference between the church and world cannot be expressed in terms of a static, spatial borderline, what conception can be used? Here the author refers us to the Bible, which has a ready answer in terms of " the four mandates."

Whether it knows it or not, the world is relative to Christ, since it is created through Christ, has Christ as its end, and consists in Christ alone. " This relativeness of the world to Christ," claims Bonhoeffer, " assumes concrete form in certain mandates of God in the world. The Scriptures name four such mandates: labor, marriage, government, and the church " (73). These divine mandates, a term that is to be preferred to " divine orders " because the term " mandate " refers more clearly to a divinely imposed task rather than to a determination of being, have been imposed by God upon all men. The first three are not " secular," in contradistinction to the fourth, but all are equally divine by virtue of their original and final relation to Christ. However, they are divine only because of this relation. Or, as Bonhoeffer expresses it: " It is not because labor, marriage, government, and church *are* that they are commanded by God, but it is because they are commanded by God that they *are*. And they are divine mandates only in so far as their being is consciously or unconsciously subordinated to the divinely imposed task " (74).

The mandates of labor and marriage confront the first man after Creation, and both permit man to share in God's creative power for the glory and service of Christ. Because both mandates are to be carried out by the race of Cain, however, a shadow falls from the outset on all human labor and on marriage and the family in this our world. The divine mandate of government presupposes those of labor and marriage; unlike them, it is not creative, but functions to preserve what has been created. Thus the governing authority is not the performer but the witness and guarantor of marriage; it is not the administrator but the inspector and supervisor of labor. " By the establishment of law and by the force of the sword the governing authority preserves the world for the reality of Jesus Christ. Everyone owes obedience to this governing authority — for Christ's sake " (76). The divine mandate of the church differs from the other three in that its task is to enable the reality of Jesus Christ to become real in the preaching and organization of the church and the Christian life. It extends to all mankind by impinging upon all the other mandates, so that the man who is simultaneously a laborer, a partner in marriage, and the subject of a government is now to be a *Christian* laborer, partner, and subject. " No division into separate spheres or spaces is permissible here," declares Bonhoeffer. " The whole man stands before the whole earthly and eternal reality, the reality which God has prepared for him in Jesus Christ " (76 f.). Only by responding fully to the totality of the offer and the claim can man live up to this reality.

Bonhoeffer now returns to his earlier affirmation that the right question is neither how one can be good nor how one can do good, but what is the will of God, and to this question he answers: " The will of God is nothing other than the becoming real of the reality of Christ with us and in our world " (77). It is not an idea still to be realized, nor is it simply identical with what is in being. It is not something hidden and unfulfilled, but something that has become manifest and that has already been fulfilled by God in his reconciliation of the world with himself in Christ. " After Christ has appeared," states Bonhoeffer, " ethics can have but one purpose, namely, the achievement of participation in the reality of the fulfilled will of God. But this participation, too, is possible only in virtue of the fact that I myself am already included in the fulfillment of the will of God in Christ, which means that I am reconciled with God " (78). Access to God's will, which embraces the whole of reality, can be gained only in faith in Jesus Christ, the sole fountainhead of all good.

The author's third section is entitled " The Last Things and the Things Before the Last." His basic presupposition is that " justification " is the " last word." " The origin and the essence of all Christian life," he says, " are comprised in the one process or event which the Reformation called justification of the sinner by grace alone " (79). Man is rescued from the abyss by the inbreaking of the word of God; his past is forgiven, his future is secure, and his life is justified and made new in the church. Yet justification is not just by grace alone, but also by faith alone. Faith sets life on the new foundation which alone can justify life before God, and this foundation is the life, death, and resurrection of Jesus Christ. " Faith," asserts Bonhoeffer, " means the finding and holding fast of this foundation. It means casting anchor upon it and being held fast by it. . . . Faith means being held captive by the sight of Jesus Christ, no longer seeing anything but him, being wrested from my imprisonment in my own self, being set free by Jesus Christ. Faith is a passive submission to an action, and in this submission alone it is itself an action " (80). Although neither hope nor love justifies, faith will always be accompanied by both.

God's justifying word is final in two respects: first, qualitatively, because it is completely free and therefore excludes man's every effort and method of achieving it on his own; second, temporally, because it is always preceded by something penultimate which remains, even though the ultimate entirely annuls and invalidates it. A way must be trodden, a span of time must elapse. Justification by grace and faith alone remains the final word, but for the sake of the ultimate Bonhoeffer now speaks of the " things before the last." His willingness to take seriously the penultimate is explained in this way:

So that this may become quite clear, let us ask why it is that precisely in thoroughly grave situations, for instance when I am with someone who has suffered a bereavement, I often decide to adopt a " penultimate " attitude, particularly when I am dealing with Christians, remaining silent as a sign that I share in the bereaved man's helplessness in the face of such a grievous event, and not speaking the Biblical words of comfort which are, in fact, known to me and available to me. Why am I often unable to open my mouth, when I ought to give expression to the ultimate? And why, instead, do I decide on an expression of thoroughly penultimate human solidarity? Is it from mistrust of the power of the ultimate word? Is it from fear of men? Or is there some good positive reason for such an attitude, namely, that my knowledge of the word, my having it at my finger tips, in other words my being, so to speak, spiritually master of the situation, bears only the appearance of the ultimate, but is in reality itself something entirely penultimate? Does one not in some cases, by remaining deliberately in the penultimate, perhaps point all the more genuinely to the ultimate, which God will speak in his own time (though indeed even then through a human mouth)? Does not this mean that, over and over again, the penultimate will be what commends itself precisely for the sake of the ultimate, and that it will have to be done not with a heavy conscience but with a clear one? (84 f.)

Bonhoeffer now points out that the problem of the relation between the ultimate and the penultimate in the Christian life can be solved either "radically" or by means of a compromise, both of which are extreme solutions. That is, one can see only the ultimate and consider everything penultimate as enmity toward Christ, or one can on principle set apart the ultimate from the penultimate, in which case the penultimate retains its right on its own account and is not imperiled by the ultimate. In the first instance the world is despised and God's final word of mercy becomes the icy hardness of the law; in the second the *status quo* is given eternal justification and God's free word of mercy becomes the law of mercy. "In both cases," explains the author, "thoughts which are in themselves equally right and necessary are in an inadmissible manner made absolute. The radical solution has as its point of departure the end of all things, God the Judge and Redeemer; the compromise solution bases itself upon the Creator and Preserver. On the one side it is the end that is regarded as absolute, and on the other side it is things as they are. Thus creation and redemption, time and eternity, confront one another in a conflict which cannot be resolved; the unity of God himself is sundered, and faith in God is broken apart " (86 f.).

Neither of these extreme solutions can suffice, for " in Jesus Christ there is neither radicalism nor compromise, but there is the reality of God and men " (87). The solution to the relationship between the ultimate and the penultimate, then, can be found solely in Jesus Christ, the incarnate, crucified, and risen God-Man. The *incarnation* means that God enters into created reality and thereby reveals his love for his creation; but even though the manhood of Jesus implies the absolute condemnation of sin and the relative condemnation of established human orders, it at the same time allows human reality to remain a penultimate which must be taken seriously in its own way. The *crucifixion* means that God pronounces the final condemnation on the fallen creation and thereby reveals his judgment upon all flesh; yet even though the cross discloses the judgment of the ultimate upon all that is penultimate, it at the same time reveals mercy toward that penultimate which bows before the judgment of the ultimate. The *resurrection* means that God sets an end to death and calls a new creation into life, thereby manifesting his will for a new world; yet even though man has already risen again with Christ to newness of life, he remains in the world of the penultimate until he passes the boundary of death. The life of the Christian with the incarnate, crucified, and risen Christ is provided with a unity which avoids both radicalism and the compromise solution. " Christian life," states Bonhoeffer, " means being a man through the efficacy of the incarnation; it means being sentenced and pardoned through the efficacy of the cross; and it means living a new life through the efficacy of the resurrection. There cannot be one of these without the rest " (91).

Since it is clear that the ultimate (the last things) leaves open a certain amount of room for the penultimate (the things before the last), Bonhoeffer now discusses what he calls " The Preparing of the Way." He claims that the penultimate, which is everything that precedes the justification of the sinner by grace alone, must be taken seriously simply on account of its relation to the ultimate, and he specifies that the two concrete things that are penultimate in relation to justification are *being man* and *being good*. Of course, it must never be forgotten that Christ's coming in grace remains the ultimate. He opens up his own way, regardless of man's preparation or readiness. Nevertheless, this does not give us any excuse for neglecting to prepare for his coming by removing every possible obstacle in his way. " There are conditions of the heart, of life, and of the world which impede the reception of grace in a special way," says Bonhoeffer, " namely, by rendering faith infinitely difficult "

(94). Hunger, injustice, loneliness, disorder — these are penultimate conditions which the Christian must continually seek to alleviate for the sake of the ultimate. Yet the preparation of the way for Christ must be more than merely an attainment of certain conditions. Everything depends upon these concrete, visible actions being at the same time a *spiritual* reality, which implies that they must be acts of humiliation before the coming of the Lord, i.e., acts of repentance. But repentance demands action, and this action should be directed toward the twin goals of " being man " and " being good."

It is the coming Lord himself who has already shed light upon what is meant by being man and being good. Bonhoeffer explains this as follows:

It is only by reference to the Lord who is to come, and who has come, that we can know what it is to be man and to be good. It is because Christ is coming that we must be men and that we must be good. For Christ is not coming to hell, but to " his own " (John 1:11); he is coming to his creation, which, in spite of its fall, is his creation still. Christ is not coming to devils but to men, certainly to men who are sinful, lost, and damned, but still to men. That the fallen creation is still the creation, and that sinful man still remains man, follows from the fact that Christ is coming to them and that Christ redeems them from sin and from the power of the devil. It is in relation to Christ that the fallen world becomes intelligible as the world which is preserved and sustained by God for the coming of Christ, the world in which we can and should live good lives as men in orders which are established. (97)

In spite of the importance of our preparations, however, Bonhoeffer emphasizes that there is no *method* for proceeding from the penultimate to the ultimate. Preparation of the way is always a way from the ultimate to the penultimate!

The spiritual situation of Western Christendom is such that the " last things " have been more and more called into question during the past two hundred years. And yet many people still hold on to the " things before the last," even though the connection of the penultimate with the ultimate has been lost. Bonhoeffer believes that we must claim this penultimate for the ultimate, since sooner or later the loss of the ultimate must necessarily lead to the collapse of the penultimate as well. Whatever humanity and goodness is found in this fallen world must be claimed for Jesus Christ, and it is Bonhoeffer's conviction that in cases where these persist as an unconscious residue of a former attachment to the ultimate, it will be more Christian not to treat the man as a non-Christian and urge him to confess his unbelief, but " to claim precisely *that* man as a Christian who would himself no longer dare to call himself a Christian, and then with much patience to help him to the profession of faith in Christ " (100).

From this perspective Bonhoeffer attempts to recover the concept of the " natural " for Protestant ethics. In the past, Protestant thought has tended to exalt grace to such an extent that everything human and natural sank into the abyss of sin, so that relative distinctions within the fallen creation were no longer made. Both the natural and the unnatural were equally damned in the presence of the word of God, and this meant that natural life suffered complete disruption.

What is the " natural " according to Bonhoeffer? It is neither the creaturely nor the sinful, but it is " that which, after the Fall, is directed toward the coming of Christ " (102). The " unnatural," on the other hand, is " that which, after the Fall, closes its doors against the coming of Christ." Through the Fall the " creature " becomes " nature," and this means that the direct dependence of the creature on God is replaced by the relative freedom of the natural life. This relative freedom, which can be used in either a true (natural) or false (unnatural) way, is not to be confused with the absolute freedom for God and for the neighbor which is imparted by the word of God alone. On the other hand, it is not to be underestimated as something penultimate which receives its validation from the ultimate, from Christ himself.

The natural, which is the form of life preserved by God for the fallen world and directed toward justification, redemption, and renewal through Christ, is determined *according to its form* through God's will to preserve it and through its being directed toward Christ. *According to its contents,* on the other hand, it is the form of the preserved life itself, the form which embraces the whole human race. Formally, the natural can be known only in its relation to Jesus Christ, but in regard to its contents it can be perceived by man's reason. The reason, stresses Bonhoeffer, is not a divine principle of knowledge. Rather, it is wholly embedded in the natural and is the conscious perception of the natural as it presents itself. "Reason," states the author, "understands the natural as something that is universally established and independent of the possibility of empirical verification." It follows from this that "the natural can never be something that is determined by any single part or any single authority within the fallen world" (104). No one can establish or decide what is natural, for the natural is already established and decided. The natural simply exists, and its innate power of existence serves to protect life against the unnatural and therefore provides "a solid basis for that optimistic view of human history which confines itself within the limits of the fallen world" (106).

The natural is form which dwells within and serves life; thus natural life is formed life. It is neither vitalism, which is an absolutization of life as an end in itself, nor mechanization, which is an absolutizing of life as means to an end. Rather, it is both at once: life as an end in itself and life as a means to an end. "In relation to Jesus Christ," explains Bonhoeffer, "the status of life as an end in itself is understood as creaturehood, and its status as a means to an end is understood as participation in the Kingdom of God; while within the framework of the natural life, the fact that life is an end in itself finds expression in the rights with which life is endowed, and the fact that life is a means to an end finds expression in the duties which are imposed on it. Thus, for the sake of Christ and his coming, natural life must be lived within the framework of certain definite rights and certain definite duties" (107). God first gives man specific rights in relation to other men, and these rights of natural life, which reflect the glory of God's creation in the midst of the fallen world, call forth duties on man's part.

Bonhoeffer believes that the Roman law dictum *suum cuique* (" to each his own ") expresses the most general formulation of the rights given with the natural, but it is misapplied either if "his own" is interpreted to mean "the same," so that the multiplicity of the natural is destroyed in favor of an abstract law, or if "his own" is defined arbitrarily and subjectively, so that the unity of rights is nullified in the interests of free self-will. Any "innate right" must be predicated on the recognition of the natural rights of others, which implies that the conflict of rights is inherent in the natural itself. This points to a limitation of the principle of *suum cuique,* since it does not take into account the fact of sin operating in the natural and therefore the unavoidable rise of conflicts that can be settled only through the application of a positive right introduced from without. Nevertheless, this does not deprive the principle of its relative correctness or its status as a penultimate.

A presupposition of *suum cuique* which is constantly being attacked by social eudaemonism is the natural right of " each man," i.e., of the individual. It is Bonhoeffer's conviction that the right of the individual must not be subordinated to the right of the community, for this can eventaully lead only to chaos. Social eudaemonism, which allies itself with a sort of blind voluntarism, can be checked only by the reason, which perceives and introduces into consciousness the reality of the fallen world. " The principle of *suum cuique,*" says the author, " is the highest possible attainment of a reason which is in accord with reality and which, within the natural life, discerns the right which is given to the individual by God (of whom reason knows nothing)" (111).

As to the question of the guarantor of the rights of natural life, Bonhoeffer answers that it is God. However, God continually makes use of *life itself* to overcome every violation of the natural. This does not necessarily mean that individuals live to see their rights restored, because in the domain of the natural life the important thing is not so much the individual as the preservation of the life of man as a species; but it does mean that life itself is man's most powerful ally in the defense of his natural rights. Bonhoeffer ends the section with a discussion of the natural rights of bodily and mental life, in which he takes up such subjects as suicide, reproduction, and nascent life, and the freedom of bodily life.

The fourth section of Bonhoeffer's *Ethics* is entitled " The Love of God and the Decay of the World." " The knowledge of good and evil seems to be the aim of all ethical reflection. The first task of Christian ethics is to invalidate this knowledge " (142). With these challenging words Bonhoeffer calls in question the underlying assumptions of all other ethics, and he does so on the grounds that " Christian ethics claims to discuss the origin of the whole problem of ethics, and thus professes to be a critique of all ethics simply as ethics" (142).

The decisive difference between Christian ethics and all other ethics is the difference between life in the unity of the knowledge of God and life in the disunity of the knowledge of good and evil. Hearkening back to the Genesis story of the Fall, Bonhoeffer relates how the eating of the forbidden fruit brings to man the knowledge of good and evil and thus makes him "like God," but at the same time against God. Man at his origin knows all things only in God and God in all things, but in knowing good and evil he falls away from the origin of God and conceives *himself* to be the origin. Man, who was made in the image of God, makes himself creator and judge, and henceforth his likeness to God is a stolen one. He is separated from the unifying, reconciling life in God, and is delivered over to death. He now lives in a world of conflicts because his life is now disunion with God, with men, with things, and with himself.

As a consequence of the Fall man's eyes are opened to his nakedness, i.e., to his disunion, and *shame* arises. "Shame," explains Bonhoeffer, " is man's ineffaceable recollection of his estrangement from the origin; it is grief for this estrangement, and the powerless longing to return to unity with the origin" (145). Unlike remorse, which arises when man feels he has been at fault, shame denotes a feeling that one lacks something, namely, the lost wholeness of life. In his shame man seeks to cover his nakedness by "making aprons," but this covering only confirms the disunion.

Whereas shame reminds man of his disunion with God and with other men, conscience presupposes this disunity and is a sign of man's disunion with himself. The call of conscience is always a prohibition, so that life is divided between what is permitted (the good) and what is prohibited (the evil). In contrast to shame, which embraces the whole of life, conscience reacts only to certain definite actions. It pretends to be the voice of God and thus the standard for the relation to other men, but it is actually *man's* judgment over God and other men and himself. All knowledge is now based upon the self-knowledge of the estranged man (which presupposes his possession of the knowledge of good and evil!), and thus all things are drawn into the process of disunion. Life is conflict and the judge is man.

Over against this world of conflict Bonhoeffer sets the world of recovered unity to which the New Testament witnesses:

Now anyone who reads the New Testament even superficially cannot but notice the complete absence of this world of disunion, conflict, and ethical problems. Not man's falling apart from God, from men, from things, and from himself, but rather the rediscovered unity, reconciliation, is now the basis of the discussion and the "point of decision of the specifically ethical experience." The life and activity of men is not all problematic or tormented or dark: it is self-evident, joyful, sure, and clear. (150)

The best Biblical example of this difference between the old and the new occurs in Jesus' encounters with the Pharisees. "The Pharisee," states Bonhoeffer, "is that extremely admirable man who subordinates his entire life to his knowledge of good and evil and is as severe a judge of himself as of his neighbor to the honor of God, whom he humbly thanks for this knowledge" (151). The Pharisees' questions arise from the world of conflict, i.e., from the disunion of the knowledge of good and evil, and Jesus' answers arise from unity with God, i.e., from the overcoming of the disunion of man with God. For that reason Jesus never allows himself to be drawn into one of their conflicts or decisions, but answers in such a way that he leaves the case of conflict behind him. In fact, the two parties speak on totally different levels. Jesus exhibits a remarkable freedom which consists not in the arbitrary choice of one among numerous possibilities, but "precisely in the complete simplicity of his action, which is never confronted by a plurality of possibilities, conflicts, or alternatives, but always only one thing. This one thing Jesus calls the will of God. . . . He lives and acts not by the knowledge of good and evil but by the will of God. There is only one will of God. In it the origin is recovered; in it there is established the freedom and the simplicity of all action" (154).

The new knowledge of reconciliation completely voids the knowledge of one's own goodness, for it is entirely transformed into action, without any reflection upon man's own self. This transformation in knowledge would be entirely misunderstood if it were regarded as psychologically observable data because the psychological view is itself always already subject to the law of disunion. "From the psychological standpoint," stresses Bonhoeffer, "the man who has become simple and free in the discipleship of Jesus can still be a man of very complicated reflection, just as, conversely, there is a psychological simplicity which has nothing whatever to do with the simplicity of life which is reconciled with God. Thus the Bible speaks of an entirely proper and necessary questioning with regard to the will of God and of an equally proper and necessary examination of oneself, without thereby coming into contradiction with the fact that those for whom the knowledge of good and evil is nullified are no longer confronted with a choice between many different possibilities, but always only with their own election to the simple performance of the one single will of God, and that for the disciples of Jesus there can no longer be any knowledge of their own goodness" (160 f.).

There must necessarily be a proving of the will of God, which may lie deeply concealed under a great number of available possibilities, and this involves one's heart, understanding, observation, and experience. "The will of God," explains the author, "is not a system of rules that is established from the outset; it is something new and different in each different situation in life, and for this reason a man must ever anew examine what the will of God may be" (161). This proving takes place solely on the basis of a "metamorphosis," namely, the overcoming of the form of the fallen man, Adam, and conformation with the form of the new man, Christ. It is based on the knowledge of God's will in Jesus Christ, which means that it implies living and increasing in love. Attention must be directed every day anew to Jesus Christ; any other supposed source of the knowledge of the will of God must be excluded. This proving presupposes one's unity with the origin which is regained in Christ, and yet it must seek to recover it anew in each concrete situation. In order to prove what is right in a given situation the whole apparatus of human powers must be called into action: intelligence, discernment, attentive observation of the given facts, all embraced and pervaded by prayer. All of this must be done in the belief that, if a man asks God humbly, God will give him certain knowledge of his will.

For the Christian there is not only a proving of the will of God, but also a proving of one's self. This consists in an examination of the self based not on the possibility of one's knowledge of good and evil and its realization in practical life, but on the possibility that Jesus Christ has entered one's life and now occupies the space that was previously occupied by one's knowledge of good and evil. " Christian self-proving," says Bonhoeffer, " is possible only on the basis of this foreknowledge that Jesus Christ is within us, and when this name is spoken in its entirety it is evident indeed that this is not some neutral concept but that it is the historical person Jesus. . . . Since he belongs to us, the question can and must certainly now arise, whether and how in our daily lives we belong to him, believe in him, and obey him " (165). But since we ourselves cannot answer this question, our self-examination will always consist precisely in our delivering ourselves up entirely to the judgment of Jesus Christ, but in so doing we will be doing the will of Christ in us.

Bonhoeffer has spoken of the simplicity of doing the will of God, and now he clarifies what the gospel intends when it speaks of "doing." He draws a clear distinction between self-justifying action, which is based upon one's own knowledge of good and evil, and action which is entirely bound up with Jesus Christ. He illuminates this distinction by introducing the irreconcilable opposite of action, namely, judgment. Judgment and action represent two mutually exclusive attitudes toward the law, for instance. One may view the law either as a criterion with which to judge others or as a summons to personal action which excludes any thought of judgment. The latter attitude, of course, marks the Christian, for whom not even the hearing of the law can be separated from its doing, because " a hearing which does not at the same instant become a doing becomes once again that 'knowing' which gives rise to judgment and so leads to the disruption of all action " (168).

In the final analysis, it is the word " love " which differentiates man in disunion and man in the origin. And what is love? None of our common human conceptions will do, declares Bonhoeffer. The Bible has one answer: *God* is love. To know God is to know what love is, and God is known only in his self-revelation in Jesus Christ. These thoughts are elaborated thusly:

Love, therefore, is the name for what God does to man in overcoming the disunion in which man lives. This deed of God is Jesus Christ, is reconciliation. And so love is something that happens to man, something passive, something over which he does not himself dispose, simply because it lies beyond his existence in disunion. Love means the undergoing of the transformation of one's entire existence by God; it means being drawn into the world as it lives and must live before God and in God. Love, therefore, is not man's choice, but it is the election of man by God. (175)

Love as a human activity is willing acceptance of God's election and his engendering in Christ. It is passive, not in a psychological but in a theological sense. Passivity does not exclude the thoughts and actions of man. " It is as whole men," states Bonhoeffer, " as men who think and who act, that we are loved by God and reconciled with God in Christ. And it is as whole men, who think and who act, that we love God and our brothers " (176).

The next section of the *Ethics* concerns " The Church and the World," and what is said here is greatly affected by the experience of the Evangelical Church in Nazi Germany. At the time this was written, when the church was undergoing severe oppression and was consequently displaying the cardinal principles of Christian belief in their hardest and most uncompromising form, an astounding thing happened. In the face of Nazi irrationalism and barbarism the defenders of such human values as reason, culture, humanity, tolerance, and self-determination, all of which concepts had heretofore been used as battle slogans against the church and Christianity, sought refuge within the sphere of the Christian church! " The children of the church, who had become independent and gone their own ways," observes Bonhoeffer, " now in the hour of danger returned to their mother " (178). They returned to their origin, to Jesus Christ, who alone has force and permanence vis-à-vis the antichrist. He alone is the center and strength not only of the Bible and the church and theology, but also of humanity, reason, justice, and culture.

This remarkable phenomenon illustrates for Bonhoeffer the total and the exclusive claim of Christ. The two sayings of Jesus: " He that is not with me is against me " and " He that is not against us is for us," which for abstract analysis are in irreconcilable contradiction, necessarily belong together in reality. That is, the more strongly the church demands exclusive adherence to Jesus Christ and confesses him as the Lord, the more fully the wide range of his dominion is disclosed to it. It is the persecution of lawfulness, truth, humanity, and freedom that has impelled men to seek the protection of Jesus Christ and has taught the church the wide extent of its responsibility. Bonhoeffer explains further:

The relationship of the church with the world today does not consist, as it did in the Middle Ages, in the calm and steady expansion of the power of the name of Christ, nor yet in an endeavor, such as was undertaken by the apologists of the first centuries of Christianity, to justify and publicize and embellish the name of Jesus Christ before the world by associating it with human names and values, but solely in that recognition of the origin which has been awakened and vouchsafed to men in this suffering, solely in the seeking of refuge from persecution in Christ. It is not Christ who must justify himself before the world by the acknowledgment of the values of justice, truth, and freedom, but it is these values which have come to need justification, and their justification can only be Jesus Christ. It is not that a " Christian culture " must make the name of Jesus Christ acceptable to the world; but the crucified Christ has become the refuge and the justification, the protection and the claim for the higher values and their defenders that have fallen victim to suffering. (180 f.)

The total claim of Christ means that both the wicked and the good belong to him. Even though before him both are sinners, who in their wickedness and in their goodness have fallen away from the origin, there is no denying the distinction between the two in our experience. Bonhoeffer is convinced that the church today must take with utter seriousness the question of the relation of the good man to Christ. Up until now it has concentrated almost exclusively on Jesus' relation to the wicked and to wickedness, and has considered the good man either as a hypocrite who needed to be convinced of his wickedness or as a converted sinner who was now enabled to do good works. To be sure, the concept of the good must be taken in its widest sense, but with this in mind it deserves the closest attention. Otherwise it is all too easy for the gospel of the sinner to become a commendation of sin.

Bonhoeffer now begins a section entitled " History and Good." He asserts that the question of good is ultimately connected with the fact

THEOLOGICAL FRAGMENTATION 231

that we are alive and therefore can never be meaningful as an abstract question. " The question of good is posed and decided in the midst of each definite, yet unconcluded, unique and transient situation of our lives, in the midst of our living relationships with men, things, institutions, and powers, in other words, in the midst of our historical existence. The question of good cannot now be separated from the question of life, the question of history " (185). This means that we have definitely abandoned the kind of ethical thought that is " largely dominated by the abstract notion of an isolated individual man who applies the absolute criterion of a good which is good in itself and has to make his decision incessantly and exclusively between this clearly recognized good and an equally clearly recognized evil " (185). This sort of ethical theory, which considers its task to be the realization of certain defined principles, never really comes to grips with life.

But what is life? Jesus said, " I am the life," and this declaration precludes any possibility of defining life in itself. Life is not a thing, an entity, or a concept, but a particular and unique person. Life is the " I " of Jesus; he is my life, our life. This is the revelation, the proclamation of Jesus Christ, that our life is outside ourselves and in him. " When we hear it," says the author, " we recognize that we have fallen away from life, from our life, and that we are living in contradiction to life, to our life. In this saying of Jesus, therefore, we hear the condemnation, the negation, of our life; for our life is not life; or, if it is life, it is life only by virtue of the fact that, even though in contradiction to it, we still live through the life which is called Jesus Christ, the origin, the essence, and the goal of all life and of our life " (189). The negation, the " no " to our apostate life, brings us to the end, to death, but precisely in this bringing the " no " becomes a mysterious " yes," the affirmation of the new life in Christ. We live now in tension between the " no " and the " yes," and only in this tension do we recognize Christ as our life. " It is the ' yes ' of creation, atonement, and redemption, and the ' no ' of the condemnation and death of the life which has fallen away from its origin, its essence, and its goal. But no one who knows Christ can hear the ' yes ' without the ' no ' or the ' no ' without the ' yes ' " (190). What Bonhoeffer means becomes clearer with these words of explanation:

It is the "yes" to what is created, to becoming and to growth, to the flower and to the fruit, to health, happiness, ability, achievement, worth, success, greatness, and honor; in short, it is the "yes" to the development of the power of life. And it is the "no" to that defection from the origin, the essence, and the goal of life which is inherent in all this existence from the outset. This "no" means dying, suffering, poverty, renunciation, resignation, humility, degradation, self-denial, and in this again it already implies the "yes" to the new life, a life which does not fall apart into a juxtaposition of "yes" and "no," a life in which there is not to be found, for example, an unrestrained expansion of vitality side by side with a wholly separate ascetic and spiritual attitude, or "creaturely" conduct side by side with "Christian" conduct. If that were so, the "yes" and the "no" would lose their unity in Jesus Christ, but this new life is one in Jesus Christ; it is in tension between the "yes" and the "no" in the sense that in every "yes" the "no" is already heard and in every "no" there is heard also the "yes." Development of the vital force and self-denial, growing and dying, health and suffering, happiness and renunciation, achievement and humility, honor and self-abasement, all these belong together in irreconcilable contradiction and yet in living unity. (190)

Returning to the question of good, Bonhoeffer asserts that good is not a quality of life, but is life itself, life as it is in reality, life in the sense of the saying " Christ is my life " (Phil. 1:21). This life assumes concrete form in the contradictory unity of " yes " and " no," which life finds outside itself in Jesus Christ, but because Jesus Christ is both man and God in one, humanity and God have thereby become integrally related to one another for eternity. The author explains what this means in this way:

Henceforward man cannot be conceived and known otherwise than in Jesus Christ, and God cannot be conceived and known otherwise than in the human form of Jesus Christ. . . . Man is the man who was accepted in the incarnation of Christ, who was loved, condemned, and reconciled in Christ; and God is God become man. There is no relation to men without a relation to God, and no relation to God without a relation to men, and it is only our relation to Jesus Christ which provides the basis for our relation to men and to God. Jesus Christ is our life, and so now, from the standpoint of Jesus Christ, we may say that our fellow man is our life and that God is our life. This means, of course, that our encounter with our fellow men and our encounter with God are subject to the same "yes" and "no" as is our encounter with Jesus Christ. We "live" when, in our encounter with men and with God, the "yes" and the "no" are combined in a unity of contradiction, a selfless self-assertion, in self-assertion in the sacrifice of ourselves to God and to men. We live by responding to the word of God which is addressed to us in Jesus Christ. Since this word is addressed to our entire life, the response, too, can only be an entire one. (192)

The term that Bonhoeffer chooses to characterize our response to the life of Jesus Christ as the "yes" and "no" to our life is "responsibility." Responsibility in this context involves the total and unified response of one's whole life, so that one's action becomes a matter of life and death. It means to confess Jesus Christ not only with one's life but also with one's lips. It is "a verbal response given at the risk of a man's life to the question asked by another man with regard to the event of Christ" (193). In answering, one stands for Christ before men and for men before Christ.

This brings the author to an exposition of the *structure of responsible life,* which he says is conditioned by two facts: first, that life is bound to man and to God, and, secondly, that a man's own life is free. Without this obligatory bond and without freedom there is no responsibility. "The obligation," states Bonhoeffer, "assumes the form of deputyship (*Stellvertretung*) and of correspondence with reality (*Wirklichkeitsgemässheit*); freedom displays itself in the self-examination of life and of action and in the venture of a concrete decision" (194).

Deputyship may be illustrated by reference to a father, who acts and works and cares and intercedes for his children. He is obliged to act in their place and thus unavoidably assumes the role of their deputy or representative. No man, as a matter of fact, can avoid deputyship, for even an isolated individual is a deputy for his own self, and that means for mankind in general. However, the full meaning of deputyship is revealed to us only in the life of Jesus Christ, who lived and acted and suffered death for all men. Deputyship consists in a total surrender of one's own life to the other man; it demands a selflessness in which the divine "yes" and "no" become one. It eschews an absolutizing of one's own ego or of the other man, either of which would deny the origin, essence, and goal of responsible life in Jesus Christ.

Another of the decisive requirements of the responsible life is that it correspond with reality. This means that responsible conduct does not arise from some pre-established principle which enjoys absolute validity on any occasion, but from the given situation itself. That is, it is in the given situation that the responsible man sees what he must grasp and do. Nevertheless, this does not imply that either servility or opposition toward the factual should determine action. " In action which is genuinely in accordance with reality," emphasizes Bonhoeffer, " there is an indissoluble link between the acknowledgment and the contradiction of the factual. The reason for this is that reality is first and last not lifeless; but it is the real man, the incarnate God . . . God became man; he accepted man in the body and therefore reconciled the world of man with God. . . . It is from this action of God, from the real man, from Jesus Christ, that reality now receives its " yes " and " no," its right and its limitations. Affirmation and contradiction are now conjoined in the concrete action of him who has recognized the real man " (198 f.).

From this, Bonhoeffer draws the conclusion that action which is in accordance with Christ is action which is in accordance with reality, and it is so because it allows the world to be the world, never forgetting, of course, that in Jesus Christ the world is loved, condemned, and reconciled by God. It would be wrong to oppose a " Christian principle " to a " secular principle," thus identifying ultimate reality with a multiplicity of irreconcilably contradictory laws; likewise, we should not regard the Christian and the secular as in principle forming a unity. " The reconciliation which is accomplished in Christ between God and the world," Bonhoeffer reminds us, " consists simply and solely in the person of Jesus Christ; it consists in him as the one who acts in the responsibility of deputyship, as the God who for love of man has become man. From him alone there proceeds human action which is not worn away and wasted in conflicts of principle but which springs from the accomplishment of the reconciliation of the world with God, an action which soberly and simply performs what is in accordance with reality, an action of responsibility in deputyship " (201 f.).

Because the world is the sphere of concrete responsibility which is given to us in and through Jesus Christ, it follows that man must live and act in *limited* responsibility and thereby allow the world ever anew to disclose its essential character to him. Responsible action is limited, first of all, by our creatureliness, and secondly, by our recognition of the responsibility of the other man. We are not the creators of the conditions under which we must act, nor can we disregard the fact that our neighbor is also a responsible agent. Our responsibility is neither infinite nor absolute, but always stands under the ultimate judgment and grace of God and within the boundary drawn by our neighbor's own responsibility. Surprisingly enough, however, it is precisely this limitation which makes our action a responsible one. " God and our neighbor, as they confront us in Jesus Christ, are not only the limit, but, as we have already perceived, they are also the origin of responsible action. Irresponsible action may be defined precisely by saying that it disregards this limit, God and our neighbor. Responsible action derives its unity, and ultimately also its certainty, from the fact that it is limited in this way by God and by our neighbor. It is precisely because it is not its own master, because it is not unlimited and arrogant but creaturely and humble, that it can be sustained by an ultimate joy and confidence, and that it can know that it is secure in its origin, its essence, and its goal, in Christ " (204 f.).

Thus far Bonhoeffer has spoken of man's responsibility to other persons, and now he turns to the impersonal realm of things. The relation between responsible man and things he calls " pertinence " ("*Sachgemässheit*"), and from this he draws two implications: first, " that attitude to things is pertinent which keeps in view their original, essential, and purposive relation to God and to men " (205); secondly, " from its origin there is inherent in every thing its own law of being (*Wesensgesetz*), no matter whether this thing is a natural object or a product of the human mind, and no matter whether it is a material or an ideal entity " (206). The former means that selfless service to man must be the goal of devotion to things or causes, and the latter requires the detection and pursuit of the particular inherent laws by which things (whether neutral or personal entities) exist.

The pursuit of the law of being, whether it be that of mathematics or of the state or of a factory, requires the mastery of a formal technique, but Bonhoeffer points out that the more involved the thing is with human existence, the clearer it becomes that the law of its being does not consist entirely in a formal technique. That is, there comes a time in historical life when the exact observance of a formal law comes into conflict with the ineluctable necessities of the lives of men, and in such a case of extreme necessity the responsible man is faced with the question of *ultima ratio,* i.e., an action that lies beyond the laws of reason. Such an abnormal situation calls forth the free venture that renounces every law and openly admits the violation of law. Yet exactly in this breaking of the law the validity of the law is acknowledged and one's action is entrusted unreservedly to the divine governance of history.

It now becomes evident that the structure of the responsible life includes both freedom and readiness to accept guilt, but only on the ground of selfless love for another man. "Jesus," explains Bonhoeffer, " took upon himself the guilt of all men, and for that reason every man who acts responsibly becomes guilty. . . . Through Jesus Christ it becomes an essential part of responsible action that the man who is without sin loves selflessly and for that reason incurs guilt " (210). All this, of course, can be called into question by those who invoke the authority of *conscience.* After all, they argue, no responsibility should oblige a man to act against his conscience, and therefore it is unthinkable to incur guilt for the sake of another man. Bonhoeffer agrees that it is inadvisable to act against one's conscience, but what does this mean?

Conscience comes as an indictment of one's loss of unity with his own self. It is primarily directed not toward a particular kind of doing but toward a particular mode of being, and it protests against any doing which imperils the unity of this being with itself. But what constitutes this unity? " The first constituent," asserts Bonhoeffer, " is the man's own ego in its claim to be ' like God,' *sicut deus,* in the knowledge of good and evil. The call of conscience in natural man is the attempt on the part of the ego to justify itself in its knowledge of good and evil before God, before men, and before itself, and to secure its own continuance in this self-justification.

Finding no support in its own contingent individuality, the ego traces its own derivation back to a universal law of good and seeks to achieve unity with itself in conformity with this law " (211 f.). In contrast with this pseudo unity, which consists in the autonomy of the natural man, the man of faith miraculously finds unity beyond his own ego and its law in Jesus Christ. True unity can never be realized by the return to an autonomy derived from the law, but only in fellowship with Jesus Christ, only in the surrender of the ego to God and to men.

It is Jesus Christ, who broke the law for the sake of God and of men, who sets conscience free for the service of God and of the neighbor. This is especially true when one responsibly enters into the fellowship of human guilt, for in an indirect way such human action shares in the action of Jesus Christ in bearing guilt for the sake of all men. Even though conscience and responsibility unite in this manner, however, the two continue to confront each other in a relation of irreducible tension. In the first place, there is a limit to the amount of guilt that conscience will permit a person to carry without breaking under the weight; care should be taken that the pursuit of responsible action does not lead to the destruction of a man's unity with himself. Furthermore, the conscience that is liberated by Christ must still reckon with the law of life, which is known, at least in a distorted and perverted way, by the natural conscience; thus there arises a conflict between concrete responsibility for the sake of Christ and a conscience that warns against the transgression of the law of life. In this situation ultimate unity can be gained only by a free decision for Christ, who is not only the foundation, essence, and goal of concrete responsibility, but also Lord of the conscience. Bonhoeffer concludes: " Thus responsibility is bound by conscience, but conscience is set free by responsibility " (216).

The author concludes his analysis of the structure of responsible life with a discussion of freedom. He begins with these assertions: " Responsibility and freedom are corresponding concepts. Factually, though not chronologically, responsibility presupposes freedom and freedom can consist only in responsibility. Responsibility is the freedom of men which is given only in the obligation to God and to our neighbor " (216 f.). The man who acts responsibly must act in the freedom of his own self. With all due consideration for the given conditions and for principles involved, a man must, in the final analysis, decide and act for himself. There is nothing that can answer for him, no law to which he can appeal and be exculpated; otherwise he would not be free. The action of the responsible man," says Bonhoeffer, " is performed in the obligation which alone gives freedom and which gives entire freedom, the obligation to God and to our neighbor as they confront us in Jesus Christ. At the same time it is performed wholly within the domain of relativity, wholly in the twilight which the historical situation spreads over good and evil " (217). For this reason it is exactly the free man who ultimately commits his action to the guidance of God; freely abandoning the knowledge of his own good, he performs the good of God.

But what is the relationship between free responsibility and obedience? Is the former category applicable only to those who have some " responsible position " in life and the latter to the common man who lives in an unexciting workaday world? Are there two ethics, one for the great and the strong, for the rulers, and another for the small and the weak, the subordinates? While recognizing the measure of truth implied in these questions, Bonhoeffer repudiates the point of view. " Even when free responsibility is more or less excluded from a man's vocational and public life, he nevertheless always stands in a responsible relation to other men; these relations extend from his family to his workmates. The fulfillment of genuine responsibility at this point affords the only sound possibility of extending the sphere of responsibility once more into vocational and public life " (219). As a matter of fact, in the concrete situation it is really impossible to distinguish where obedience leaves off and responsibility begins, because obedience is rendered in responsibility. There is an undeniable tension between obedience and freedom; *both* are realized when the responsible man delivers up himself and his deed to God.

Now that the author has spoken of the structure of the responsible life, he proceeds to a consideration of the place of responsibility. What is the locus and what are the limits of responsible activity? Here the discussion centers around the concept of " the calling " or " vocation." It is Bonhoeffer's belief that the New Testament concept of the calling has nothing to do with Max Weber's definition in terms of a " limited field of accomplishments " or with the pseudo-Lutheran view which simply provides the justification and sanctification of secular institutions; instead, it concerns the gracious calling of God to live in the fellowship of Jesus Christ. It is the call to discipleship, and God himself designates the place of responsibility. Man does not seek out grace in its own place, but it is grace that seeks and finds man in *his* place, a place, to be sure, which is laden with sin and guilt, no matter whether it is a royal throne or a miserable hovel, and regardless of whether the person is Jew or Gentile, free man or slave, man or woman, married or single. "This visitation of man by grace," asserts Bonhoeffer, " occurred in the incarnation of Jesus Christ, and it occurs in the word of Jesus Christ which is brought by the Holy Ghost " (223). Only through this call can one live a life justified before God. " From the standpoint of Christ," continues the author, " this life is now my calling; from my own standpoint it is my responsibility " (223).

Bonhoeffer points out two misunderstandings of the calling which are prominent in the history of the church. It was the misunderstanding of secular Protestantism to identify the calling with the loyal discharge of worldly obligations, whereas the misunderstanding of medieval monasticism involved the attempt to find a place withdrawn from the world where the call could be answered more appropriately. In the light of the New Testament, monasticism fails to understand either God's " no " to the entire world, including the monastery, or his reconciling " yes "; on the other hand, pseudo-Lutheranism fails to recognize that God's " yes " to the world includes at the same time an extremely emphatic " no." Neither realizes that Jesus Christ calls man to unite in concrete responsibility the " yes " and the " no " to life in the world. Bonhoeffer illustrates what he means by referring to Luther: " Luther's return from the monastery to the world, to the ' calling,' is, in the true New Testament sense, the fiercest attack and assault to be launched against the world since primitive Christianity. Now a man takes up his position against the world *in* the world; the calling is the place at which the call of Christ is answered, the place at which a man lives responsibly. Thus the task which is appointed for me in my calling is a limited one, but at the same time the responsibility to the call of Jesus Christ breaks through all limits " (223 f.).

In a final section on " The ' Ethical ' and the ' Christian ' as a

Theme," Bonhoeffer begins with a consideration of the *warrant* for ethical discourse. Against the moralist, who so blithely treats the " ethical " and the " Christian " as a theme, he states: " We cannot, in fact, even set foot in the field of Christian ethics until we have first of all recognized how extremely questionable a course we are pursuing if we take the ' ethical ' and the ' Christian ' as a theme for our consideration or discussion or even as a subject for scientific exposition " (231). The " ethical " as a theme is bound to a definite time and a definite place, namely, the sphere of everyday happenings, and here general moral principles prove to be completely inadequate and unfitting. Bonhoeffer elaborates his meaning in these words:

That is so because man is a living and mortal creature in a finite and destructible world and because he is not essentially or exclusively a student of ethics. It is one of the great naïvetés, or, more exactly, one of the great follies, of the moralists that they deliberately overlook this fact and start out from the fiction that at every moment of his life man has to make a final and infinite choice, the fiction that every moment of life involves a conscious decision between good and evil. They seem to imagine that every human action has had a clearly lettered notice attached to it by some divine police authority, a notice which reads either " permitted " or " forbidden." They assume that a man must continually be doing something decisive, fulfilling some higher purpose and discharging some ultimate duty. This represents a failure to understand that in historical human existence everything has its time (Eccl., ch. 3), eating, drinking, and sleeping as well as deliberate resolve and action, rest as well as work, purposelessness as well as the fulfillment of purpose, inclination as well as duty, play as well as earnest endeavor, joy as well as renunciation. Their presumptuous misjudgment of this creaturely existence leads either to the most mendacious hypocrisy or else to madness. It turns the moralist into a dangerous tormentor, tyrant, and clown, a figure of tragicomedy. (232 f.)

The so-called " ethical phenomenon " most assuredly has its place in the life of man, but it would be destructive of the creaturely wholeness of life to raise the experience of obligation to the level of an exclusive and all-embracing claim. " To confine the ethical phenomenon to its proper place and time is not to invalidate it," explains Bonhoeffer; " it is, on the contrary, to render it fully operative. Big guns are not the right weapons for shooting sparrows " (233).

In respect to the normal daily life and activity of a community or an individual, where morality simply " goes without saying," the ethical phenomenon is strictly a peripheral event. It comes into play only when fellowship is disrupted or organization is endangered, and as soon as order is restored it becomes dormant. The occasions when the ethical is made a theme of discussion purify and restore the human community and are necessary for it, but they must be followed by times when man's activity lies not merely on the periphery but in the center and in the fullness of everyday life. Otherwise the ethical phenomenon, which brings into play " shall " or " should " as an " ultimate " word, all too easily loses its quality as an ultimate and becomes a penultimate, a pedagogical method.

In terms of what he has said thus far, Bonhoeffer now tries to define an ethic and an ethicist. He first declares what they cannot be:

An ethic cannot be a book in which there is set out how everything in the world actually ought to be but unfortunately is not, and an ethicist cannot be a man who always knows better than others what is to be done and how it is to be done. An ethic cannot be a work of reference for moral action which is guaranteed to be unexceptionable, and the ethicist cannot be the competent critic and judge of every human activity. An ethic cannot be a retort in which ethical or Christian human beings are produced, and the ethicist cannot be the embodiment or ideal type of a life which is, on principle, moral. (236)

Then he moves to some positive characteristics:

Ethics and ethicists do not intervene continuously in life. They draw attention to the disturbance and interruption of life by the " shall " and the " should " which impinge on all life from its periphery. Ethics and ethicists do not wish to represent goodness as such, that is to say, as an end in itself, but, precisely by speaking strictly from the standpoint of the " ethical," from the standpoint of the peripheral event of " shall " and " should," they wish to help people to learn to share in life, to share in life within the limits of the obligation of " shall " and " should," and not hold themselves aloof from the processes of life as spectators, critics, and judges; to share in life not out of the motive of " shall " and " should," but from the full abundance of vital motives, from the natural and the organic, and from free acceptance and will, not in humorless hostility toward every vital force and toward every weakness and disorder . . . , to share in life . . . in the abundant fullness of the concrete tasks and processes of life with all their infinite multiplicity of different motives. (236 f.)

The author next approaches the problem of the warrant (*Ermächtigung*) for ethical discourse. He cites the familiar phenomenon that correct words from the mouth of an immature youth do not carry equal authority with the same words uttered by an experienced and mature man. That is, in ethical discourse it is not only what is said that matters, but also who says it. No one can win for himself the warrant for ethical discourse; it is rather assigned to him, primarily on the basis of the position or office he holds. " Thus the authorization for ethical discourse is conferred upon the old man and not upon the young one, upon the father and not the child, the master and not the servant, the teacher and not the pupil, the judge and not the accused, the ruler and not the subject, the preacher and not the parishioner " (239). In other words, inherent and essential in the ethical is a disparity between the superior and inferior, an objective subordination of the lower to the higher. The ethical implies a definite structure of human society, certain concrete sociological relations which involve authority.

Again, authority can be grounded neither in abstract propositions or timeless and placeless systems, nor in the given itself. Neither an empirical positivism, which bases its warrant on reality as it is given, nor a metaphysical or religious positivism, which constructs a system of orders and values on the basis of philosophical or religious criteria, provides an adequate warrant for ethical discourse. Both represent attempts to ground authority from below.

For Bonhoeffer there is only one warrant for ethical discourse, only one possible object of a " Christian ethic," an object which lies beyond the " ethical," namely, *the commandment of God.* " The commandment of God," he asserts, " is the total and concrete claim laid to man by the merciful and holy God in Jesus Christ " (244). It is not an abstract principle or a timeless truth, but in both form and content it is the concrete speech of God to the concrete man at a particular time and in a specific place. " If God's commandment is not clear, definite, and concrete to the last detail, then it is not God's commandment " (245). Its concreteness consists in its historicity, which means that it is always heard in a definite historical form. And what is this form? Bonhoeffer answers: "God's commandment, which is manifested in Jesus Christ, comes to us in the church, in the family, in labor, and in government" (245).

Even though the commandment of God comes to us in these various historical forms, however, Bonhoeffer insists that God's commandment is and always remains that which is revealed in Jesus Christ. It does not spring from the created world, but comes down from above and establishes on earth an inviolable superiority and inferiority. In establishing the superiority it confers the warrant for ethical discourse, or, more comprehensively, the warrant to proclaim the divine commandment. Since God's commandment is the commandment that is revealed in Christ, neither the church nor the family nor labor nor government can claim to speak with absolute authority or to identify itself with the commandment of God. Only in conjunction and collaboration with one another do they give effect to that commandment.

Bonhoeffer elucidates his concept of the commandment of God by contrasting it with the ethical:

> God's commandment, revealed in Jesus Christ, embraces the whole of life. It does not only, like the ethical, keep watch on the untransgressible frontier of life, but it is at the same time the center and the fullness of life. It is not only obligation but also permission. It does not only forbid, but it also sets free for life; it sets free for unreflected doing. It does not only interrupt the process of life when this process goes astray, but it guides and conducts this process even though there is not always need for consciousness of this fact. . . . The commandment of God becomes the element in which one lives without always being conscious of it, and thus it implies freedom of movement and of action, freedom from the fear of decision, freedom from fear to act; it implies certainty, quietude, confidence, balance, and peace. I honor my parents, I am faithful in marriage, I respect the lives and property of others, not because at the frontiers of my life there is a threatening "thou shalt not," but because I accept as holy institutions of God these realities, parents, marriage, life, and property, which confront me in the midst and in the fullness of life. (247)

Bonhoeffer defines the commandment of God as "the permission to live as man before God" (248). In contrast to all human laws it commands freedom, and precisely in the overcoming of this contradiction it manifests itself to be God's commandment. Freedom is its true object, not that God now allows man a realm in which he can act according to his own choice, but that freedom derives solely from the commandment itself, i.e., from God's permission! No longer does man always stand like Hercules at the crossroads, no longer is he tormented by the hopeless question of his motives, no longer does he wear himself out trying to make the right decision. " He can now have the right decision really behind him, and not always before him " (250). The commandment of God fully takes into account the darkness that veils the roots of human life and action, the interconnection of activity and passivity, the conscious and the unconscious, but it is precisely by taking advantage of the divine permission that light comes to man from above and allows him to live as a man before God.

It is now evident that for Bonhoeffer the " ethical " and the " commandment of God " occupy entirely different positions relative to the life of man. The ethical impinges upon life from its periphery, whereas God's commandment embraces the center and fullness of life. The ethical defines the boundary with a " thou shalt not "; the commandment of God renders possible a positive " sharing in life." The ethical is encompassed by the commandment, but the opposite of this proposition is never true. And in a like manner, if the philosophical notion of the " ethical " is replaced by the Biblical concept of the " law," it follows that the commandment of God and the law are inseparably linked together, but that the law is comprised within the commandment, arises from it, and must be understood by reference to it.

The author now begins a subsection on " The Concrete Commandment and the Divine Mandates." He first defines the concept of the mandate and then turns to a discussion of the various mandates, namely, the church, marriage and the family, labor (or culture), and government. Unfortunately, his work was interrupted, and he never reached his interpretation of the latter three mandates.[21]

"By the term ' mandate,' " he explains, " we understand the con-

---

[21] Bonhoeffer's thought about these mandates, especially the mandate of government, is available to a limited extent in his essay on " State and Church" in Part Two of the *Ethics*.

crete divine commission which has its foundation in the revelation of Christ and which is evidenced by Scripture; it is the legitimation and warrant for the execution of a definite divine commandment, the conferment of divine authority on an earthly agent. The term ' mandate' must also be taken to imply the claiming, the seizure, and the formation of a definite earthly domain by the divine commandment. The bearer of the mandate acts as a deputy in the place of Him who assigns him his commission " (254). Bonhoeffer prefers the term " mandate " to that of " order " or " institution " or " estate " or " office " because these notions no longer connote their pristine meaning, namely, that they are *divine* commissions and in no sense the products of history. Because this commission comes from above, i.e., from God, an unalterable relation of superiority and inferiority is established in the sphere of the mandate. This relation is not to be confused with an earthly relation of superior and inferior power, however, because the superior derives its authority solely from above. Furthermore, this superiority established by any one of the mandates has several limitations. It is limited by God, by the relation of inferiority, and by the other mandates. The latter limitation is explained in this way:

The mandates are *conjoined;* otherwise they are not mandates of God. In their conjunction they are not isolated or separated from one another, but they are directed toward one another. They are " for " one another; otherwise they are not God's mandates. Moreover, within this relation of mutual support this limitation is necessarily experienced as a relation of mutual opposition. Wherever this mutual opposition no longer exists there is no longer a mandate of God. (257)

Now what of the mandate of the church? This, says Bonhoeffer, is the word of God, the proclamation of the revelation of God in Jesus Christ. The commandment of God in the church confronts men in both a public and a private way, namely, in the preaching of the word and in the confession or ecclesiastical discipline. Both forms of the commandment must go together. If preaching is emphasized and the confession or discipline neglected, then the commandment becomes devoid of any concrete claim (the situation in Protestantism!); if the confession is emphasized and the preaching neglected, a legalistic casuistry will result (the situation in Roman Catholicism!).

The word of God proclaimed in the church establishes a clear relationship of superiority (the office of proclamation) and inferiority (the listening congregation). The preacher stands before the congregation in the place of God and of Jesus Christ. His office is instituted by Jesus Christ himself. "It is established *in* the congregation and not *by* the congregation, and at the same time it is *with* the congregation" (259). The bearer of the spiritual office is both preacher and pastor of the flock, with authority to teach, to admonish and to comfort, to forgive sin, but also to retain sin. The congregation responds to the proclamation of the word of God in faith and service.

The office of proclamation, of course, is inseparably bound up with Holy Scripture. "At this point," says Bonhoeffer, "we must venture to advance the proposition that Scripture is essentially the property of the office of preaching and that it is the preaching which properly belongs to the congregation. Scripture requires to be interpreted and preached" (260). Or again: "The book of homilies and the prayer book are the principal books for the congregation; the Holy Scripture is the book for the preacher" (261). This by no means implies that the Bible should be withheld from the laity, of course. Bonhoeffer merely wants to emphasize the essential and primary relation of the Scripture to the office of proclamation.

On the basis of Holy Scripture the preacher proclaims the same message for both believers and unbelievers: Jesus Christ as the Lord and Savior of the world. Likewise he proclaims one and the same commandment for both the Christian congregation and the world, the one commandment of God revealed in Jesus Christ. "The church proclaims the commandment by testifying to Jesus Christ as the Lord and Savior of his people and of the whole world, and so by summoning all men to fellowship with him" (262). That Jesus Christ is *the eternal Son* means that no created thing can be conceived or understood apart from Christ, the Mediator of creation. That Jesus Christ is *the incarnate God* means that God has taken upon himself bodily all human being, that henceforth divine being cannot be found otherwise than in human form, that in Jesus Christ man is made free to be really man before God, that God does not wish to exist for himself but "for us." That Jesus Christ is *the crucified Reconciler* means that all the world has become godless in its rejection of Christ, that it is precisely this godless world which has been reconciled to God, that only through the proclamation of Christ crucified is a life in genuine worldliness possible. That Jesus Christ is *the risen and ascended Lord* means that he has overcome sin and death, that he is the living Lord to whom all power is given in heaven and on earth, that all the powers of the world are made subject to him and must serve him, that his commandment sets creation free for the fulfillment of the law which is its own, namely, the law which is inherent in it by virtue of its having its origin, its goal, and its essence in Jesus Christ.

At this point Bonhoeffer must introduce the notion of the church, for the name Jesus Christ does not only designate an individual man, but mysteriously embraces at the same time the whole of human nature. In Jesus Christ is the new humanity, the congregation of God, so that through him the word of God and the congregation of God are inseparately united. The word of God dominates and rules the whole world; in contrast, the congregation does not dominate but serves the world, stands as a deputy for the world. The church has its own "law," and this can never become the law of the worldly order, just as the law of the worldly order can never become the law of the church. Yet both are subject to the Lordship of Christ.

The church as a self-contained community fulfills its mandate of proclamation by being at the same time a *means to an end* and an *end in itself*. That is, it organizes itself to be an effective instrument for the proclamation of Christ, and exactly in this action on behalf of the world its purpose is achieved: the congregation has become the goal and the center of all God's dealing with the world. " The concept of deputyship characterizes this twofold relationship most clearly," concludes Bonhoeffer. "The Christian congregation stands at the point at which the whole world ought to be standing; to this extent it serves as deputy for the world and exists for the sake of the world. On the other hand, the world achieves its own fulfillment at the point at which the congregation stands. The earth is the ' new creation,' the ' new creature,' the goal of the ways of God on earth. The congregation stands in this twofold relation of deputyship entirely in the fellowship and discipleship of its Lord, who was Christ precisely in this, that he existed not for his own sake but wholly for the sake of the world " (266).[22]

2. "Prisoner for God"[23]

During his imprisonment at Tegel Prison in Berlin, Dietrich Bonhoeffer had a great deal of time for reading and study and thought, and he was more and more forced back upon basic questions. What is Christianity, or even who is Christ, for us today — really? What do I myself believe — really? How can Christ become the Lord even of the nonreligious world? To those who have followed the development of Bonhoeffer's thought to this point, his answers to these questions will not be too surprising. To those who have not, they may seem startling. In any case, Bonhoeffer's message is extremely provocative and challenging.

It is Dietrich Bonhoeffer's conviction that our world has " come of age," by which he means that the time of " religion " is over. " The time when men could be told everything by means of words, whether theological or simply pious, is over," he remarks, " and so is the time of inwardness and conscience, which is to say the time of religion as such " (122). We stand near the completion of a long development toward the autonomy of man and the world, and we are moving

---

[22] The writer does not think it necessary to condense the five essays which comprise Part Two of the *Ethics*, since they were written by Bonhoeffer on various occasions and were not intended as an integral part of the book. However, the importance of these essays in shedding more light upon specific areas of Bonhoeffer's thought is fully appreciated, and the omission is due solely to the writer's conviction that the essays agree with and add nothing essentially new to the thoughts developed in Part One. The titles of the essays are as follows: " The Doctrine of the *Primus Usus Legis* according to the Lutheran Symbolic Writings "; " Personal and 'Real' Ethos "; " State and Church "; " On the Possibility of the Word of the Church to the World "; " What Is Meant by 'Telling the Truth'? "

[23] Unless otherwise specified, quotations will be cited from the English translation of Reginald H. Fuller, which was published in England under the title *Letters and Papers from Prison* (S.C.M. Press, Ltd., London, 1953), and in America as *Prisoner for God* (The Macmillan Company, 1954; used by permission of the publisher). Except for occasional alterations the following summary of Bonhoeffer's thought in his letters and papers from prison is taken from the writer's essay entitled " Theology from a Prison Cell," which appeared in *The Drew Gateway*, Vol. XXVIII, No. 3, Spring, 1957, pp. 139–154.

rapidly into a time of radical religionlessness. Beginning as early as the secular impulses of the thirteenth century, man has more and more been able to answer his important questions without recourse to God as a " working hypothesis." As the frontiers of knowledge have gradually been pushed back, what we call " God " has been losing more and more ground. Man has discovered the laws that govern the world's existence, laws that would be valid, *etsi deus non daretur,* though there were no God — to use a phrase from Hugo Grotius. That " God " has become superfluous as an answer to questions in the fields of science, art, politics, and even ethics, is hardly debatable today, and Bonhoeffer believes this is becoming increasingly true of religious questions also.

Whenever Bonhoeffer explains what he means by " religious," he connects it with such terms as " metaphysical," " inwardness," " subjective," and " individualistic." A religious interpretation of Christianity would be a metaphysical or an individualistic one, i.e., one which turned it into a system of abstract truths to be communicated to men by words, or one which turned it into an individualistic concern for the " salvation of souls " for a world beyond the boundary of death. But what if man is no longer " religious," no longer concerned with the answers given by a religious interpretation of things? What if man is not inherently religious? What happens if the " religious Apriori " of man, this *a priori* premise upon which Christian preaching and theology have rested for nineteen hundred years, simply does not exist? Bonhoeffer is convinced that modern man *cannot* be religious even if he thinks he is and wants to be. If he describes himself as religious, it is obvious that he does not live up to it, or that he means something quite different. If religion was no more than a " garment of Christianity," which must now be cast aside because it has lost its meaning in a world which has come of age, if the real problem facing Christianity today is not so much that of religionlessness, but precisely that of *religion,* then what does all this mean for the church? Before giving Bonhoeffer's answer, let us look at what he thinks has happened up till now.

What has been the reaction of the church to the development whereby the " God " of religion has been edged out of the world as the world has come to a self-assured adulthood? The worst possible!

claims Bonhoeffer. The whole movement has been viewed as "the great defection from God and from Christ," and the more that "God" and "Christ" have been used in opposition to the development, the more it has considered itself to be anti-Christian! Thus the tragic irrelevance of the church in the modern world! Christian apologetic has tried to prove to the world that it could not live without the tutelage of "God," but it has been fighting rear-guard actions, surrendering one battlefield after another. This apologetic has been carried on by religious people, who have used God as a "stopgap for their incompleteness of knowledge." Bonhoeffer gives this insight into his own reaction to "religious" and to "religionless" people.

> I often ask myself why a Christian instinct frequently draws me more to the religionless than to the religious, by which I mean not with any intention of evangelizing them, but rather, I might almost say, in "brotherhood." While I often shrink with religious people from speaking of God by name — because that Name somehow seems to me here not to ring true, and I strike myself as rather dishonest (it is especially bad when others start talking in religious jargon: then I dry up completely and feel somehow oppressed and ill at ease) — with people who have no religion I am able on occasion to speak of God quite openly and as it were naturally. Religious people speak of God when human perception is (often just from laziness) at an end, or human resources fail: it is always the *deus ex machina* they call to their aid, either for the so-called solving of insoluble problems or as support in human failure — always, that is to say, helping out human weakness or on the borders of human existence. (123 f.)

Even though God was driven out of the world by the surrender of the church in one area after another, there seemed to be one sphere in which religious answers remained secure, and that was the sphere of the so-called ultimate questions (death, suffering, guilt, etc.), that is, the sphere of man's "inner life." If "God" alone can furnish an answer to the ultimate questions, then at least (or at last!) there is some reason why God and the church and the pastor are needed. But, asks Bonhoeffer, if we can only talk of God on the "borders of human existence," in the "boundary situations," are we not in the final analysis frantically seeking to make room for God in the world? Or worse yet, are we not assigning him his place in the world? And even in these areas, Bonhoeffer reminds us, answers are to be found nowadays that leave God right out of the picture. It simply isn't true that " Christianity alone has the answers." In fact, it is Bonhoeffer's opinion that the Christian answers are no more conclusive or compelling than any of the others.

Here the church that has clung to its religious interpretation and has restricted God to the private life of man comes face to face with what Bonhoeffer calls " the secularized offshoots of Christian theology," the existential philosophers and the psychotherapists! They, too, have the "answer" to life's problems, the solution to its distresses and conflicts, and their answer does not depend on " God." They pry into the secret recesses of man's inner, personal life and try to demonstrate to secure, happy, contented mankind that it is really unhappy and desperate, that its health is sickness, its vigor and vitality despair. For Bonhoeffer this is a " revolt of inferiority " characterized by an attitude of mistrust and suspicion toward mankind, and while it touches a few intellectuals and degenerates and egotists, it completely passes by the ordinary man, who has neither the time nor inclination for thinking about his intellectual despair or regarding his modest share of happiness as a trial, trouble, or disaster. This sort of " secularized methodism " has its ecclesiastical counterpart in the clergy's " priestly " snuffing around in the lives of men to bring to light their sins of weakness. Bonhoeffer believes there is a twofold theological error here: first, the idea that man can be addressed as a sinner only on the basis of his weaknesses; secondly, the notion that man's essential nature consists of his inner life. Jesus did not make every man a sinner first; he called men out of their sin, not into it. Again, the Bible does not recognize our distinction between outer and inner, but is concerned with the *whole* man in his relation to God. Bonhoeffer believes it is imperative that the church give up all " clerical subterfuge " and the regarding of psychotherapy and existentialism as " precursors of God." It must take an entirely different approach to a world come of age. " I should like to speak of God," he says, " not on the borders of life but at its center, not in weakness but in strength, not, therefore, in man's suffering and death but in his life and prosperity. On the borders it seems to me better to hold our peace and leave the problem unsolved. . . . The church stands not where human powers give out, on the borders, but in the center of the village " (124).

When all is said and done, Bonhoeffer considers the attack by Christian apologetic upon the adulthood of the world to be "pointless," "ignoble," and "unchristian." Pointless because it " looks to me like an attempt to put a grown-up man back into adolescence "; ignoble because this " amounts to an effort to exploit the weakness of man for purposes alien to him and not freely subscribed to by him "; unchristian because " for Christ himself is being substituted one particular stage in the religiousness of man, i.e., a human law " (147).

What has been the attitude of modern theology toward the question of Christ and the newly matured world? In his letter of June 8, 1944, Bonhoeffer presents this amazingly concise and penetrating sketch of recent developments in theology:

It was the weak point of liberal theology that it allowed the world the right to assign Christ his place in that world; in the dispute between Christ and the world it accepted the comparatively clement peace dictated by the world. It was its strong point that it did not seek to put back the clock, and genuinely accepted the battle (Troeltsch), even though this came to an end with its overthrow. Overthrow was succeeded by capitulation and an attempt at a completely fresh start based on consideration of the Bible and Reformation fundamentals of the faith. Heim sought, along Pietist and Methodist lines, to convince individual man that he was faced with the alternative " either despair or Jesus." He gained " hearts." Althaus, carrying forward the modern and positive line with a strong confessional emphasis, endeavored to wring from the world a place for Lutheran teaching (ministry) and Lutheran worship, and otherwise left the world to its own devices. Tillich set out to interpret the evolution of the world itself — against its will — in a religious sense, to give it its whole shape through religion. That was very courageous of him, but the world unseated him and went on by itself: he too sought to understand the world better than it understood itself, but it felt entirely *mis*understood, and rejected the imputation. (Of course the world does need to be understood better than it understands itself, but not " religiously," as the religious socialists desired.) Barth was the first to realize the mistake that all these efforts (which were all unintentionally sailing in the channel of liberal theology) were making in having as their objective the clearing of a space for religion in the world or against the world. He called the God of Jesus Christ into the lists against religion, "*pneuma* against *sarx*." That was and is his greatest service. (147 f.)

Bonhoeffer's objection to Barth's theology is that in the place of religion there appears a " positivist doctrine of revelation " which says in effect that everything (virgin birth, Trinity, etc.) must be swallowed as a whole or not at all. Bonhoeffer does not believe that this accords with the Bible, where there are " degrees of perception and degrees of significance." A " positivism of revelation " which sets up a " law of faith " and says, " Take it or leave it," makes it too easy for itself, for the world is left to go its own way, and that is all wrong. Barth's real limitation, asserts Bonhoeffer, is that he has given no concrete guidance on the " nonreligious interpretation of theological concepts " (148).

Bultmann would seem to have felt Barth's limitation, but Bonhoeffer thinks he misconstrued it in the light of liberal theology, reverting to the typical liberal reduction process whereby Christianity is reduced to its " essence " by stripping off its " mythological elements." But for Bonhoeffer it is not the mythological concepts that are problematic, but the " religious " ones, so that in one sense Bultmann, with his call for demythologizing, did not go far enough. What Bultmann calls mythology (resurrection, etc.) is for Bonhoeffer " the thing itself," so that the full content of the New Testament must be maintained, but the concepts must be interpreted in a way that does not make religion a precondition of faith. Only in this way will liberal theology be overcome and, at the same time, the question it raises be genuinely taken up and answered.

What are the implications of Bonhoeffer's thought about the relationship of Christianity to the world come of age? Bonhoeffer believes that the fact that the world has come of age means that " the linchpin is removed from the whole structure of our Christianity to date," and he interprets this as God's way of telling the church that it has misinterpreted the gospel. It has failed to understand the true meaning and implication of the incarnation, which destroyed once and for all the idea of religion. It consequently made the world's coming of age an occasion for polemics and apologetics which were based on a false " religious " premise, and the world rightly resisted the church's attempt to impose intellectually dishonest answers to its questions. Bonhoeffer even toys with the idea that perhaps the world, which has become religionless and " godless," is in fact thereby closer to God, although he in no way means to imply that modern man's shallow self-understanding is identical to the profound illumination of human existence provided by God's revelation in Jesus Christ. Their only point of similarity is that neither (if the Christian faith is rightly interpreted!) bases its view on a " religious Apriori," and for this reason Bonhoeffer believes that the church today, with its message which proclaims the end of all religion, stands in an exceedingly hopeful situation for communicating to a religionless world.

Bonhoeffer suggests that the question of whether religion is a condition of salvation parallels the Pauline question as to whether circumcision is a condition of justification, and in the light of Christ both must receive a negative answer. Christ is not an object of religion, but is in truth the living Lord of the world! It is only because of his understanding of Jesus Christ, and therewith an apprehension of the depth of God's involvement in the world, that Bonhoeffer comes to a new appreciation of the true " worldliness " of Christianity, " not in the anthropocentric sense of liberal, pietistic, ethical theology, but in the Bible sense of the creation and of the incarnation, crucifixion, and resurrection of Jesus Christ " (126).

But the " worldliness " of Christianity is only one pole of Bonhoeffer's total thought as it comes to expression in his letters from prison, for over against it he insists that Christians must rediscover what he calls an *Arkandisziplin,* an arcane, or secret, discipline that would preserve the mysteries of the Christian faith from profanation. Bonhoeffer connects this notion of a secret discipline with his thoughts about the ultimate and the penultimate, the last things and the things before the last. In contrast to the visible, " worldly " life of the Christian in the realm of the " things before the last," there must be a hidden, disciplined life of devotion and prayer that is grounded in belief on the " last things." These form the dialectical poles of Christian existence, the worldly life always requiring the nourishment of the secret discipline and the secret discipline always sending a man back into the world.

In the letters and papers from prison Bonhoeffer gives us no systematic treatment of traditional theological concepts, but in what follows an effort is made to bring some of his thoughts into focus. At this point it should be re-emphasized that Bonhoeffer's thinking never got beyond the initial stage and is available to us only in an intimate and fragmentary form.

God: The religious person thinks of God either in such abstract terms as " omnipotent," " omniscient," etc., or as an " answer " to life's problems. That is, he either confuses God with an idea of God or makes God peripheral by assigning him a place on the " borders of human existence." In the first instance man treats God as if he could be known apart from the world, and in the second he makes a bit of space for God in the world. For Bonhoeffer both understandings are false, because here God is placed at the disposal of man. What is lacking is an adequate appreciation of God's *transcendence,* and in a brief outline of a book that he hoped to write someday Bonhoeffer explains what this notion involves:

> Our relation to God is not a religious relationship to a supreme Being, absolute in power and goodness, which is a spurious conception of transcendence, but a new life for others, through participation in the being of God. The transcendence consists not in tasks beyond our scope and power, but in the nearest thing to hand. God in human form, not, as in other religions, in animal form — the monstrous, chaotic, remote, and terrifying — nor yet in abstract form — the absolute, metaphysical, infinite, etc., nor yet in the Greek divine-human of autonomous man, but man existing for others, and hence the Crucified. (179)

Bonhoeffer is convinced that we cannot know God as an " object " of our perceptual faculties, as if we could separate him from the world and use him as a standpoint from which to assault the world. An epistemological transcendence has nothing to do with the transcendence of God, for God is the " beyond " in the midst of our life! The transcendence of God is a *this-worldly transcendence,* so that God is only known in a concrete living for others, a participation in the being of Jesus for others.

God is not a " stopgap " or a *deus ex machina* that we can use to answer our " ultimate questions " or our unsolved problems, for this leaves God a place only on the borders of human existence. Bonhoeffer believes we should find God in what we *do* know, not in what we do not; in the problems we *have* solved, not in those outstanding. God "must be found at the center of life: in life, and not only in death; in health and vigor, and not only in suffering; in activity, and not only in sin. The ground for this lies in the revelation of God in Christ. Christ is the center of life, and in no sense did he come to answer our unsolved problems" (143). The fact that God is not a "working hypothesis," even in religion, gives support to the world's coming of age and its dispensing with this "God." But if we must live in the world *etsi deus non daretur,* as if there were no God, then how is God to be found in the center of life? In answer, Bonhoeffer gives this surprising and radical explanation:

Our coming of age forces us to a true recognition of our situation vis-à-vis God. God is teaching us that we must live as men who can get along very well without him. The God who is with us is the God who forsakes us (Mark 15:34). The God who makes us live in this world without using him as a working hypothesis is the God before whom we are ever standing. Before God and with him we live without God. God allows himself to be edged out of the world and on to the cross. God is weak and powerless in the world, and that is exactly the way, the only way, in which he can be with us and help us. Matthew 8:17 makes it crystal-clear that it is not by his omnipotence that Christ helps us, but by his weakness and suffering. This is the decisive difference between Christianity and all other religions. Man's religiosity makes him look in his distress to the power of God in the world; he uses God as a *deus ex machina.* The Bible, however, directs him to the powerlessness and suffering of God; only a suffering God can help. To this extent we may say that the process we have described by which the world came of age was an abandonment of a false conception of God, and a clearing of the decks for the God of the Bible, who conquers power and space in the world by his weakness. This must be the starting point for our "worldly" interpretation. (163 f.)

Salvation: The religious person has an individualistic concern for the salvation of souls "from cares and need, from fears and longing, from sin and death into a better world beyond the grave" (154). The emphasis falls on the other side of the boundary drawn by death. But the Old Testament is not concerned with the "saving of souls" at all, and the real interest in the whole Bible centers on *righteousness* and the *Kingdom of God on earth*. " It is not with the next world that we are concerned," asserts Bonhoeffer, " but with this world as created and preserved and set subject to laws and atoned for and made new " (126). Bonhoeffer believes it has been a cardinal error to interpret Christ in the light of the myths of salvation of various Oriental religions, and thus to conceive of Christianity as a " religion of salvation " that emphasizes release from this world. Such an interpretation divorces Christ from the Old Testament, which speaks of *historical* redemption, i.e., redemption on *this* side of death. But, someone will object, what about the Christian proclamation of the resurrection hope? Does this not confirm the otherworldly character of the Christian faith? No, declares Bonhoeffer; the Christian hope of resurrection differs from a mythological hope in that the Christian hope " sends a man back to his life on earth in a wholly new way which is even more sharply defined than it is in the Old Testament " (154). The Christian does not write off this world prematurely, but " like Christ himself he must drink the earthly cup to the lees, and only in his doing that is the crucified and risen Lord with him, and he crucified and risen with Christ " (154).

The Christian Life: The Christian lives a life of faith, and faith is defined by Bonhoeffer as participation in the being of Jesus as one whose only concern is for others. Unlike the religious act, which is always something partial, faith is always something whole, an act involving one's whole life. " Jesus does not call men to a new religion," Bonhoeffer points out, " but to life " (167). Jesus claims for himself the whole of human life in all its manifestations, and faith makes possible a total response that is characterized by what Bonhoeffer terms the " polyphony of life." By this he means that " God requires that we should love him eternally with our whole hearts, yet not so as to compromise or diminish our earthly affections, but as a kind of *cantus firmus* to which the other melodies of life provide the counterpoint " (131). The Christian faith plunges one into many different dimensions of life at the same time, but this multidimensioned life obtains a wholeness because of its polyphonous nature.

The Christian, then, lives a " worldly " life. Indeed, it is only by living completely in this world that one learns to believe, for only thus can one participate in the sufferings of God at the hands of a godless world. And this, claims Bonhoeffer, is the only difference between Christians and unbelievers: " Christians range themselves with God in his suffering. . . . As Jesus asked in Gethsemane, ' Could ye not watch with me one hour? ' That is the exact opposite of what the religious man expects from God " (166). This is *repentance:* " not in the first instance bothering about one's own needs, problems, sins, and fears, but allowing oneself to be caught up in the way of Christ, into the Messianic event, and thus fulfilling Isaiah, ch. 53 " (166). The Christian does not try to make something out of himself (a saint, a penitent, a churchman, etc.), does not try to become a *homo religiosus,* but is content to be a man, pure and simple — a man who takes life in his stride, with all its duties and problems, its successes and failures, its joys and sorrows; a man in whom an arcane discipline and true worldliness interact to produce a life lived completely " before God."

The Church: How can the church as *ekklēsia* — " those who are called forth " — understand itself, not religiously as specially favored, but as wholly belonging to the world? First of all, states Bonhoeffer, " the church must get out of her stagnation. We must move out again into the open air of intellectual discussion with the world " (177). Furthermore, the church must cease making the defense of its own existence its primary concern. It is Bonhoeffer's opinion that the Confessing Church, which began with such a valiant stand against the German Christians, ended by fighting for self-preservation as though it were an end in itself, and thereby it " lost its chance to speak a word of reconciliation to mankind and the world at large " (140). Finally, the people of God must proclaim their own real and personal belief in all honesty. " To say, ' It's the church's faith, not mine,' can be a clerical subterfuge, and outsiders always regard it as such " (180). By entrenching itself behind the so-called " faith of the church " and evading the question of its real and personal belief, the proclamation of the Confessing Church became powerless. In this situation Bonhoeffer believed that the Confessing Church should remain silent, confining itself to praying for and doing right by its fellow men, and then the day would again come when God would call men to utter his word with power, but in a new and startling language, a language which reflected a nonreligious interpretation of the Christian faith.

Bonhoeffer gives this advice to any church that lets its interest in self-preservation obscure its *raison d'être:*

The church is her true self only when she exists for humanity. As a fresh start she should give away all her endowments to the poor and needy. The clergy should live solely on the freewill offerings of their congregations, or possibly engage in some secular calling. She must take part in the social life of the world, not lording over men, but helping and serving them. She must tell men, whatever their calling, what it means to live in Christ, to exist for others. . . . She will have to speak of moderation, purity, confidence, loyalty, steadfastness, patience, discipline, humility, content, and modesty. She must not underestimate the importance of human example, which has its origin in the humanity of Jesus, and which is so important in the teaching of St. Paul. It is not abstract argument, but concrete example which gives her word emphasis and power. (180 f.)

" To exist for others " — this is Dietrich Bonhoeffer's ringing challenge to the church, and to discover what this means in its entirety is the task before which we stand.

Chapter IV

Theological Evaluation

A. THE PROBLEM

The problem of Bonhoeffer's theology lies in its development during the final period, especially during the time of his imprisonment, and in the relation of the thought of this period to that of the two preceding periods. Are the fragmentary insights of the third period continuous or discontinuous with the development of his theology up to that time? The connection between the concentration on the sociological phenomenon of the church during the initial period and the stress on the ethical demands of discipleship during the second is obvious, but how do these relate to the emphasis on the world come of age and the nonreligious character of the Christian faith during the third? Does the third period represent a break with the former periods, or is it possible to discover a fundamental unifying element that provides continuity to Bonhoeffer's theology from beginning to end?

It is certainly easy to demonstrate how many prominent concepts in the last period of Bonhoeffer's theology are traceable to concepts found in the former periods. For instance, the notion that the church is not a religious community of worshipers of Christ but rather Christ himself taking form among men (E 20) finds its antecedent in the concept of the " body of Christ " in *The Cost of Discipleship* and the definition of the church as " Christ existing as community " in *Sanctorum Communio*. The ideas of " being there for the other " (PFG 179) and " deputyship " (E 194) may be traced back to " the ministry of bearing " in *Life Together*, " bearing the cross " in *The Cost of Discipleship*, *pati* in *Act and Being*, and " the principle of vicarious representation " in *Sanctorum Communio.* His concern for an " arcane discipline " (PFG 126) has its roots in the chapter on " The Day Alone " in *Life Together* and the exposition of " the hidden character of the Christian life " in *The Cost of Discipleship,* whereas his thoughts about the " penultimate " and " preparing the way " (E 84 ff.) are foreshadowed in the discussion about " taking the first step " in *The Cost of Discipleship* (54 ff.).

Further, Bonhoeffer's denial of a " religious Apriori " in man (PFG 122) hearkens back to his polemic in *Act and Being* against Seeberg's use of the concept (AS 35 f.), and his distinction between the " world of conflict " and the " world of recovered unity " (E 142 ff.) cannot be understood apart from the book *Creation and Fall.* The notion of the " mandates " (E 73 ff.) derives from his doctrine of the " orders of preservation," which he develops in " Concerning the Theological Foundation of the Work of the World Alliance " (an address from 1932!), and in this same address may be found his insistence on the concreteness of the commandment of God (E 23 ff., 244 ff.) and his conviction that responsible action includes the acceptance of guilt (E 209 f.). Bonhoeffer's understanding of the relation of church and state (E 297 ff.) depends upon his development of this theme in another early address: " Thy Kingdom Come! " Many other concepts could be traced in a similar manner, but the above should be sufficient to prove the point.

Having demonstrated this wealth of continuity, however, we still have the problem of the surprisingly new concepts that emerge in the third period of Bonhoeffer's life. Certain statements in Bonhoeffer's letters from prison seem to indicate that the new dimensions in his thinking signified a rather decisive turning point in his theological development. For instance, he writes the following to Eberhard Bethge on April 30, 1944, " You would be surprised and perhaps disturbed if you knew how my ideas on theology are taking shape " (PFG 121 f.). In August of the same year, while working on the book that was to delineate his new ideas, he writes, "I am often shocked at the things I am saying, especially in the first part, which is mainly critical " (PFG 185). After reading W. F. Otto's book on the Greek gods, which is about " this world of faith, which sprang from the wealth and depth of human existence, rather than from its cares and longings," Bonhoeffer remarks: "I wonder if you will understand me when I say I find something attractive in this theme and the way it is treated in this book. In fact, I find these gods — *horrible dictu* — less offensive when treated like this than certain brands of Christianity! I believe I could pretty nearly claim these gods for Christ" (PFG 150).

Perhaps the best insight into the nature of the change that had taken place in Bonhoeffer's thinking comes in a letter written the day following the fateful failure of the attempt to assassinate Hitler. Here he relates his conversation with a young French pastor (Jean Lasserre) thirteen years earlier:

> We were discussing what our real purpose was in life. He said he would like to become a saint. I think it is quite likely he did become one. At the time I was very much impressed, though I disagreed with him, and said that I should prefer to learn to have faith, or words to that effect. For a long time I did not realize how far we were apart. I thought I could acquire faith by trying to live a holy life, or something like it. It was in this phase that I wrote *The Cost of Discipleship*. Today I can see the dangers of this book, though I am prepared to stand by what I wrote. Later I discovered and am still discovering up to this very moment that it is only by living completely in this world that one learns to believe. One must abandon every attempt to make something of oneself, whether it be a saint, a converted sinner, a churchman (the priestly type, so-called!), a righteous man or an unrighteous one, a sick man or a healthy one. This is what I mean by worldliness (*Diesseitigkeit*) — taking life in one's stride, with all its duties and problems, its successes and failures, its experiences and perplexities. It is in such a life that we throw ourselves utterly into the arms of God, that we take seriously not our own but God's suffering in the world, that we watch with Christ in Gethsemane. And I think that this is faith, this is *metanoia* (repentance), and it is in this way that one becomes a man, a Christian (cf. Jer., ch. 45!).[1]

What are we to conclude about the new direction of Bonhoeffer's thought, namely, the growing appreciation of the this-worldly, nonreligious character of Christian faith? It would be ludicrous to agree with a well-meaning German pastor, who, remembering Bonhoeffer's thoughts about a religionless Christianity, felt obliged to say,

[1] PFG 168 f. Translation slightly altered by the writer.

"One may still hope that at the very end Bonhoeffer regained his faith."[2] Hardly more discerning, in our estimation, is the conclusion of Erich Müller-Gangloff, who asserts that in Bonhoeffer's fragmentary thoughts about a theology for a mature world, "he, in resolute opposition to Karl Barth, for whom all thinking is related to God, thinks emphatically from the standpoint of man."[3] Karl Barth himself, who is deeply appreciative of Bonhoeffer's thought, is inclined to stress the enigmatic character of the thoughts from prison, pointing out that Bonhoeffer tended to be an impulsive, visionary thinker, who would suddenly become consumed by an idea (in this case an idea grounded in a particular philosophy of history!), only later to stop at some penultimate thesis and turn to another.[4] Eberhard Bethge interprets the final period as another illustration of Bonhoeffer's ever-burning concern for the "concretion of the revelation," that is, where and how the revelation of God becomes concrete.[5] Gerhard Ebeling, on the other hand, believes that Bonhoeffer, whose theology he interprets as a *theologia crucis,* was concerned with the problem of law and gospel — a nonreligious interpretation of Christianity being one that distinguishes between law and gospel, whereas a religious interpretation is one according to law.[6]

One could point to many factors in Bonhoeffer's life during his last years that must have made deep impressions upon his mind and directed his thoughts toward "worldliness." One factor is his envolvement in the resistance movement, where he came in contact with completely "secular" men who were willing to suffer and even to die for their fellow men. Another is his disappointment with the Confessing Church, which in the later years worried too much about its own existence and thus neglected its responsibilities in and for the world. A third factor is the raw reality of prison life, where he was daily in contact with men who belonged to the "unchurched masses" but for whom Christ died. Finally, there is the searching

[2] MW I, p. 19.
[3] "Theologie für die mündige Welt," *Die neue Furche,* Jahrgang 6, Heft 8, August, 1952, p. 530.
[4] See Barth's letter of December 21, 1952, to Landessuperintendent P. W. Herrenbrück, MW I, pp. 121 f.
[5] Epilogue to the second edition of *Dein Reich komme!* pp. 40 ff.
[6] "Die 'nicht-religiöse Interpretation biblischer Begriffe,'" MW II, p. 53 ff., 70.

study, which Bonhoeffer undertook in prison, especially his research in the Old Testament, with its emphasis on God's blessing upon all life, and its stress on *historical* redemption and the Kingdom of God *on earth,* and in the history of Western civilization, which revealed that the movement toward the present age of man's unprecedented technological mastery over the world was paralleled by a gradual defection from Christ.

Granting that these factors undoubtedly played a significant catalytic role, and admitting the possibility of the above-mentioned interpretations, the writer must now disclose his own conviction that the last development in Bonhoeffer's theology, while indeed unexpected, does in no sense represent a break with the theology of the former periods, but rather a bold consummation of the same! That is, the unifying element in Bonhoeffer's theology is his Christology, and it is precisely the Christology that impelled his theological development. The following section will be an attempt to validate this thesis.

B. The Clue to Bonhoeffer

The cohesive and elucidative element in the theology of Dietrich Bonhoeffer is his steadfast concentration upon the revelation of God in Jesus Christ. Throughout the continuing development of his theology, as he faced the various situations of his life, it was the figure of the incarnate, crucified, and risen Lord that captivated his attention and evoked his faithful obedience. For Bonhoeffer theology was essentially Christology, but because Christ is not without his body, Christology includes ecclesiology within itself. This explains Bonhoeffer's insistence that revelation is always concrete revelation. The word of God, Jesus Christ, became not an idea but flesh! God revealed himself in a concrete, historical life, and Bonhoeffer passionately believed that revelation continues to take place only in a concrete form, namely, as Jesus Christ lives and takes form in a concrete community, in his church.

Bethge has shown how Bonhoeffer's passion for the concreteness of revelation provides an explanation for his distinctive attitudes and actions.[7] It led to his interest in the *sociological* form of the church in *Sanctorum Communio,* his questioning in *Act and Being* of the

[7] Epilogue to second edition of *Dein Reich kommel* pp. 40 ff.

dialectical theologians about how the revelation that is free and not at man's disposal ever becomes *concrete* revelation, his criticism that in his ethics Emil Brunner neglected to investigate whether the church must risk the proclamation of quite concrete commandments. It explains his continual plea at ecumenical conferences for the risking of a concrete commandment, his concern about the Sermon on the Mount and discipleship, his intransigent position in regard to the ecclesio-political decisions of the Confessing Church. Further, the question drove him to work on his *Ethics,* which asks how the reality of God becomes real on earth and answers that it is only in the context of real life that revelation becomes attached to the penultimate things, that there can be no static separation of the sphere of the world from the sphere of the church. Finally, it brought him to a denial that Christianity was a religion of salvation emphasizing release from this world, and to an affirmation of the " this-worldly " character of the Christian faith.

Although Bethge's schema is undeniably true and discloses a motif that is indispensable for a proper understanding of Bonhoeffer, it seems to us that behind this continual demand for the concretion of revelation stands a more basic clue to the development of Bonhoeffer's life and thought, namely, the " content " of the revelation itself. It is his Christological concentration, that is, his meditation upon and understanding of the person and work of the living Christ, which accounts for his drive toward concretion. In fact, the Christocentric focus and the demand that revelation be concrete are characteristics of Bonhoeffer's theology from the beginning, but it is his *understanding* of the revelation of God in Jesus Christ which develops and thus provides the real clue to the development within his theology itself. It is the ever-increasing apprehension of the implications involved in this Name, the growing awareness of the total meaning of Jesus Christ, which of course is not *un*related to the external events of his own life, that accounts for the different emphases and the development in Bonhoeffer's theology.

At the risk of oversimplification, the writer would like to propose the following schema, which is presented in terms of an unfolding of Bonhoeffer's comprehension of Christology, as the proper guide to the three periods that are discernible in his theological development.

During the first period his thought centered on *Jesus Christ as the revelational reality of the church.* During the second period his emphasis was upon *Jesus Christ as the Lord over the church.* In the third period Bonhoeffer concentrated his attention upon *Jesus Christ as the Lord over the world.* Of course, it must be admitted from the outset that all these aspects of Christology are to be found in some degree in each period, but the thesis here proposed has this twofold implication: first, that one of the aspects was dominant in each period, and, second, that each succeeding period represents an expansion of Bonhoeffer's Christological understanding. From this perspective we are able to view the striking contrast between his original emphasis on the church and his final emphasis on the world, not as a break in his theology, but as the two poles of a development. In what follows we shall endeavor to confirm this thesis by a short analysis of each period.

In the first period Bonhoeffer's main interest is in the relation of Jesus Christ to the sociological phenomenon of the church, and this relation he defines in terms of Christ's *presence.* Just as Christ is the presence of God, the church is the presence of Christ, which means that " the New Testament knows a form of revelation ' Christ existing as community ' " (SC 92). Thus a concrete community of persons is to be looked upon as a collective person, and this rests upon the principle of representation or substitution, since Christ as the Second Adam bears the guilt and sin of the old humanity unto death on the cross and establishes a New Humanity in his body. In this very act, however, Christ restores the broken fellowship and creates a fellowship of love, which is based upon the life-principle of vicariousness (SC 98). This is a fellowship *sui generis,* because it is a fellowship of the Holy Spirit (SC 204), who in the preaching of the word of justification makes Christ present and so awakens faith and love in the hearts of the hearers. God rules through his word, but the paradoxical fact about God's rulership is that he rules by serving (SC 126)! His will to rule is his will to love, that is, to establish a fellowship of love, so the congregation is at once a means to an end (an instrument of spreading the word of God's sovereign claim) and an end in itself (God claims man precisely for this fellowship of love). The members of the fellowship live " for one another," which means that in their actions they become "like Christ," or, as Luther put it, one becomes a Christ to another (SC 127).

The problem of this *Christus praesens*-ecclesiology, with its stress on the being of the Christ-Person in the fellowship of persons (AS 104), is to avoid an identification of Christ with the church. Bonhoeffer recognizes that the New Testament will allow no total identification, since Christ has ascended and will come again, but he contends that the problem of the relation between "Christ existing as community" and "Christ in heaven" remains unsolved (SC 92). In the second period this problem is overcome by his concentration upon the Lordship of the risen Christ over his body.

This new emphasis is already evident in May, 1932, when Bonhoeffer preached a memorable Exaudi sermon in which he used these words of II Chron. 20:12 as his text: "We do not know what to do, but our eyes are upon thee" (GS I, pp. 133 ff.). In the sermon Bonhoeffer explains that the church is faced with grave ethical problems, and for direction it must look to the resurrected Lord! More and more this young German theologian became engrossed with the problem of following Christ in the modern world. What does the Lord command? That we be disciples! And what does it mean to be disciples? To adhere to Christ bodily (CD 51)! And where can one find bodily communion with him? In the body of Christ, which is to say, the church (CD 180)! All of Bonhoeffer's thinking about the problem of how we can live the Christian life in the modern world comes to fruition in *The Cost of Discipleship,* the heart of which is his profound exposition of the Sermon on the Mount. Here his thoughts are still revolving around the problem of the relation between Jesus Christ and his church, but now he is carefully thinking through that relationship from the standpoint of Christ's Lordship over the church, Christ as the Lord who calls us to faithful obedience. What was implicit in *Sanctorum Communio* is now made explicit, and in the process Bonhoeffer's Christology, that is, his understanding of the meaning of Jesus Christ, is expanding. Now the concern is not so much "Christ in the church," but "Christ over the church"; not so much "faith and fellowship," but "faith and obedience." Bonhoeffer's ethical concern made imperative a working through of the problem of grace and discipleship, of justification and sanctification, and so he centers his attention upon the figure of Jesus Christ, whose word is not only gospel but also law, not only grace but also commandment — and, to be sure, never one without the other!

The chief danger in the second period of Bonhoeffer's theological development is that of turning the gospel of grace into a new law. His sharp polemic against "cheap grace" and his unmitigated emphasis upon obedience might be *mis*interpreted in the direction of a new legalism, which could lead either to despair or to pride. Bonhoeffer was willing to run this risk, however, because he was convinced that "the word of cheap grace has been the ruin of more Christians than any commandment of works" (CD 48). It seems to us that this danger was overcome in the third period by Bonhoeffer's doctrine of Christian "worldliness," which is a profound exposition of the *freedom* that comes to those who are obedient, a freedom for a life of genuine worldliness.

The final period of Bonhoeffer's theology is a gradual thinking through of the tremendous fact that Jesus Christ is not only Lord of the church, but is at the same time Lord of the world. Yes, even the godless world stands under his Lordship, and because of its positive relation to him, it is not without hope. This new concentration in Bonhoeffer's thought is clearly evident in his *Ethics,* particularly in his discussions of "reality" and of "ultimate and penultimate" and of "church and world," but it becomes ever more intense in the letters and papers from prison. At this point it is important to recognize, however, that his work remains unfinished. He never had the opportunity fully to develop his thoughts about the relation of the world to Christ, but he points the way and challenges the church to finish the task!

Just as all of the theology of the first period is carried into the second, the accumulated wisdom of both periods is present in the third. What is new is the emphasis, the investigation and elaboration of an area that has heretofore received only slight treatment. There are foreshadowings of the new interest in *The Cost of Discipleship,* where Bonhoeffer states that Christ is the Mediator between man and reality (CD 79) and that Christians must love the world "with the love wherewith God loved it in Jesus Christ" (CD 82), but the main burden of this book is to stress the *distinction* between the church and the world. The call of Christ demands a breach with the world! To be sure, Christians must continue to live in the world, but because their citizenship is in heaven, they can live in the world without being of the world (CD 49). They tread " on the razoredge between this world and the Kingdom of Heaven " (CD 163). Here the emphasis is on the movement from the world to the church, whereas in the third period Bonhoeffer's concern is with precisely the opposite movement. Indeed, the church can never want to be separated from the world, because only by its complete involvement in and for the world can it be the church! Church and world are not to be identified, but " the church is divided from the world solely by the fact that it affirms in faith the reality of God's acceptance of man, a reality which is the property of the whole world. By allowing this reality to take effect within itself, it testifies that it is effectual for the whole world " (E 72).

It is his Christocentric concept of reality, which Bonhoeffer develops in the *Ethics,* that perhaps best illustrates the motif of the third period and, at the same time, acts as a springboard into his thoughts from prison. Bonhoeffer declares that there is only *one* ultimate reality, and that is the reality in Jesus Christ. In the person of Christ the reality of God and the reality of the world are united and help together in a " polemical unity," so that in him there is no possibility of partaking in one without the other. " The reality of God discloses itself only by setting me entirely in the reality of the world," says Bonhoeffer, " and when I encounter the reality of the world it is always already sustained, accepted, and reconciled in the reality of God. This is the inner meaning of the revelation of God in the man Jesus Christ " (E 61). Because both divine and cosmic reality are in Christ, Bonhoeffer called upon the church to cease thinking in terms of two static spheres, e.g., the " Christian " and the " worldly," the " sacred " and the " secular," the " supernatural " and the " natural," the " revelational " and the " rational." On the other hand, the spheres are not to be identified, but their unity in Christ means that the " Christian " is to be found only in the " worldly," the " sacred " only in the " secular," etc. The church is not to act as if the spheres stood side by side and as if the main problem of history is the conflict between them. Rather, the church is to take with full seriousness the fact that the whole reality of the world is already drawn into Christ and bound together in him, and that the movement of history consists in the world's " being accepted and becoming accepted by God in Christ " (E 65). The Christian is not a man of eternal conflict, but sharing in the unity of the spheres in Jesus Christ, he himself becomes an undivided whole. " His worldliness does not divide him from Christ, and his Christianity does not divide him from the world. Belonging wholly to Christ, he stands at the same time wholly in the world " (E 67).

It is from *this* perspective that Bonhoeffer developed his thoughts about the " worldliness " of Christianity. They did not simply drop from heaven while he was in prison, but these fresh and original insights are dependent upon, and a development of, all that has gone before! Christian " worldliness " is a Christological judgment, a judgment deriving from Bonhoeffer's understanding of the incarnation, crucifixion, and resurrection of Jesus Christ. This can also be illustrated from the *Ethics,* where he asserts that the *incarnation* means that " God has taken upon himself bodily all human being," that " henceforth divine being cannot be found otherwise than in human form " and that " in Jesus Christ man is made free to be really man before God." The *crucifixion* means that " the whole world has become godless by its rejection of Jesus Christ," but that " the godless world bears at the same time the mark of reconciliation as the free ordinance of God," which means that " the cross of atonement is the setting free for life in genuine worldliness." The *resurrection* and *ascension* mean that " Jesus Christ has overcome sin and death and that he is the living Lord to whom all power is given in heaven and on earth," and that his Lordship " sets creation free for the fulfillment of the law which is its own, that is to say, the law which is inherent in it by virtue of its having its origin, its goal and its essence in Jesus Christ " (E 262 ff.).

It is from this deep understanding of God's love and involvement in the world that Bonhoeffer speaks of " worldliness," and not from some desire to compromise the Christian gospel. We should be clear about this from the outset, or else everything that Bonhoeffer says in his letters will be distorted. The " worldliness " of which he speaks is *not* the world's understanding of worldliness, not the " shallow this-worldliness of the enlightened, of the busy, the comfortable, or the lascivious" (PFG 168), but a worldliness deriving from the knowledge of Christ, a knowledge in which death and resurrection is ever present. Bonhoeffer's desire is not to " gloss over the ungodliness of the world," but to " expose it in a new light" (PFG 167). Furthermore, he does not mean that in becoming "worldly" the church would cease to be the church, but that it can only *be* the church in the true sense when its own attitude toward the world parallels God's attitude, when its life in the world is patterned according to Christ's life, when it takes with utmost seriousness its role as vicarious representative and deputy for the world. That the notion of Christian worldliness does not dissolve the identity of the church nor exclude its essential functions is easily proved, because Bonhoeffer speaks of its ongoing task of proclaiming the word of God (PFG 140), its secret discipline (PFG 126), its cultus (PFG 179), and its task of intellectual discussion with the world (PFG 177).

Bonhoeffer's polemic against "religious" interpretations of the faith arises precisely because they either diminish God's concern for the world or refuse to recognize Christ's Lordship over the world. That is, " religious " interpretations, which for Bonhoeffer means " metaphysical " or " individualistic " interpretations, separate the reality of God from the reality of the world, continue to think in terms of two spheres, and thus deny their unity in Christ. Metaphysical interpretations fabricate a " God " to be a " working hypothesis " (PFG 163), a " stopgap for the incompleteness of our knowledge " (PFG 142), a *deus ex machina* that people call to their aid, " either for the so-called solving of insoluble problems or as support in human failure — always, that is to say, helping out human weakness or on the borders of human existence " (PFG 124). Thus God is removed from the center of the world and is relegated to a diminishing role on the periphery of life. Christ is turned into an " object of religion " instead of being recognized as the Lord of the world (PFG 123), who in no sense came " to answer our unsolved problems " (PFG 143), but " takes hold of man in the center of his life " (PFG 154). Individualistic interpretations, on the other hand, make of Christianity a " religion of redemption " (*Erlösungsreligion*), which emphasizes salvation of souls for another world, and thus history is denied " in the interests of an eternity after death " (PFG 153). Here there is a failure to discern that the gospel's primary concern is with " this world as created and preserved and set subject to laws and atoned for and made new " (PFG 126). God's transcendence is neither an epistemological nor an other-worldly, but a *this-worldly* transcendence, because he is " the 'beyond' in the midst of our life " (PFG 124). " What is beyond the world is, in the gospel," declares Bonhoeffer, " intended to exist *for* this world — I mean that not in the anthropocentric sense of liberal, pietistic, ethical theology, but in the Bible sense of the creation and of the incarnation, crucifixion, and resurrection of Jesus Christ " (PFG 126). For example, even the Christian hope of resurrection " sends a man back to his life on earth in a wholly new way " (PFG 154). " To live in the light of the resurrection — that is the meaning of Easter " (PFG 116)!

Now we can see why Bonhoeffer could take a positive attitude toward the modern technological age, which no longer looked to " God " for its answers and therefore was not " religious." By the use of his reason man has gradually discovered the laws by which the world lives and manages, not only in science, but also in social and political affairs, art, ethics, and religion, and in the name of intellectual honesty he no longer uses " God " as a working hypothesis. Since he has ceased to be religious and since the laws which he has discovered have their origin, goal, and essence in Jesus Christ (E 264), today's godless, secular man is ripe for the Christian message that Jesus Christ is the Lord of the world, that the world stands ever before God, the one God who is Creator, Reconciler, and Redeemer and who refuses to be a *deus ex machina*. This is what Bonhoeffer means when he asserts that " now that it has come of age, the world is more godless, and perhaps it is for that very reason nearer to God than ever before." This is no sanctioning of the world's godlessness, but rather a recognition that it is a *hopeful* godlessness. " Our coming of age," says Bonhoeffer, " forces us to a true recognition of our situation vis-à-vis God " (PFG 163). It is by this reasoning, namely, by a bold effort to answer the question of how Jesus Christ can become Lord even of the religionless, that Bonhoeffer arrived at his plea that the church work out and proclaim a " nonreligious " interpretation of the central Biblical concepts.

C. QUESTIONS

Because of the fragmentary and incomplete character of the theology that was taking form during the final period of his life, Bonhoeffer has left many questions unanswered, and we must accept them as open questions. No one knows exactly what the finished product would have been, had he had enough time to work through and to organize his *Ethics* and the book he outlined in prison (PFG 178 ff.).

One open question, for instance, is what form he thought the church should take in a religionless Christianity. In his " Thoughts on the Baptism of D. W. R." he writes: " By the time you are grown up, the form of the church will have changed beyond recognition. We are not yet out of the melting pot, and every attempt to hasten matters will only delay the church's conversion and purgation " (PFG 140). As it turned out, Bonhoeffer apparently underestimated the church's inertia, but this makes us inquire even more urgently about what he had in mind. We can be certain of one thing, namely, that the new form would be structured in such a way that the church would most effectively exist for humanity. Conditions that encourage clerical arrogance and ecclesiastical self-interest would have to be eliminated and measures instituted to ensure the church's involvement in the social and political life of the world (PFG 180). The church must learn to live the gospel and not just preach it, for only its example will empower its words. It must be the instrument for proclaiming God's word (in a " nonreligious " language!), but beyond that Bonhoeffer believed that the Protestant Church had to regain its own peculiar life as an end in itself. This is evident not only from what he says about the need for an arcane discipline, but also from this passage in the *Ethics:*

The danger of the Reformation . . . lies in the fact that it devotes its whole attention to the mandate of the proclamation of the word and, consequently, almost entirely neglects the proper domain and function of the church as an end in itself, and this consists precisely in her existence for the sake of the world. One need only call to mind the liturgical poverty and uncertainty of our present-day Protestant services, the feebleness of our ecclesiastical organization and law, the almost complete absence of any genuine ecclesiastical discipline, and the inability of most Protestants even to understand the significance of such disciplinary practices as spiritual exercises, asceticism, meditation, and contemplation. One need only consider the general uncertainty about the special functions of the clergy, or the startlingly confused or presumptuous attitude of countless Protestant Christians toward those Christians who refuse to perform military service, etc., and one cannot help perceiving at once where the Protestant Church is at fault. Exclusive interest in the divine mandate of proclamation, and, together with this, interest in the church's mission in the world, has resulted in failure to perceive the inner connection between this mission and the church's internal function. (E 267)

Another open question, to which we have previously alluded, is exactly what Bonhoeffer meant by a " nonreligious interpretation of Biblical concepts." It is much easier to grasp what he meant by " religious " than " nonreligious "! Nevertheless, he does give us the starting point for a " worldly " or " nonreligious " interpretation when he directs our view to the God of the Bible, " who conquers power and space in the world by his weakness . . . God is weak and powerless in the world, and that is exactly the way, the only way, in which he can be with us and help us " (PFG 164). A nonreligious interpretation would call men to participate in the suffering of God in the life of the world, " not in the first instance bothering about one's own needs, problems, sins, and fears, but allowing oneself to be caught up in the way of Christ, into the Messianic event, and thus fulfilling Isa., ch. 53 " (PFG 166). The problem of a nonreligious interpretation is not merely a hermeneutical one, but involves the whole existence of the church itself. It is an interpretation that is not concerned with religion, but with *life*. It is by living in the midst of the world, by taking life in our stride, " that we throw ourselves utterly into the arms of God and participate in his sufferings in the world and watch with Christ in Gethsemane " (PFG 169). Bonhoeffer, then, would interpret the central Biblical concepts, not in terms of metaphysics or psychology, not in terms of an abstract system of doctrine or the experience of the inner self, but in terms of responsible involvement in life itself. Since we have no specific example from the pen of Bonhoeffer, perhaps we should consider Oscar Hammelsbeck's suggestion that Bonhoeffer's own death is a piece of " worldly interpretation" of the gospel (MW I, p. 61)!

In connection with this same problem, it seems advisable to ask about Bonhoeffer's criticism of the psychotherapists and existentialists, whom he usually lumps together, and of such theologians as Karl Barth and Rudolf Bultmann. The exponents of psychotherapy and existential philosophy are the target of Bonhoeffer's sharpest attack. When we try to analyze the reason for this, his basic objection appears to be their invasion of man's private, intimate life. They are professionally dedicated to making man aware of and own up to his inner weaknesses, problems, needs, and conflicts. In Bonhoeffer's opinion this is bad per se, but it becomes calamitous when this is perpetrated in the name of religion, particularly when clergy follow this approach, because now these weaknesses are interpreted as sin and used to demonstrate man's need of God. This is calling man into his sin instead of out of it, and this is the exact opposite of Jesus' approach! In fact, Bonhoeffer thinks this is nothing but religious blackmail and clerical subterfuge — " religious interpretation " at its very worst. It relegates God to man's inner life and makes the mistake of thinking that " a man can be addressed as a sinner only after his weaknesses and meannesses have been spied out " (PFG 159). Bonhoeffer is convinced that man's sin is to be found in his strength, not in his weakness.

Instead of uncovering the " dirty linen " in the closets of men's lives, an action that he feels is a mark of cynicism, Bonhoeffer believes that " since the Fall reticence and secrecy are essential," that *"in statu corruptionis* many things in man are to remain concealed, and that if it is too late to eradicate evil, it is at least to be kept hidden " (PFG 80, E 334). Although we can understand Bonhoeffer's attitude toward pastors who prey on the secret sins of men, it is impossible to accept his general broadside against psychotherapy and existentialism. Psychotherapy, for instance, can hardly be accused of desiring to " spy things out " for their own sake. Rather, this discipline is dedicated to helping men overcome the subconscious " demons " that prevent them from living mature lives. It is concerned with mental illness and plays an important role within the medical profession. Likewise, existentialism is not born primarily of distrust and suspicion of mankind, but is a philosophical attempt to advocate the primacy of life over thought — a priority that Bonhoeffer himself would affirm. Therefore, we believe that Bonhoeffer was censuring these disciplines only in so far as they were being *mis*used to impose a *religious* interpretation of Christianity upon the world come of age, i.e., in so far as they represent religious ideologies that prey on human weakness.

Now what of Bonhoeffer's criticism of Karl Barth? These two theologians have a great deal in common, and they maintained a friendly relation of mutual respect and admiration from the early 1930's onward. They share a decidedly Christocentric point of view, and Bonhoeffer made it clear that he stood *within* the theology of revelation advocated by Barth. Although they both accept the same starting point, however, their theologies are by no means the same. Bonhoeffer believed that Barth had started on the right line of thought, namely, away from liberal theology and the identification of Christianity with religion, but had failed to carry it through to its logical conclusion. That is, instead of proceeding to a nonreligious interpretation of theological concepts, he had stopped at a sort of halfway point, which Bonhoeffer called a "positivism of revelation." What does he mean? This is difficult to say, especially because Bonhoeffer connects Barth so closely with the Confessing Church, which took the Barthian approach, but "lapsed from positivism into conservative restoration" (PFG 148). Nevertheless, it would seem that by "positivism of revelation" Bonhoeffer meant that, on the basis of the Bible, Barth had reformulated the traditional doctrines of the church into a dogmatic system, all parts of which (Trinity, virgin birth, etc.) were of equal importance and had to be accepted as a whole or not at all (PFG 126). The church, then, could proclaim the whole as "revelation" and more or less say to the world, " Take it or leave it." Bonhoeffer was convinced that this made it too easy for the church, because the mature world, which could no longer understand the traditional terminology, would usually " leave it." The church would feel that it had done its duty, and the world would go its own way and be left to its own devices.

Bonhoeffer does not believe that words alone, even words informed by a theology of revelation, will have much impact upon a mature world. What is needed is a church that takes seriously its call to participate in the being of Christ in the world, a church that loves the world so much that it does not try to impose upon it some absolute, but rather shares willingly and joyously in its immediate, relative realities. Only a community that is willing to live and suffer in, for, and with the world in its common life will be able to speak God's reconciling word.

Bonhoeffer would also question whether the church should live exclusively from the New Testament message of the sovereign triumph of God's grace. In contrast to Barth, who sees everything in the light of the " last things," Bonhoeffer emphasizes that we must take seriously the " things which go before the last things," that is, the penultimate manifestations of humanity and goodness which are preparatory to the ultimate message of justification by grace and faith alone. He is convinced that the last word must not be spoken before the next to last, because we live on the next to last word, and believe on the last. This is why Christians must not neglect the Old Testament:

It is only when one knows the ineffability of the name of God that one can utter the name of Jesus Christ. It is only when one loves life and the world so much that without them everything would be gone, that one can believe in the resurrection and a new world. It is only when one submits to the law that one can speak of grace, and only when one sees the anger and wrath of God hanging like grim realities over the head of one's enemies that one can know something of what it means to love them and forgive them. I don't think it is Christian to want to get to the New Testament too soon and too directly. (PFG 79)

One may question whether Bonhoeffer's criticism of Barth hits the mark. To be sure, Barth uses traditional language and takes seriously all of the time-honored doctrines of the church, but he has never tried to *impose* his theology on either church or world. Barth has as little regard for religion as Bonhoeffer and would never dream of making religion a precondition of faith, but he would not agree with Bonhoeffer's judgment about the world's having come of age and would put more reliance upon the Holy Spirit's speaking through the traditional language of the church. It is our conviction that Bonhoeffer probably blamed Barth for the attitude and actions of the Confessing Church, which in its later years " fought for self-preservation as though it were an end in itself " (PFG 140), entrenched itself behind the "faith of the church," and avoided the honest question of real and personal belief (PFG 180). What he never knew was that Barth himself was critical of these developments within the Confessing Church. This is not the place for an investigation of the real differences which exist in the theologies of these two men, but it is important at this point to sound a warning against those who use the slogan "positivism of revelation" to separate them into opposing camps.

Whereas Bonhoeffer believed that Barth had moved in the right direction, he thinks that Bultmann intended to go beyond Barth but actually slipped back in the direction of liberal theology. In this regard, however, we must question whether Bonhoeffer really understood Bultmann's view of "demythologizing" when he considers it a typical liberal reduction process aimed at eliminating myth in order to expose the essence of Christianity. Here Bonhoeffer clearly misunderstands the *intention* of Bultmann, who has repeatedly declared that he is not interested in eliminating the mythological elements, but in *interpreting* them. It is another question, of course, whether Bultmann has fulfilled his intention or whether Bonhoeffer's instinctive judgment is correct after all, but we must admit that the two men actually share a common interest in interpreting the Christian faith to twentieth-century man. Bultmann calls for an "existential" interpretation, Bonhoeffer a "nonreligious" one; but it is by no means self-evident that the two theologians mean the same thing. Bultmann thinks in the anthropological terms of man's self-understanding, Bonhoeffer in the "theanthropological" terms of the *new reality* eternally uniting God and the world in Jesus Christ.

For Bultmann "demythologizing" involves the academic question of hermeneutics, namely, the question of interpreting the Bible by means of the "existentials" of Heidegger's existentialist philosophy in order to disclose the Biblical understanding of human existence. On the other hand, Bonhoeffer's "dereligionizing" is concerned not only with the hermeneutical question, but with the question of the existence of the church itself. Only a church whose message is a part of its own being, a church that in obedience witnesses to its own ultimate concern through its actions, is able to exegete and proclaim the word of God to a world come of age. For Bonhoeffer, Bultmann's interpretation is too introspective and individualistic, and thus too "religious." Furthermore, from the very first, Bonhoeffer objected to Bultmann's importation of Heidegger's concept of "possibility" into theology. It is Bonhoeffer's contention that theology does not deal with possibilities (even man's existentialistic-ontological possibilities!) but only reality.[8]

There are many other questions which we wish Bonhoeffer had answered. For instance, in view of his concept of "this-worldly transcendence," it would be interesting to know how he would develop a doctrine of the Trinity. Further, what notion of eschatology is implicit in a worldly or nonreligious interpretation of the Christian faith? What place has the doctrine of the "adversary" or evil in a world that is solely and entirely the world of Christ? What does Bonhoeffer have in mind when he speaks of "natural" piety and "unconscious Christianity," which he links with the differentiation that the old Lutheran dogmaticians made between *fides directa* and *fides reflexa* (PFG 172)? These must all remain tantalizing questions for us, but perhaps this is not a misfortune. Indeed, perhaps one of the reasons why Bonhoeffer's theology is so fascinating and stimulating is because it was cut off in the midst of a great thrust of creativity, because we do *not* have all the answers!

D. Conclusion

The life and work of Dietrich Bonhoeffer is finished, but his influence on the Christian church is steadily extending around the world. What is it about his thought that commands attention and speaks to people in a way that is almost uncanny? Why is it that his name is being mentioned in the same breath with such theological giants as Barth and Bultmann and Tillich?[9] What is it that distinguishes his theology?

---

[8] See especially AS 55 f., 72 ff. Bonhoeffer's strongest polemic against the notion of "possibility" is found in his matriculation address at the University of Berlin, entitled "Die Frage nach dem Menschen in der gegenwärtigen Philosophie und Theologie."

[9] See, for instance, the address delivered at Union Theological Seminary, New York City, by the eminent Scottish theologian Dr. John Baillie, entitled "Some Reflections on the Changing Theological Scene," *Union Seminary Quarterly Review*, Vol. XII, No. 2, January, 1957, pp. 3–9.

We have already pointed out that the clue to Bonhoeffer is the Christocentric focus of his thought, that is, his constant reference to Jesus Christ, who is at once the Incarnate, the Crucified, and the Risen One. In his theology he consciously endeavored to hold in balance all three elements, because he believed " it would be quite wrong to establish a separate theology of the incarnation, a theology of the cross, or a theology of the resurrection, each in opposition to the others, by a misconceived absolutization of one of these parts " (E 89). Bonhoeffer has bequeathed the church an exceedingly rich doctrine of the person and work of Christ. His doctrine of the incarnation emphasizes that the eternal Son of God took upon himself our entire human nature, but in doing so he became not only man but *a* man (an affirmation of both *anhypostasia* and *enhypostasia!*). His doctrine of the atonement resembles Irenaeus' notion of recapitulation, that is, that Christ came as the Second Adam and recapitulated the life of the first Adam *without* disobeying and thus fulfilled the covenant, but Bonhoeffer adds to this Luther's emphasis on Christ's vicarious suffering on the cross for the sins of the whole world. The resurrection becomes the basis for all that Bonhoeffer says about the life in the New Humanity and the Lordship of Christ over the church and the world.

Furthermore, Bonhoeffer has quite simply and clearly called the church to new obedience to the commandment of Jesus Christ. He has not been afraid to speak of good works, but has done so on the basis of a sound evangelical theology. He has made Protestantism again conscious of the cost of discipleship, and he speaks with the authority of one who practiced what he preached. Within the theology of the Word of God he has introduced what might be called an *imitatio Christi* theology, which means that the community that is established by the hearing of the word must pattern its life after Christ's own life and thus be transformed into his image. It is not enough for the church to have a proper dogmatics or a sound hermeneutic or a venerable liturgy — important as these are! — but there must be obedience. This will take place in two areas: first, in the church's interior life as a community of faith and, second, in the life of the members who are scattered in the workaday world.

In the final period of his theology Bonhoeffer was breaking fresh ground in his concept of "worldly" Christianity, and it is here that he is helping the church to a new understanding on the relation between God and the world. In the long run this will undoubtedly be Bonhoeffer's greatest contribution, and it is possible that his thought will lead to a significant revolution of the understanding of the Christian faith. If the experience of transcendence is found only in a new life for others, that is, by participating in the being of Jesus as one whose only concern is for others, then this means that our abstract ideas of God in terms of his omnipotence, omniscience, and omnipresence must be discarded once and for all. We can never know God as an idea, but only in and through our concrete encounter with others in our life in the world. God is not to be known except in human form, as man existing for others, and the sole ground for his omnipotence, omniscience, and omnipresence is his freedom from self, maintained to the point of death. It is from this new understanding of transcendence that Bonhoeffer would have us reinterpret the Biblical concepts of Creation, Fall, atonement, repentance, faith, the new life, and the last things.

Bonhoeffer's theology is one of commitment and involvement. To be a Christian means to be committed to and involved in a way of life in the world, and this is God's own way, which he has revealed in Jesus Christ. This precludes any "spectator" attitude toward the world and any "prescriptive and perceptual approach"[10] to the ministry. The church must reassess the context and compass of redemption and come to a more realistic appraisal of the humble (but vital!) role that it plays in God's scheme of things. It must learn afresh that God's *primary* concern is with *this world*. It must be willing to risk its own existence for the sake of the world. It must be ready to act responsibly for mankind, even unto the death of many of its cherished ideas and traditions. Only by losing itself, namely, by not bothering about its own needs, problems, sins, and fears, will it be caught up in the way of God, into the Messianic event.

Perhaps the most impressive thing about Dietrich Bonhoeffer is the way in which his own life provides the commentary on his theology. He lived close to God and out of the depth of involvement, and he learned the secret of freedom. Shortly after he heard the news

[10] We are indebted to Paul Lehmann for this well-suited phrase.

of the failure of the plot against Hitler, he outlined these "Stations on the Way to Freedom":

SELF-DISCIPLINE

If you set out to seek freedom, you must learn before all things
Mastery over sense and soul, lest your wayward desirings,
Lest your undisciplined members lead you now this way, now that way.
Chaste be your mind and your body, and subject to you and obedient,
Serving solely to seek their appointed goal and objective.
None learns the secret of freedom save only by way of control.

ACTION

Do and dare what is right, not swayed by the whim of the moment.
Bravely take hold of the real, not dallying now with what might be.
Not in the flight of ideas but only in action is freedom.
Make up your mind and come out into the tempest of living.
God's command is enough and your faith in him to sustain you.
Then at last freedom will welcome your spirit amid great rejoicing.

SUFFERING

See what a transformation! These hands so active and powerful
Now are tied, and alone and fainting, you see where your work ends.
Yet you are confident still, and gladly commit what is rightful
Into a stronger hand, and say that you are contented.
You were free for a moment of bliss, then you yielded your freedom
Into the hand of God, that he might perfect it in glory.

DEATH

Come now, highest of feasts on the way to freedom eternal,
Death, strike off the fetters, break down the walls that oppress us,
Our bedazzled soul and our ephemeral body,
That we may see at last the sight which here was not vouchsafed us.
Freedom, we sought you long in discipline, action, suffering.
Now as we die we see you and know you at last face to face. (E xii.)

The witness of Dietrich Bonhoeffer is sealed. "The blood of the martyrs is the seed of the church."

Bibliography

Primary Works

A complete bibliography of the works of Bonhoeffer published up until the year 1956 is to be found at the conclusion of *Die mündige Welt II*. Almost all these and also most of the unpublished works now being edited in the *Gesammelte Schriften* have been read by the writer, but the following list has been limited to those books and essays most immediately connected with this study.

Akt und Sein: Transzendentalphilosophie und Ontologie in der systematischen Theologie. Beiträge zur Förderung christlicher Theologie, 34. Band, 2. Heft, Gütersloh, 1931. 2d ed., *Theologische Bücherei*, Band V, Kaiser, Munich, 1956.
"Die Bekennende Kirche und die Oekumene," *Evangelische Theologie*, Heft 7, August, 1935, pp. 245–261. Reprinted in *Gesammelte Schriften I*, pp. 240–261.
"Concerning the Christian Idea of God," *The Journal of Religion*, Vol. XII, No. 2, April, 1932, pp. 177–185.
Dein Reich komme! Das Gebet der Gemeinde um Gottes Reich auf Erden. Stimmen aus der deutschen christlichen Studentenbewegung, Heft 78, Furche, Berlin, 1933, pp. 29–42. 2d ed., with the addition of "Die erste Tafel: Eine Auslegung der ersten drei Gebote" (written in 1944), Furche, Hamburg, 1957.
"Die Erhöhung Jesu Christi," *Unterwegs,* Heft 2, 1950, pp. 66–71.
Ethik. Zusammengestellt und herausgegeben von E. Bethge, Kaiser, Munich, 1949. Trans. by N. Horton Smith as *Ethics,* S.C.M. Press, Ltd., London, 1955; The Macmillan Company, 1955.

Das Gebetbuch der Bibel: Eine Einführung in die Psalmen, MBK, Salzuflen, 1940. 5th ed., 1956.

"Geheimnis der Menschwerdung," *Unterwegs,* Heft 6, 1949, pp. 325–331.

Gemeinsames Leben. Theologische Existenz heute, Heft 61, Kaiser, Munich, 1939. 8th ed., 1955. Trans. by John W. Doberstein as *Life Together,* Harper & Brothers, 1954; S.C.M. Press, Ltd., London, 1955.

Gesammelte Schriften. Band I (Oekumene). Herausgegeben von Eberhard Bethge, Kaiser, Munich, 1958.

Glaubst Du, so hast Du. Versuch eines Lutherischen Katechismus (written with Franz Hildebrandt). Monatsschrift für Pastoraltheologie, Heft 5/6, 28. Jhg., 1932, pp. 167–172.

" Glück und Macht ": Gespräche aus Romanfragment, *Unterwegs,* Heft 4, 1954, pp. 196–205. Trans. by Miss H. M. Bishop as " Happiness and Power," *The Bridge,* April, 1955, pp. 4–15.

" Die Kirche und die Völker der Welt," *Unterwegs,* Heft 3, 1954, pp. 129–131. Trans. as " The Church and Peoples of the World," *Gesammelte Schriften I,* pp. 447–449.

" Die Kirche vor der Judenfrage," *Der Vormarsch,* Heft 6, 3. Jhg., June, 1933, pp. 171–176.

" König David: Drei Stunden Bibelarbeit," *Junge Kirche,* 4. Jhg, 1936, Heft 2, pp. 64–69, Heft 4, pp. 157–161, Heft 5, pp. 197–203.

Nachfolge. Kaiser, Munich, 1937. 5th ed., 1955. Trans. by R. H. Fuller as *The Cost of Discipleship,* S.C.M. Press, Ltd., London, 1948; The Macmillan Company, 1949.

"Protestantismus ohne Reformation," *Unterwegs,* Heft 1, 1949, pp. 3–17. Reprinted in *Gesammelte Schriften I,* pp. 323–354.

Sanctorum Communio: Eine dogmatische Untersuchung zur Soziologie der Kirche. Trowitzsch und Sohn, Berlin u. Frankfort/Oder, 1930. 2d ed., *Theologische Bücherei,* Band III, Kaiser, Munich, 1954.

Schöpfung und Fall: Theologische Auslegung von Genesis 1–3. Kaiser, Munich, 1933. 3d ed., 1955.

Versuchung. Bearbeitet und herausgegeben von E. Bethge, Kaiser, Munich, 1953. 2d ed., 1954. Trans. by Kathleen Downham as *Temptation,* S.C.M. Press, Ltd., London, 1955; The Macmillan Company, 1955.

"Von der Dankbarkeit," *Unterwegs,* Heft 1, 1950, pp. 2–3.

"Was ist Kirche?", *Der Vormarsch,* Heft 1, 3. Jhg., January, 1933, pp. 8–10.

"Der Wiederaufbau Jerusalems nach Esra und Nehemia," *Junge Kirche,* 4. Jhg., 1936, Heft 14, pp. 653–661.

Widerstand und Ergebung: Briefe und Aufzeichnungen aus der Haft. Herausgegeben von E. Bethge, Kaiser, Munich, 1951. 6th expanded ed., 1955. Trans. by R. H. Fuller as *Letters and Papers from Prison,* S.C.M. Press, Ltd., London, 1953; as *Prisoner for God,* The Macmillan Company, 1954.

"Zu Karl Heim's: Glauben und Denken," *Christentum und Wissenschaft,* Heft 12, 8. Jhg., December, 1932, pp. 441–454.

"Zur Frage nach der Kirchengemeinschaft," *Evangelische Theologie,* 3. Jhg., 1936, pp. 214–233. II. "Fragen," pp. 405–410. Reprinted in MW I.

"Zur Tauffrage," *Unterwegs,* Heft 6, 1948, pp. 3–13.

"Zur theologischen Begründung der Weltbundarbeit," *Die Eiche,* 20. Jhg., Nr. 4, 1932, pp. 334–344. Reprinted in *Gesammelte Schriften* I, pp. 140–158.

Works About Bonhoeffer

The best secondary sources are to be found in the two volumes of collected essays, *Die mündige Welt I und II.* Most of the essays in *Die mündige Welt I* were also published in *Evangelische Theologie,* Heft 4/5, 15. Jhg., 1955. Two other small volumes that contain valuable essays are the *Bonhoeffer Gedenkheft* and *Dietrich Bonhoeffer: Einführung in seine Botschaft.* A memorial volume published by the World Council of Churches, entitled *Das Zeugnis eines Boten,* contains interesting introductory material. Because it would unnecessarily lengthen the bibliography, the individual authors and essays in these volumes are not listed below.

Bethge, Eberhard. "Dietrich Bonhoeffer," *German Life and Letters,* Basil Blackwell, Oxford, 1957, pp. 126–130. Also published in *World Dominion,* Vol. XXXV, No. 2, April, 1957, pp. 77–81.

———. "Dietrich Bonhoeffer," *The Student Movement,* Vol. LVI, No. 3, 1954, pp. 24–26. Also published in *Campus Lutheran,* Vol. VI, No. 3, December, 1954, pp. 20–23.

―――― " Dietrich Bonhoeffer. An Account of His Life," *The Plough,* Vol. III, No. 2, 1955, pp. 35–42.

―――― " In Memoriam Dietrich Bonhoeffer. Zum 50. Geburtstag am 4. Februar 1956," *Stimme der Gemeinde,* Heft 3, 8. Jhg., February, 1956, Darmstadt, pp. 67–69.

―――― "Die Tat der freien Verantwortung. Zum Thema: Dietrich Bonhoeffer," *Unterwegs,* Heft 6, 1947, pp. 5–10.

Bonhoeffer Gedenkheft. Herausgegeben von Eberhard Bethge, Haus und Schule, Berlin, 1947.

Brunner, Hans Heinrich. " Am Ende des religiösen Zeitalters. Versuch einer Standortbestimmung zehn Jahre nach der Hinrichtung von Dietrich Bonhoeffer," *Reformatio,* Heft 8, IV. Jhg., August, 1955, pp. 419–435.

Dietrich Bonhoeffer: Einführung in seine Botschaft. Herausgegeben von Presseverband der Evangelischen Kirche im Rheinland, Fr. Staats GmbH, Wt.-Barmen, 1956.

Ebeling, Gerhard. " Die ' night-religiöse Interpretation biblischer Begriffe,' " *Zeitschrift für Theologie und Kirche,* Heft 3, 52. Jhg., December, 1955, pp. 296–360. Reprinted in MW II.

Glenthøj, Jørgen. " Dietrich Bonhoeffers Konfirmanden," *Die Tür des Wortes: Evangelischer Almanach auf das Jahr 1957,* Evangelischer Verlagsanstalt, Berlin, pp. 136–151. Shortened edition in *Die Zeichen der Zeit,* Heft 6, 1957, pp. 213–218.

―――― *Efterfølgelse. Nogle Indtryk af Dietrich Bonhoeffers Bog Nachfolge.* Saertryk af Diakonissehuset Sankt Lukas Stiftelsens Aarsberetning, 1956–1957.

Godsey, John D. " Theology from a Prison Cell," *The Drew Gateway,* Vol. XXVII, No. 3, Spring, 1957, pp. 139–154.

Hammelsbeck, O. "Begegnung mit Dietrich Bonhoeffer," *Evangelische Erziehung,* June, 1949, pp. 29–30.

Harbsmeier, Götz. " Die ' nicht-religiöse Interpretation biblischer Begriffe' bei Bonhoeffer und die Entmythologisierung," *Antwort: Karl Barth zum siebzigsten Geburtstag,* Evangelischer Verlag, Zollikon-Zürich, 1956, pp. 545–561. Reprinted in MW II.

Hill, George G. " Bonhoeffer: Bridge Between Liberalism and Orthodoxy," *The New Christian Advocate,* June, 1957, pp. 80–83.

Müller-Gangloff, Erich. " Theologie für die mündige Welt — Die-

trich Bonhoeffer und die geistesgechichtliche Situation der Gegenwart," *Die neue Furche,* Heft 8, 6 Jhg., August, 1952, pp. 525–530.
Die mündige Welt: Dem Andenken Dietrich Bonhoeffers. Kaiser, Munich, 1955.
Die mündige Welt: II. Band. Kaiser, Munich, 1956.
Niebuhr, Reinhold. "The Death of a Martyr," *Christianity and Crisis,* Vol. V, No. 11, June 25, 1945, pp. 6–7.
Schlingensiepen, Hermann. "Zum Vermächtnis Dietrich Bonhoeffers," *Evangelische Theologie,* 13. Jhg., 1953, pp. 97–106. Reprinted in MW I.
Schönherr, Albrecht. "Diesseitigkeit: Ein Gedenkwort für Bonhoeffer," *Die Zeichen der Zeit,* Heft 8/9, 1947, pp. 307–312.
Sutz, Erwin. "Dietrich Bonhoeffer," *Reformatio,* Heft 4, IV. Jhg., April, 1955, pp. 163–166.
West, Charles. "Dietrich Bonhoeffer — the Theologian," *The Student Movement,* Vol. LVI, No. 3, 1954, pp. 27–29. Also published in *Campus Lutheran,* Vol. VI, No. 3, December, 1954, pp. 23–25.
Das Zeugnis eines Boten. Zum Gedächtnis von Dietrich Bonhoeffer. Oekumenische Kommission für die Pastoration der Kriegsgefangenen, Geneva, 1945.

Related Works

The following books and articles have been read wholly or in part by the writer and provide helpful background material for Bonhoeffer's life and thought.

Barth, Karl. *Kirchliche Dogmatik,* III/4 (1951), IV/2 (1955). Evangelischer Verlag, Zollikon-Zürich.
Bekennende Kirche: Martin Niemöller zum 60. Geburtstag. Kaiser, Munich, 1952.
Bell, G. K. A. *The Church and Humanity, 1939–1946.* Longmans, Green & Co., Inc., London, 1946.
——— "The Church and the Resistance Movement in Germany," *The Wiener Library Bulletin,* Vol. XI, Nos. 3–4, pp. 21–23. Reprinted in GS I.
Best, S. Payne. *The Venlo Incident.* Hutchinson & Co., Ltd., London, 1950.

Duncan-Jones, A. S. *The Struggle for Religious Freedom in Germany.* Victor Gollancz, Ltd., London, 1946.
Forck, Bernhard H. (ed.). "Und folget ihrem Glauben nach": *Gedenkbuch für die Blutzeugen der Bekennenden Kirche.* Evangelisches Verlagswerk, Stuttgart, 1949.
Frey, Arthur. *Der Kampf der evangelischen Kirche in Deutschland.* Evangelischer Verlag, Zollikon-Zürich, 1937.
Gaevernitz, Gero v. S. (ed.). *They Almost Killed Hitler.* The Macmillan Company, 1947.
Gollwitzer, H., Kuhn, K., and Schneider, R. (eds.). *Dying We Live.* Pantheon Books, 1956.
Grob, Rudolf. *Der Kirchenkampf in Deutschland.* Zwingli Verlag, Zürich, 1937.
Hammelsbeck, O. *Die veränderte Weltsituation des modernen Menschen als religiöses Problem.* Theologische Existenz heute, Neue Folge Nr. 45, Kaiser, Munich, 1955.
Karl Barth zum Kirchenkampf. Theologische Existenz heute, Neue Folge Nr. 49, Kaiser, Munich, 1956.
Kupisch, Karl. *Zwischen Idealismus und Massendemokratie.* Lettner, Berlin, 1955.
Lieb, Fritz. *Christ und Antichrist im dritten Reich.* Editions du Carrefour, Paris, 1936.
Otto, W. F. *The Homeric Gods.* Thames & Hudson, Ltd., London, 1954.
Rouse, Ruth, and Neil, Stephen C. (eds.). *A History of the Ecumenical Movement 1517–1948.* The Westminster Press, 1954.
Schmidt, Kurt D. (ed.). *Die Bekenntnisse und grundsätzlichen Aeusserungen zur Kirchenfrage.* Band I (das Jahr 1933), Band II (1934), Band III (1935). Vandenhoeck & Ruprecht, Göttingen, 1934–1936.
Smith, Ronald G. *The New Man.* Harper & Brothers, 1956.
"Studienreise des Predigerseminars der Bekennende Kirche zu Finkenwalde in Pommern nach Dänemark und Schweden vom 29.2.-11.3.1936," *Junge Kirche,* Heft 9, 4. Jhg., May, 1936, pp. 420–426.
von Weizsäcker, C. F. *The World View of Physics.* University of Chicago Press, 1952.

The Author

John Drew Godsey was born in Bristol, Tennessee, on October 10, 1922, to William Clinton Godsey, a proprietor and executive in the dairy industry, and Mary Lynn, nee Corns. He attended the Bristol Public School, 1928–1938, and The McCallie School in Chattanooga, Tennessee, from 1938 to 1940. He entered Virginia Polytechnic Institute in 1940 and studied until 1943, when he left to serve in the United States Army. In 1946 he returned to V.P.I., graduating with honors in 1947. He worked in industry from 1947 until 1950, when he entered the ministry of The Methodist Church.

From 1950 to 1953 he studied at Drew Theological Seminary, Madison, New Jersey, graduating with honors. From 1953 to 1956 he studied at the University of Basel in Basel, Switzerland, under Professor Karl Barth. Having received a call to teach systematic theology at Drew, he returned with his wife, Emalee, whom he married in 1943, and his son and three daughters, two of whom were born in Basel, to Madison, New Jersey. In the summer of 1958 he returned to the University of Basel to complete his work for the Doctor of Theology degree. At present he is Assistant Professor of Systematic Theology and Assistant to the Dean at The Theological School of Drew University.

Indexes

SUBJECTS

Act (*Akt*), 56
  actus directus, 56, 70, 78
  actus reflexus, 56, 78
America, 24, 94 f.
American Christendom, 25 f., 195
American Revolution, 209
Analogia entis, 62, 124
Analogia relationis, 124
Apologetics, 250, 252
Apostles' Creed, 52 f.
Arcane discipline, 254, 261, 273
Authority, 50, 98, 242

Beatitudes, 156 f.
Being (*Sein*), 56
Bible. *See* Holy Scripture

Calling (vocation), 37, 238 f.
Care of souls, 50
Christian, the
  cross of, 155
  as deputy, 247
  as example, 50, 259
  as formed by Christ, 171, 205, 206, 227
  ministry of, 185 ff.
  priestly duties of, 50
  righteousness of, 161
  as saint, 169 f.
  suffering of, 155, 159, 169, 177, 193, 282
Christian life, 42 f., 160 f., 169, 171, 180 ff., 220, 257 f., 281
Christianity
  religious interpretation of, 17, 249, 271
  nonreligious interpretation of, 253 f., 256, 272, 274, 281
Christology, 264 ff., 280
Church, 27, 34 f., 52, 57, 67, 156, 192, 206, 211, 214 f., 258 f.
  actualization of, 35, 38, 40 ff.
  authority of, 50 f.
  as body of Christ, 17, 47, 52, 147, 166 f., 169, 206, 216, 260, 267
  boundary of, 111 ff.
  as "Christ existing as community," 22, 43, 45, 51, 55, 67, 260, 266
  empirical form of, 44, 46 f.
  as " end in itself " and " means to an end," 51, 247, 266
  and faith, 57
  as fellowship of love, 42, 51, 266
  as fellowship of persons, 68
  as fellowship of the Spirit, 22, 41, 42 f., 51, 266
  founding of, 37 f.

Church (*cont.*)
  in statu confessionis, 110, 116
  as Kingdom of Christ, 46, 55, 215
  and Kingdom of God, 46, 55
  life-principle of, 36, 39, 51
  mandate of, 245 f.
  misunderstandings of, 34
  as new humanity, 35, 38, 105, 266
  objective spirit of, 44 f.
  order of, 115 f.
  and politics, 109 f., 159, 273
  predestinarian view of, 41
  as presence of Christ, 40, 51, 98, 168, 266
  realization of, 35 ff.
  as revelational reality, 34 f., 266
  as *sanctorum communio,* 28, 33 ff., 42
  sin in, 44 f., 74 f.
  and state, 107 ff., 210
  unity of, 43, 106, 207
  and word of God, 47 f., 51, 245 f.
  and world, 53, 162, 215, 216, 230, 247, 269, 281
Confession (Creed), 106 f., 112 f.
Confession, practice of, 187 f., 211, 245
Confessional Synods, 91
  Augsburg, 91
  Barmen, 91, 92, 111, 114, 116, 117
  Dahlem, 91, 92, 111, 114, 116, 117
  Oeynhausen, 91, 115
Conscience, 74 f., 76 f., 79, 139, 225, 236
Consciousness, 56, 64
Creation, 119 ff., 126 f., 192, 212 f.

Death, 36, 129, 140 f., 282
Demythologizing, 253, 278

Deputyship, 233 f., 247, 260
Discipleship, 151, 153, 155, 164, 167, 239

Ecumenical movement, 15, 16, 81, 96 ff., 104, 106
  Faith and Order, 15, 16
  Life and Work, 16, 86, 90, 97, 105
  World Alliance, 16, 81, 86, 97, 102, 103
Eschatology, 53, 58 f., 78, 194
  apocatastasis, 54, 78
  eternal life, 54 f.
  Last Judgment, 53 f., 162
  resurrection of body, 54
Ethical, the, 240 ff., 243
Ethics
  as formation, 205
  point of departure of, 206, 212
  positivistic view, 213
  purpose of, 217
  warrant for, 242
Evil, 132, 137, 159
Existential philosophy, 251, 275 f.
Extant (*Seiendes*), 56

Faith, 41 f., 51, 52, 65, 69 f., 77, 154, 218, 257, 262
  as act, 55
  as experience, 52
  fides directa, 49, 77, 279
  fides reflexa, 279
Fellowship. *See Gemeinschaft* and Church
Finkenwalde seminary, 17, 87 f., 92
  Scandinavian trip of, 89
Forgiveness of sins, 149, 155, 193
French Revolution, 208

Gemeinschaft (fellowship or community), 27, 30 f., 53, 68
German Church Struggle, 16 f., 86, 107 ff., 117 f., 153
  Confessing Church, 16 f., 86 f., 92 f., 106 f., 114 f., 117, 258, 263, 276 ff.
  German Christians, 16 f., 84, 86, 106 f., 111, 258
Gesellschaft (society), 30 f., 53
God, 62, 250, 255
  commandment of, 98 f., 100 f., 104, 242 ff., 245
  as Creator, 60, 119 ff., 192
  curse and promise of, 139 f.
  as *deus ex machina,* 250, 255, 256, 271, 272
  freedom of, 64, 67, 123 ff.
  grace of, 54, 176
  judgment of, 149
  Kingdom of, 46, 55, 107 ff., 161, 212 f., 223, 257, 264
  knowledge of, 70, 225
  as love, 228 f.
  omnipotence of, 22, 281
  orders (ordinances) of, 16, 82
  as Preserver, 101, 122, 141
  righteousness of, 161
  transcendence of, 62, 255, 272, 281
  as Trinity, 123, 171
  will of, 35, 217, 226, 227 ff., 266
  word of, 14, 41, 46 f., 50 f., 63, 73, 98, 121, 149, 174 f., 233, 245 f.
  as "working hypothesis," 249, 256, 271
  wrath of, 54, 176
Good, the, 212, 230 f., 232
Good works, 157
Grace, 218, 239

cheap grace, 18, 152, 268
costly grace, 152

History, 36 f., 38, 45, 53, 206, 231
  sacred history, 192
Holy Scripture, 48, 65, 119, 182, 189, 246, 253
Holy Spirit, 35, 39 ff., 44, 48, 70, 123, 165
  and human spirit, 26
  at Pentecost, 38
  social activity of, 44
  spatial activity of, 39
  and word of God, 48
  work of, 40 ff., 45

Idealism, 26, 29, 31, 55, 58, 59, 60, 61
I-Thou relation, 27 ff.

Jesus Christ
  ascension of, 38, 168, 247, 270
  claim of, 229 f.
  commandment of, 154, 164 f.
  crucifixion (cross) of, 37, 107, 120, 143, 155, 205, 207, 220, 247, 270, 280
  as Example, 38, 50
  as Foundation of church, 38 f.
  as Head of body, 168, 267
  historical activity of, 39, 44
  incarnation, 107, 156, 166 f., 168, 205, 207, 219 f., 232, 234, 239, 246, 253, 270, 280
  law of, 186
  as lord, 97, 203, 215, 246 f., 254, 267 268, 280
  as Mediator, 156, 180, 246
  as New Man (Second Adam), 67, 167

Jesus Christ (*cont.*)
  person of, 68, 234
  as Reconciler, 204, 234, 247
  as Representative (*Stellvertreter*), 36, 39 f., 261
  resurrection of, 37 f., 107, 120, 205, 220, 247, 270, 272, 280
  Second Coming of, 168, 194
  suffering of, 155, 193
  temptation of, 174 f.
  as Vicarious Substitute (*Stellvertreter*), 39 f., 42
  as Word of God, 34, 40
  work of, 36, 38, 39 f., 171, 236
Justice, 102 f., 105
Justification, 218, 254
  justified sinner, 149, 151

Knowledge, 58 f., 63
  of faith (believing), 70, 72
  of good and evil, 28, 128 f., 134, 225
  preaching, 71 f.
  theological, 71 f.

Last Supper, 37
Law, the, 37, 76, 100, 157 f., 192, 237, 244
Life, 224, 231 f.
  tree of, 128 f., 142 f., 192 f.
Lord's Prayer, 190
Love, 41, 42, 43, 159, 161, 181, 228 f.
Lutheran, Lutheranism, 15, 17, 91, 115, 153, 213, 238, 239, 279

Man
  as "Adam," "in Adam," 28, 32 f., 36, 73 ff., 127 ff., 167
  as body and soul, 127
  as *Dasein*, 62
  Fall of, 32 f., 36, 107, 132 ff., 170, 173 f., 225, 275
  freedom of, 123 ff., 243 f.
  guilt of, 32, 193
  "in Christ," as new humanity, 22, 33, 35 f., 38, 40, 67, 76
  as *imago Dei* (image of God), 122 ff., 127, 170 f., 225
  as single person and collective person, 29 f., 75
  original sin of, 32, 138
  original state of, 28 ff., 127 ff.
  self-understanding of, 63, 73, 278
  as *sicut deus* (like God), 134 ff., 140 f., 170, 225, 236
  temptation of, 75 f., 132 ff., 172 ff.
  will of, 30 f.
Mandates, 216 f., 244 ff., 261
Marriage, 131, 139, 158
Meditation, 183 f.

Natural, the, 222 f.
Negro spirituals, 24, 88
Nonresistance, 159

Obedience, 154, 171, 280
Objective spirit, 31 f., 44 f.
Ontology, 56, 60 ff., 66
Orders of creation, 16, 82, 100 ff., 141
Orders of preservation, 82, 101 ff., 141, 261

Pati, 69, 260
Peace, 102 f., 104 f.
Penultimate, 218 ff., 261, 277
Perisson, 160
Person, idea of, 27 f., 68 f., 70
  individual person, 29, 32 f., 53
  collective person, 22, 29, 32 f., 53

Pharisees, 226
Phenomenology, 61 f.
Prayer, 161 f., 183, 184, 189 f.
Preaching, 22, 46, 48, 68, 71 f., 167, 210, 245 f.
Psalms, 181, 189 ff.
Psychotherapy, 251, 275 f.

Reality, 204, 212, 214, 269, 278
Reason (Logos), 60, 222 f.
  corruption of, 61
"Religious Apriori," 249, 254, 261
Reformation, Reformers, 51, 112, 153, 159, 207, 218, 273
Repentance, 77, 258, 262
Responsibility, 233 ff.
  and freedom, 237
  and obedience, 238
Revelation, 35, 55, 57, 67 f., 269
  as "act," 55, 63 f.
  as "being," 55, 64 f.
  continuity of, 68
  positivism of, 253, 276, 278
Roman Catholic, Catholicism, 15, 34, 52, 62, 65, 111, 112, 152, 207, 208, 246

Sacraments, 49, 77, 100, 164
  Baptism, 49, 77, 78, 100, 112, 155, 165 f., 167 f., 171
  Lord's Supper, 49, 100, 112, 127, 167 f., 188 f.
Salvation, 256 f.

Self-examination, 227 f.
Sermon on the Mount, 86, 100, 151, 156 ff.
Sexuality, 131, 138 f.
Shame, 131, 138, 225
Sin (*see also* Man), 32, 45, 74 f., 147, 178
  punishment of, 39, 149 f.
Social philosophy, 27, 29, 47
Society. *See Gesellschaft*
Sociology, 27, 30
Suum cuique, 223 f.

Theology, 71, 97
  "consciousness," 26
  dialectical, 14 f., 22, 24, 64
  liberal, 15, 27, 252, 253, 254, 276
  Catholic-Thomistic, 61 f.
  natural, 16
Transcendence, transcendent, 58 ff., 62
Transcendentalism, 56, 58 ff., 63
Truth, 63, 73, 102, 104, 105
Two kingdoms (two realms), doctrine of, 17, 159, 208, 213 ff., 269

Union Theological Seminary, 23, 24, 80, 94

World come of age (*die mündige Welt*), 248, 252, 253, 272
Worldliness, 262, 263, 268, 270 f.
Worship service, 48

NAMES

Althaus, Paul, 252
Andrews, C. F., 87
Asmussen, Hans, 85

Baillie, John, 196, 279
Barth, Karl, 14, 17, 21, 24, 64, 81, 85, 86, 199, 252, 253, 263, 275, 276 ff., 279
Beck, Ludwig, 197, 201
Bell, George, Bishop of Chichester, 86, 87, 93, 197, 198, 199, 201, 203
Bernard of Clairvaux, 43
Best, Payne, 202
Bethge, Eberhard, 19, 23, 80, 83, 88, 89, 90, 92, 93, 95, 195, 196, 197, 200, 203, 261, 263, 264, 265
Böhm, Hans, 90
Bonhoeffer, Karl Ludwig, 19
Bonhoeffer, Klaus, 197, 203
Bonhoeffer, Sabine, 19
Brunner, Emil, 14, 265
Bultmann, Rudolf, 14, 17, 65, 253, 275, 278 f.

Canaris, Wilhelm, 197, 203
Coffin, Henry Sloane, 94
Cyprian, 115

Deissmann, Adolf, 20
Delbrück, Hans, 19
Delitzsch, Franz, 78
Dibelius, Otto, 85
Dilthey, Wilhelm, 56
Dohnanyi, Hans von, 197, 200, 203
Duncan-Jones, A. S., 87

Ebeling, Gerhard, 263

Falconer, Hugh, 202
Falkenhausen, General von, 202
Frank, Franz R. von, 21
Fritsch, Werner von, 197

Gandhi, Mahatma, 87
Gehre, Captain, 202
Gerstenmaier, Eugen, 90
Glenthøj, Jørgen, 197
Goerdeler, Karl, 201
Gogarten, Friedrich, 14, 65
Gollwitzer, Helmut, 91
Grisebach, Eberhard, 65
Groos, Karl, 20
Grotius, Hugo, 249

Hammelsbeck, Oscar, 274
Harnack, Adolf von, 14, 19, 20, 23
Hase, Karl von, 19
Hase, Paula von, 19
Heckel, Theodor, 87, 90
Hegel, G. W. F., 29, 31, 57, 60
Heidegger, Martin, 15, 61, 62, 65, 278, 279
Heim, Karl, 20, 252
Heitmüller, Wilhelm, 20
Herrenbrück, P. W., 263
Heuss, Theodor, 85
Hildebrandt, Franz, 87
Himmler, Heinrich, 92, 197
Hitler, Adolf, 13, 16, 17, 80, 84, 85, 90, 92, 107, 116, 117, 195, 196, 197, 198, 199, 201, 262, 282
Hodgson, Leonard, 93

Holl, Karl, 20
Hollaz, David, 78
Husserl, Edmund, 61, 62

Irenaeus, 280

Kant, Immanuel, 55, 58, 59
Kerrl, Hanns, 91
Kleist, Frau von, 196
Koch, Karl, 87, 90
Kokorin, Wassilli, 202
Kupisch, Karl, 90

Lasserre, Jean, 24, 262
Lehmann, Paul, 24, 95, 281
Leibholz, Gerhard, 19
Leiper, Henry, 94
Liedig, Franz, 202
Lietzmann, Hans, 20
Lütgert, Wilhelm, 23
Luther, Martin, 20, 39, 60, 73, 74, 76, 119, 152, 153, 208, 209, 214, 239, 267, 280
Lyman, Eugene W., 24

Marahrens, August, 91
Meiser, Hans, 91
Molotov, V. M., 202
Müller, Josef, 202
Müller, Ludwig, 85, 91
Müller-Gangloff, Erich, 263

Niebuhr, Reinhold, 17, 24, 93, 94, 95, 203
Niemoeller, Martin, 85
Nygren, Anders, 84

Oster, Hans, 197, 203
Otto, Walter F., 261

Paton, William, 198
Peter, Friedrich, 82
Przywara, Erich, 61, 62
Pünder, Hermann, 202

Rabenau, General von, 202
Ranke, Leopold von, 53
Richards, G. C., 84
Rössler, Helmut, 23
Rosenberg, Alfred, 80
Rott, Wilhelm, 89

Scheler, Max, 30, 61, 62
Schlabrendorff, Fabian von, 201
Schlatter, Adolf, 20, 23
Schleicher, Rüdiger, 197, 203
Seeberg, Reinhold, 14, 20, 21, 44
Sellin, Ernst, 20
Stählin, Wilhelm, 82
Sutz, Erwin, 24, 81, 90

Thurneysen, Eduard, 14
Tillich, Paul, 252, 279
Tönnies, Ferdinand, 30
Troeltsch, Ernst, 51, 252

Visser 't Hooft, W. A., 93, 197, 198

Ward, Harry F., 24
Webber, Charles C., 24
Weber, Max, 51, 238
Wedemeyer, Maria von, 200
Wolf, Ernst, 21
Wurm, Theophil, 91

Zöllner, Wilhelm, 82, 90
Zwingli, Huldreich, 47

SCRIPTURE REFERENCES

Genesis
chs. 1 to 2:4a . . . . 119 ff.
2:4b–25 . . . . 126 ff.
3:1–24 . . . . 132 ff.
4:1–16 . . . . 142 f.

Leviticus
19:2 170

Deuteronomy
12:10–11 146

I Samuel
chs. 16 to 31 . . . . 143 ff.

II Samuel
chs. 1 to 24 . . . . 145 ff.
7:5, 11 146

II Chronicles
20:12 267

Job
chs. 38 to 41 22

Isaiah
ch. 53 258
53:5 202
55:11 . . . . 48, 51

Jeremiah
ch. 45 262

Matthew
4:1–11 . . . . 174 f.
ch. 5 . . . . 156 ff.
5:47 160
ch. 6 . . . . 160 f.
6:13 . . . . 172, 175
ch. 7 . . . . 161 ff.
8:17 256
9:35 to 10:42 . . . . 163 ff.
10:16 163
11:21 ff. 53
12:30 229
19:16–22 154
26:40 258

Mark
9:40 229
10:43 197
15:34 . . . . 174, 256

Luke
11:4 . . . . 172, 175
22:28 f. 179

John
1:11 221

Romans
6:23 36
8:2 f. 171
8:3 149
8:29 170

I Corinthians
12:4–6 43

Galatians
4:19 205
6:2 186

Ephesians
4:4–6 43
5:1 172

Philippians
1:21 232
2:5 ff. 171

Colossians
3:3 205

I Thessalonians
5:17 183

I Timothy
3:1 ff. 187

Hebrews
2:12 190
3:7 190
10:5 190
13:12 150

James
1:13 ff. 175
5:16 187

I Peter
1:3 202
4:13 177
4:19 177

Revelation
chs. 2; 3 53
3:10, 16 53

www.ingramcontent.com/pod-product-compliance
Lightning Source LLC
Chambersburg PA
CBHW071236230426
43668CB00011B/1463